KT-546-189

REEL HISTORY

Also by Alex von Tunzelmann

Indian Summer: The Secret History of the End of an Empire
Red Heat: Conspiracy, Murder and the Cold War in the Caribbean

Reel HISTORY

The World According to the Movies

ALEX VON TUNZELMANN

Atlantic Books
London

First published in hardback in Great Britain in 2015 by Atlantic Books,
an imprint of Atlantic Books Ltd.

1 2 3 4 5 6 7 8 9

A CIP catalogue record for this book is available from the British Library.

Hardback ISBN: 978-1-78239-646-8
E-book ISBN: 978-1-78239-647-5
Paperback ISBN: 978-1-78239-648-2

Printed and bound by CPI Group (UK) Ltd, Croydon, CR0 4YY

Atlantic Books
An Imprint of Atlantic Books Ltd
Ormond House
26–27 Boswell Street
London
WC1N 3JZ

www.atlantic-books.co.uk

For Eugénie

CONTENTS

INTRODUCTION

What would the history of the world look like if you learned it all from watching movies? According to some of the films in this book, birth control pills have been available for 1,600 years; everyone in the Middle Ages could read, but William Shakespeare was illiterate; Scottish rebel Sir William Wallace managed to father King Edward III of England, even though he never met Edward's mother and died seven years before Edward was born; Mozart was murdered by a jealous rival; champions of democracy have included the ancient Mauryan emperor Asoka, the nation of Sparta, Marcus Aurelius, Lady Jane Grey and Oliver Cromwell; the American war in Vietnam was awesome; all American wars were awesome; and a crew of plucky Americans including Jon Bon Jovi captured the first Enigma machine from the Nazis in World War II.

Unless you make an effort to read history books or watch high-quality television documentaries on historical subjects, the chances are that as an adult you will consume all your history from fictional feature films and television dramas. Maybe, if you paid attention in school, you'll know they get some things wrong. But it will be difficult to stop deeper and broader misconceptions finding their way into your consciousness.

If you get it from the movies, your history of the world will be strongly focused on Western Europe and North America, and on the doings of white, heterosexual, Christian men of the upper classes. The women you know about will mostly be queens and mistresses, if they have characters at all beyond the ability to wear (and perhaps swiftly remove) sparkly, flimsy outfits. Even when you watch something about, say, ancient Egyptians, Mongols or Arabs, they will frequently be played by white people. Even if you watch films that are not made in Hollywood, this might still be true. In the Pakistani movie *Jinnah* (1998), Mohammad Ali Jinnah was played by Christopher Lee; in the Libyan movie *Lion of the Desert* (1981), Sharif al-Ghariyani was played by John Gielgud. Most historical characters will present themselves to you with a comforting simplicity, either as heroes or villains. Most historical stories will seem to have a satisfying beginning, middle and end. The good guys will mostly win, at least morally; for filmmakers know that if you leave the cinema uplifted or invigorated you will recommend the film to your friends. History onscreen becomes legend, myth, fable, propaganda.

Since 2008, I've been the historian behind Reel History, a column on historical films for the *Guardian*'s website. Every week, I watch one, then try to work out how it relates to the truth of what happened – aware, of course, that truth itself is slippery and subjective. It's not always a bad thing to learn about history from films. I've certainly broadened and deepened my knowledge by watching such fine examples as *The Lion in Winter* (1968), a razor-sharp Plantagenet comedy with Peter O'Toole as Henry II and Katharine Hepburn as Eleanor of Aquitaine; *The Killing Fields* (1984), a moving tale of Cambodia under the Khmer Rouge; *Ran* (1985), Akira Kurosawa's synthesis of *King Lear* and the real story of sixteenth-century Japanese daimyo Mori Motonari; and *Twelve Years a Slave* (2013), Steve McQueen's searingly brilliant retelling of the story of Solomon Northup. In all of these cases, and many more, filmmakers have taken resonant stories and told them within a setting of well-researched period detail which does not suffocate meaning but enhances it. They get the facts right, or approximately right; but they also go beyond a simple retelling of the facts to find poignancy, tragedy, drama or humour. These films have a feeling for their time, but also a sense of what matters in ours.

Many filmmakers go to great lengths in pursuit of accuracy. Historian Justin Pollard has consulted on films including *Elizabeth* (1998) as well as the TV series *The Tudors* and *Vikings*. He spent two years researching *Vikings* from primary sources. 'We translate lines into Old Norse and Old English, use pre-Conquest missals for religious scenes and reconstruct locations and events from contemporary chronicles – inasmuch as that's possible in the ninth century!' he told me. 'We do make mistakes but often what are called "mistakes" are conscious decisions made for reasons of budget, logistics or narrative, like compressing time frames, shooting in a different location to the actual event, or reducing the cast of characters.'

Reel History goes easy on such 'mistakes' that are really just storytelling choices. Real life doesn't fit neatly into three-act structures, nor into the approximately 90–240-minute run-time of feature films. Most filmmakers working in a commercially driven industry have to work within these conventions. Restructuring stories to be more compelling and more easily understood is part of a screenwriter's job.

Changes that have been made for deliberate comic effect don't tend to get slapped down in Reel History either, if they're funny. Greg Jenner was historical consultant to the terrifically enjoyable *Horrible Histories* TV series, beloved of many usually serious historians. 'We had to balance the post-modern comic whimsy, complete with time-travelling devices and modern TV references, with communicating 4,000 historical facts, and then flagging up which were the jokes and which were the true bits,' he says. 'We had a puppet rat to do that.' In one of my favourite semi-historical films, *Bill & Ted's Excellent Adventure* (1989), two Californian teenagers with a time machine establish that Napoleon is 'a short dead dude', Julius Caesar is 'a salad-dressing dude', and Genghis Khan is 'a dude who, 700 years ago, *totally* ravaged China'. Some of us passed History GCSE with less. Jenner's master's thesis was on the reactions of medieval historians to films about King Arthur: 'Everyone decided *Monty Python's Holy Grail* was the best because it's full of historical in-jokes.'

'Humour is vital in helping us engage with the past,' adds Professor Kate Williams, who presents history programmes on radio and TV. 'Even if historical films are inaccurate, they get audiences involved.' Justin Pollard agrees: 'I hope historical drama serves as an inspiration for people to go and find out more. If you look at how well sales of popular Tudor history books did after *The Tudors* then I think that was the case.'

This is a very positive effect – but there is a darker side to some historical filmmaking. Many of the films in this book were made, officially or unofficially, for the purpose of advancing a specific political agenda. Some of these qualify as official propaganda, financed by governments or militaries; others are just trying to push a case because the filmmakers strongly believe it, whether that's Roland Emmerich advancing his oddball Shakespeare conspiracy theories in *Anonymous* (2011) or Cecil B. DeMille bigging up McCarthyism in *The Ten Commandments* (1956). From *Alexander Nevsky* (1938) to *Zero Dark Thirty* (2012), some films are meant to influence the way we think.

Every week, somebody says to me: 'It's a fictional movie, not a documentary.' Well, yes, of course it is – but some films deliberately blur the line. Paul Greengrass's *United 93* (2006) and Oliver Stone's *JFK* (1991) both use a documentary style to present heavily fictionalized – and heavily politicized – historical cases. Even in less overtly political films, the versions of history shown often have a substantial and long-lasting impact. The iconic cultural images of such figures as Henry VIII, Robin Hood and Richard III were set by *The Private Life of Henry VIII* (1933), *The Adventures of Robin Hood* (1938) and Laurence Olivier's production of *Richard III* (1955) respectively. The myth that Jewish slaves built Egypt's pyramids – controversially repeated by Israeli politician Menachem Begin in the twentieth century – does not appear in the Bible and is a historical impossibility: the great pyramids were built before Judaism existed. Yet it has been cemented in many people's minds by generations of fanciful Hollywood movies about Moses. The myth that galley slaves were the norm in the Roman Empire can largely be traced to *Ben-Hur* (1959). The myth that Vikings wore helmets with two horns stems from the costume designs for the 1876 Bayreuth opera festival performance of Wagner's *Der Ring des Nibelungen*, but has been kept alive by films like *The Norsemen* (1978). The words 'Follow the money' were never said by Deep Throat (Mark Felt), the key source in the Watergate scandal, though they are often attributed to him by journalists and even historians; they were written by screenwriter William Goldman for the movie *All the President's Men* (1976). Hollywood history can itself become the commonly accepted definition of history: the one most people know. 'What is history but a fable agreed upon?' asked Napoleon (paraphrasing Voltaire), and he hadn't even seen *Braveheart* (1995).

One of the most striking things I've learned since writing Reel History is that, actually, a lot of people can and do believe some of the things they see in the movies. Many of us will know that a particularly outlandish claim is tosh when we watch it, but years later it may have taken root in our imaginations – and we don't always remember that we first saw it in a fictional film. Some films have an immediate and terrifying effect. In the wake of the release of gung-ho Iraq War drama *American Sniper* (2014), social media filled up with violent, racist messages inspired by the movie. One example from Twitter: 'Great fucking movie and now I really want to kill some fucking ragheads.' The American-Arab Anti-Discrimination Committee reported that threats against Muslims and Arabs in the United States tripled following the movie's release. It's easier to argue 'it's a fictional film, not a documentary' if no one is threatening to murder you after watching it.

Evidently, not all audiences can tell the difference between fact and fiction. And this doesn't necessarily make them stupid: perhaps they could have done with a better education, but unfortunately many educational systems don't encourage people to challenge what they're being told. Film is an incredibly persuasive medium, which is why governments across the world, led by figures as politically diverse as Joseph Stalin, Winston Churchill, Richard Nixon, Kim Jong-un and Sayyid Ali Khamenei, have expended substantial amounts of time, money and effort making films, or interfering with other people's films. 'Filmmakers have a great responsibility,' says Kate Williams. 'How they present the past is how it gets remembered.'

As the historian Professor Richard Evans wrote in 2013: 'History isn't a myth-making discipline, it's a myth-busting discipline, and it needs to be taught as such in our schools.' The most essential principle of historical analysis is to question everything you are told and shown. That's what Reel History wants you to do. Engage with what you're watching. Ask questions and seek answers. There is nothing wrong with fictionalizing historical figures and events. It's a fine literary tradition, from William Shakespeare to *War and Peace* to *Wolf Hall*: it can be creative and it can be fun. Also, everyone makes mistakes. My most embarrassing was in reviewing *Elizabeth* (1998). I stated that Elizabeth's mother Anne Boleyn had been beheaded with an axe. Commenters rightly leapt on my blunder. Anne was beheaded by a French swordsman. Everyone knows that. I know that, too. Yet somehow, when I wrote it down, I messed it up. All the other historians pointed and laughed, and made me move my seat in the British Library next to the strange man who researches UFO conspiracies and smells of eels.

The government of Egypt banned Ridley Scott's film *Exodus: Gods and Kings* (2014), saying it was 'historically inaccurate'. It is. Even in the cases of the most egregiously and deliberately falsified historical films – I'm looking at you, Mel Gibson, and you, Oliver Stone – I have certainly never suggested they should be banned, nor that filmmakers should stop making them, nor that they be forced instead to make movies that a supreme council of historians deems accurate. I would hope any filmmaker would act intelligently when dealing with real material, be aware of the influence their film may have and take responsibility for the decisions they make – but that's an aspiration, not a rule.

Films should be made and seen in an atmosphere of creative and intellectual freedom. Then they should be debated by historians, pulled apart, analysed, and, where necessary, mocked loudly and in public. If all else fails, just remember the unintentionally honest tagline of *U-571* (2000), the film in which Jon Bon Jovi rescues the Enigma machine: 'Nine men are about to change history.'

1

The Ancient World

The history of the world presented in cinema stretches back hundreds of millions of years. Animated dinosaur adventure *The Land Before Time* (1988) follows an orphaned Apatosaurus through the Cretaceous, 145–66 million years ago; the *Ice Age* films (from 2002) recount the adventures of Sid the sloth and friends, between 110,000 and 12,000 years ago. Sid the sloth was not, as far as we know, a real historical character.

Some filmmakers have had a go at caveman stories, though these are limited by their lack of language – and by the assumption that cavemen of all sorts were painfully literal and a bit dull. Jean-Jacques Annaud's *Quest for Fire* (1981) employed *A Clockwork Orange* author Anthony Burgess to write a grunty language for its Neanderthals, and zoologist Desmond Morris to advise them on how to shuffle around and pick each other's fleas off. Prehistoric flop *The Clan of the Cave Bear* (1986) subtitled a warpainted, Cro-Magnon Daryl Hannah.

The Birth of a Nation (1915) director D. W. Griffith was fascinated by prehistory, telling caveman tales in shorts *Man's Genesis* (1912) and *Brute Force* (1914). In the latter, cavemen were pitted against dinosaurs. The earliest fossil remains of our species, *Homo sapiens sapiens*, date from around 200,000 years ago, during the Palaeolithic era – millions of years after the last dinosaur. Yet pitting plucky little humans against an angry T. Rex has often proved too tempting for filmmakers to resist.

1,000,000 BCE

One Million Years B.C. (1966)

Director: Don Chaffey • Entertainment grade: D • History grade: Fail

Dates: 'This is a story of long, long ago, when the world was just beginning,' intones a voiceover over images of swirling clouds and burping lava. Well, no. The film is ostensibly set in 1 million years BC, which would put it over 4.5 billion years after the world was just beginning. If by 'the world' it means hominid society, it's not quite so far out: only 1.5 million years or so. It opens with the Rock Tribe, a band of loincloth-wearing, warthog-eating cavemen. They are clearly *Homo sapiens* with slightly mussed-up hair. Finding genuine *Homo erectus* would be a casting challenge – though one does occasionally wonder about the exact species of Mickey Rourke – but *Homo sapiens* actors without suitable prosthetics date the film to 200,000 BC at the earliest.

Fauna: A caveman, Tumak (John Richardson), is exiled from the Rock Tribe, and wanders the land encountering local wildlife. In 1 million years BC, you might expect a mammoth, a sabre-toothed tiger or a glyptodon. Instead, Tumak hears a roar, and there looms before him a really big iguana. Finding genuine dinosaurs would be another casting challenge, but a really big iguana does not look like a dinosaur. It looks like a really big iguana. Or a normal-sized iguana chasing a tiny caveman. Things get even sillier a few minutes later, when a really big tarantula shows up. It is four times Tumak's height. The biggest true spider ever to walk the earth is the goliath birdeater. It's still knocking around in South America and, while finding one in the bathtub would be alarming, even it is no bigger than your hand. Fortunately, Ray Harryhausen's beautifully animated stop-motion dinosaurs are on their way to rescue the film's visual credibility. Real dinosaurs, of course, died out 65 million years ago. Which makes them something of an anachronism in 1 million BC.

Culture: Exhausted, Tumak collapses on a beach, conveniently situated in the territory of the Tribe of Hot Blonde Women Who Wear Furry Bikinis. These folk are more advanced than the Rock Tribe. In addition to two-piece swimwear, they have invented embroidery, conch shell trumpets, cave-painting workshops, bouffants, false eyelashes, spear aerodynamics, laughing at foreigners, and the small-scale manufacture of boho costume jewellery. At one point, a turnip is lifted triumphantly aloft. Presumably they must have foraged for it rather than actually working out how to farm, which would catapult them forward into the Neolithic. Meanwhile, the Rock Tribe sit around banging sticks together, thumping each other and grunting, while a nubile young woman is forced to do a sexy dance. So all they seem to have managed to invent is patriarchy.

Survival: For all the Hot Blonde Tribe's innovations, they are still prey to an Allosaur, a Rhamphorhynchus and an angry turtle the size of a bus. If you're thinking this last may be from the same pet shop as the iguana and the tarantula, you're underestimating Harryhausen. It's Archelon ischyros, a gigantic testudinate of the late Cretaceous. In life less gigantic than it looks here, admittedly, and again 64 million years out of date – but it was, in some sense, real. Loana (Raquel Welch) points at it, shouting, 'Archelon! Archelon!', which is clever of her, seeing as it was named by palaeontologist G. R. Wieland in 1896.

Verdict: Harryhausen's dinosaurs are well worth a look, but the rest of *One Million Years B.C.* will bore the furry pants off anyone more advanced than a Neanderthal.

After the Ice Age, early civilizations began to form. By around 2500 BCE, there would be more for later filmmakers to work with: cities and trade networks, complete with forms of writing, numeracy, transport and exchange, across Mesopotamia and the valleys of the Nile and Indus rivers.

According to American and European cinema, ancient Egypt was populated and ruled by white people, though the occasional black actor is allowed a non-speaking role:

usually as a spear carrier or leopardskin-clad trumpeter. The English rose complexion of Jeanne Crain passed for fourteenth- century BCE Queen Nefertiti in Italian adventure flick *Nefertiti, Queen of the Nile* (1961), opposite Vincent Price as a high priest. Nefertiti's husband, the pharaoh Akhenaton, was played by Michael Wilding in *The Egyptian* (1954), with other Egyptian roles filled by Jean Simmons, Gene Tierney, Peter Ustinov and Victor Mature. Even in the more recent *Exodus: Gods and Kings* (2014), almost all the speaking parts were occupied by conspicuously white people.

2560 BCE

Land of the Pharaohs (1955)

Director: Howard Hawks • Entertainment grade: C– • History grade: D–

Khufu, or Cheops, was an Egyptian pharaoh of the fourth dynasty. He is remembered for building the Great Pyramid of Giza in the twenty-sixth century BC, the only surviving wonder of the Seven Wonders of the World.

Casting: Khufu returns from a war, rich with treasure and slaves. In 1955, Hollywood knew how to stage this sort of thing: scores of marching trumpeters, drummers, pipers and maraca players, hundreds of cavalry camels, and almost 10,000 extras supplied by the Egyptian government of Gamal Abdel Nasser. This spectacle made an impact on the then thirteen-year-old Martin Scorsese: 'When I first saw it as a kid,' he said, '*Land of the Pharaohs* became my favourite film.' Unfortunately, when

Khufu descends from his litter, he is Jack Hawkins. Clipped, uptight and as English as a rained-off cricket match, Hawkins is hopelessly miscast as the passionate, obsessive, despotic Khufu. The only Hollywood actor who could have pulled this off at the time was Marlon Brando.

Tyranny: Khufu's people labour for years on a pyramid for him. Eventually, they start getting ticked off. There's a nod to Herodotus here, who wrote of Khufu that his fixation on pyramid construction brought his people 'every kind of evil… [he] bade all the Egyptians work for him… they worked by a hundred thousand men at a time, for each three months continually'. The film leaves out the part where Herodotus says Khufu came 'to such a pitch of wickedness, that being in want of money he caused his own daughter to sit in the stews' – or brothels.

Romance: Khufu's lands end up so poor that some can't pay their annual tribute. One – Cyprus – instead sends Princess Nellifer (Joan Collins). It takes Khufu ages to work out that Nellifer doesn't like him, even after she has him stabbed. 'So it was you!' he gasps. 'Yes!' she hisses, with the same delicious venom she will later bring to Alexis Carrington Colby. 'You can know now! I planned it all, and it's all turned out as I hoped it would!'

Dialogue: 'I don't know how a pharaoh talks,' director Howard Hawks admitted later. 'And [screenwriter and Nobel laureate William] Faulkner didn't know. None of us knew. We thought it'd be an interesting story, the building of a pyramid, but then we had to have a plot, and we didn't really feel close to any of it.' If they'd all followed Collins's lead and stopped taking it so seriously, *Land* *of the Pharaohs* still wouldn't have been any good – but it might have been fun.

Verdict: Next time, less fourth dynasty; more just *Dynasty*.

Many of Hollywood's ancient Egyptian movies take inspiration from the biblical story of Moses, painting the pharaohs as proud and despotic. Historians are divided on whether Moses actually existed in the form that has been passed down in religious texts. Some suggest his stories may have been inherited and rewritten from even older traditions, or made up entirely. If he was real, he is usually dated to some time between the fourteenth and thirteenth century BCE.

Moses is popular with filmmakers nonetheless, though Ridley Scott's 2014 epic *Exodus: Gods and Kings*, starring Christian Bale, drew critical snark for its pompous tone. Hollywood films like *Exodus: Gods and Kings* are also largely responsible for sustaining the belief that Jewish slaves built the pyramids. It makes for a great cinematic visual, but the famous pyramids at Giza, Sakkara, Abu Sir and other major Egyptian locations were mostly built between the twenty-seventh and twenty-fourth century BC – hundreds of years before any Jews arrived in Egypt and at least a millennium before Moses. The Bible claims that Jewish slaves built the cities of Pithom and Rameses, not the pyramids, and many modern historians and archaeologists dispute the idea that the pyramids were built by slave labour at all.

1250 BCE

The Prince of Egypt (1998)

Director: Brenda Chapman, Steve Hickner, Simon Wells • Entertainment grade: A • History grade: C

Family: To save her son from an Egyptian cull of Hebrew baby boys, Moses's mother seals him in a basket and floats him off down the Nile. The pharaoh's queen plucks him out of the waters. The story bears a glancing similarity to the legend of Sargon of Akkad, a Sumerian king of the twenty-fourth century BC (around a millennium before Moses). Sargon was sealed in a basket by his mother and floated off down the Euphrates, arrived at the palace of the goddess Ishtar, was adopted, and grew up to become king.

Class: Moses is brought up thinking he's Egyptian. This isn't obvious from Exodus, but it does create a satisfying character arc for him – he'll go from spoilt brat to a leader of humanity. The film invents a daredevil race through the city, with Moses and his brother Rameses sending slaves scuttling into doorways as they gallop around in their shiny gold chariots, guffawing with princely entitlement. At one point, they knock the nose off the Great Sphinx of Giza, which appears to be under construction. In real life, the Sphinx was built at around the time of Sargon of Akkad. Its nose probably wasn't knocked off until around three millennia after Moses: possibly by British or French troops in Napoleon's time.

Disease: Pharaoh won't free the slaves, so God sends plagues. There are lice, locusts, frogs, hail (upgraded to massive bolts of fire plummeting out of the sky), dead cows, boils, and a new and horrifying eleventh plague of people bursting into song. Or maybe that's just because this is a musical. As is the Book of Exodus: there's a song in chapter fifteen. The plagues were not recorded in Egyptian texts, but this doesn't mean they didn't happen. Egyptian royal inscriptions tended to stick to the happy stories.

Escape: Moses leads the Hebrews to the Red Sea, which whooshes back to allow them through. It's superbly done – the shadow of a whale shark looming through the parted sea is a nice touch – but not particularly accurate. Scholars have pointed out that the Hebrew text of Exodus refers not to the Red Sea but to *yam sûf*, the 'Reed Sea', possibly a marsh or lake. A bit small to accommodate a whale shark.

Mythology: There's a triumphal final shot of Moses's face as he comes down from the mountain with the Ten Commandments. In Exodus, after meeting God, Moses's face radiated light, forcing him to wear a veil. Owing to another mistranslation, 'radiated light' appeared in the Latin Bible for centuries as 'grew horns'. There's even a statue of Moses by Michelangelo complete with a lovely set of horns. *Prince of Egypt*'s Moses has a face that is neither glowing nor horned. Overall, though, this is a stunning film – certainly the most watchable cinematic version of the Moses story yet.

1250 BCE

The Ten Commandments (1956)

Director: Cecil B. DeMille • Entertainment grade: C+ • History grade: C–

Sources: DeMille himself strolls on screen at the beginning of the film, to explain how he has filled the gaps in the biblical story of Moses's life with the work of historians such as Josephus and Philo. He claims they had access to ancient documents, which have since been destroyed. In reality, there's no evidence that there were ever any such documents, and both Josephus and Philo were writing over a millennium after Moses's death. Other historians of that era, including Tacitus, treated Moses as a legendary figure.

People: One of the reasons that putting a date to Moses's life is so difficult is that the Book of Exodus isn't specific about which pharaohs it describes. The film plumps for Seti I as Moses's adoptive father and Rameses II as his brother, though there's a slip-up when Moses congratulates Seti on his victory at Kadesh, a battle actually fought by Rameses. As for the love triangle between Moses, Nefretiri and Rameses, that doesn't appear in scriptures or history. Bad luck, Josephus and Philo: DeMille also filled the gaps in Moses's life from a stack of pulp novels.

Technology: The film won an Oscar for rising to the special effects challenges of religious, rather than historical, imagery, most famously the pillar of fire and the parting of the Red Sea. But there's disappointment in store when Rameses refuses to listen to Moses's plea to let his people go, and Egypt is visited by… four plagues. The other six are only mentioned in passing, because DeMille couldn't work out how to do frogs, flies, lice, boils, locusts or the death of livestock. These days, of course, it would be easy: just set up a camera outside the toilet block at the Glastonbury Festival.

Politics: 'Are men the property of the state?' thunders DeMille. 'Or are they free souls under God? This same battle continues throughout the world today.' In his analogy, the repressive pharaohs are the Soviets, while the brave Hebrews are the Americans. A historian may wonder with horror whether Moses is supposed to be Senator Joseph McCarthy. At the time of filming, one of the stars, Edward G. Robinson, and its composer, Elmer Bernstein, had been persecuted by McCarthy's investigations, and were in the process of being rehabilitated – a process mirrored by the redemption of Robinson's entirely fictional character, Dathan. DeMille was one of Hollywood's most prominent conservatives.

Verdict: *The Ten Commandments* is a fascinating historical film – not for what it says about Moses, but for what it says about Cold War America. 'Go!' commands Moses. 'Proclaim liberty throughout all the lands, unto all the inhabitants thereof!' The original line, attributed to God in Leviticus 25:10, has 'land' in the singular. It seems that didn't make the case for spreading American-style freedom and democracy clearly enough.

After the ancient Egyptians came the ancient Greeks. Special and visual effects technologies have limited cinema's efforts at translating Homer's possibly historical *Iliad* and mostly fantastical *Odyssey* to the screen, though there have been attempts. Kirk Douglas starred in *Ulysses* (1954), and Greek singer Irene Papas in *Iphigenia* (1977). Historians have mixed feelings about the extent to which the Trojan War actually happened, though it does match up date-wise with evidence of a city known to archaeologists as Troy VII, at Hisarlik in Turkey. Troy VII was burned to the ground in around the twelfth or eleventh century BCE, roughly the right date for Homer's war.

1250 BCE

Troy (2004)

Director: Wolfgang Petersen • Entertainment grade: D • History grade: D–

Scandal: In Sparta, King Menelaus holds a banquet for the Trojan princes, Hector and Paris. Paris sneaks off to make whoopee with Menelaus's wife, Helen. The next day, she runs away with him. This puts Menelaus in a bate, and gives his brother Agamemnon an excuse to start a war. 'Sparta was never my home,' Helen explains. 'My parents sent me there when I was sixteen, to marry Menelaus.' Actually, in Homeric tradition, her parents were king and queen of Sparta and it was her home. Helen herself chose Menelaus, a prince of Mycenae, to be her husband, and he gained the throne of Sparta by marrying her. This film is already a right old mess.

People: War obliges Agamemnon to enlist Greece's best warrior and biggest pain in the backside, Achilles (Brad Pitt). Pitt's Achilles is a hero with an attitude problem the size of Asia Minor, who spends most of his time lounging around in a kaftan and getting laid. Not a million miles from the Homeric depiction, but much more annoying. In classical history, Achilles was disguised as a girl to avoid going to war. The film wimps out of putting Pitt in a dress, and instead has him in a cobalt-blue sarong, necklace of shells and tousled honey-blonde wig. He looks like a creepy yoga teacher.

Sex: Achilles is sparring with his lover Patroclus, whom the film insists is just his cousin. It seems the Greek hero has undergone a radical straightening process – and we're not talking about his hair any more. The filmmakers have edited out all the gay sex from the *Iliad*, along with the presence of the gods. You have to wonder why they bothered making a film about ancient Greece in the first place.

Zoology: As the Greek ships arrive at Troy, the people start panicking in their marketplace, running past the camera with a donkey, a birdcage and two llamas. That's right: llamas. From Peru. First visited by Europeans in the sixteenth century CE. It is impossible that there would have been any llamas in Europe or Asia for at least another 2,800 years. Unless these ones were really good swimmers and just bobbed over the Atlantic of their own accord.

Violence: Paris challenges Menelaus to a duel. Being a big girl's blouse, the prince of Troy is no match for the Spartan king, who lumbers around whacking him with a sword for about thirty seconds until the bleeding Paris scuttles away to hide behind Hector's skirts. Menelaus goes in for the kill, but Hector gets him first with a stab through the chest. The real (or real-ish) Menelaus survived the Trojan War, and was happily reunited with Helen afterwards. Director Wolfgang Petersen also prematurely bumps off Ajax and Agamemnon. At least all these deaths rule out the sequel.

In the forties, fifties and sixties, there was a fashion for biblical epics. Though many of these featured Hollywood stars and were filmed in English, they were often produced in Italy. Italy made the first feature-length ancient epic, *The Last Days of Pompeii* (1908), and the most influential, Punic War story *Cabiria* (1914), a hodge-podge of historical fiction and real-life characters, who included Hannibal and Archimedes.

Hollywood's ancient stories were often drawn from the Old Testament, which records tales of the ancient near east around a millennium BCE. Paulette Goddard was Jezebel in *Sins of Jezebel* (1953); Orson Welles played King Saul in *David and Goliath* (1960); Joan Collins turned up again in *Esther and the King* (1960). The ludicrous *Solomon and Sheba* (1959) tempted in audiences with the promise of an Old Testament orgy scene, though being 1959 this merely consisted of the Queen of Sheba (Gina Lollobrigida) doing the funky chicken in a gold bikini while her acolytes formed a conga line and then ran off giggling into the undergrowth.

1000 BCE

Samson and Delilah (1949)

Director: Cecil B. DeMille • Entertainment grade: B • History grade: B

The story of Samson is recorded in the Book of Judges, thought to have been written in about the seventh or sixth century BCE.

People: Samson (Victor Mature), hero of the Danites, macks on hot Philistine blonde Semadar (Angela Lansbury). Meanwhile, Semadar's sister Delilah burns with lust for him. She is played by the gorgeous real-life mathematician Hedy Lamarr, sometimes credited as the inventor of wi-fi. Historians and scientists might be happier with the statement that she was one of the inventors of frequency hopping, which was subsequently used in military and civilian communications technology. None of this is much use to her in tenth-century BCE Gaza.

Romance: Delilah drags Samson out to the desert, where they are waylaid by a lion. Bravely, Samson leaps at it. Or, rather, his stunt double does. Cecil B. DeMille was furious with Victor Mature for refusing to wrestle the actual clapped-out old lion he procured for the scene, though the leading man gamely rolled around with a stuffed version in the close-ups. 'You killed him with your hands!' gasps Delilah. 'Oh, Samson!' She leaps upon him, considerably more rapacious than either the real or the fake lion. No dice: he still marries the blonde.

Arson: The marriage doesn't work out. Aggrieved, Samson sets fire to the fields of the Philistines, though fortunately for some foxes DeMille did not attempt to film the novel method of arson as described in the Book of Judges: 'Samson went and caught three hundred foxes, and took firebrands, and turned tail to tail, and put a firebrand in the midst between two tails. And when he had set the brands on fire, he let them go into the standing corn of the Philistines.'

Costume: Delilah seduces Samson, so as to betray him to the Philistines. The Philistines take him to be humiliated at the temple of their god, Dagon. Delilah turns up in a fabulous cloak of peacock feathers. Just as no foxes were inconvenienced in the making of this film, nor were any peacocks. DeMille had pet ones, and is said to have spent a decade collecting their shed plumes from his grounds to make Lamarr's costume.

Love: Samson still loves Delilah, even if it is her fault that he has now been imprisoned, blinded, subjected to hard labour, and attacked by miniature gladiators (no, that bit isn't in the Bible, but this is a long film and somebody got creative). 'Wherever you go, my love is with you,' he tells her. Well, she did invent wi-fi. Kind of. His strength returns and he destroys the temple. It's a striking sequence, even though some of the blocks of falling stone bounce.

Verdict: 'I am sometimes accused of gingering up the Bible with large and lavish infusions of sex and violence,' wrote Cecil B. DeMille in his autobiography. 'I can only wonder if my accusers have ever read certain parts of the Bible.' Hollywood may taketh away flaming foxes with one hand, but it giveth miniature gladiators with the other.

The Battle of Thermopylae in 480 BC is seen by some historians as a pivotal moment in the relationship between East and West. For three days, Greek forces, under the command of King Leonidas of Sparta and his 300 warriors, held back the entire Persian army, under the Achaemenid emperor Xerxes. The main source on Thermopylae is the Greek historian Herodotus, who was alive (though very young) at the time. He is often considered unreliable, preferring to tell a good story than to stick to the facts – making his work ideal material for Hollywood adaptation twenty-four centuries later.

Thermopylae has been filmed as *The 300 Spartans* (1962), with Richard Egan and Ralph Richardson, and more recently as an adaptation of Frank Miller's graphic novel *300* (2007). To be fair, some historians appreciated *300*. Tom Holland, author of such terrific ancient history books as *Rubicon* and *Persian Fire*, argued that Zack Snyder's movie is 'profoundly unsettling, to be sure, but is also the most authentic rendering of an ancient culture's *mores* yet achieved by a Hollywood director'. He noted: 'What few jokes do intrude all derive from Herodotus, Xenophon, or Plutarch. Otherwise, the film is solemn to an almost muscle-bound degree. It really does seem to argue that militarism is a thing of glory. Which is precisely, of course, what makes it so convincing as a portrait of the Spartan *mentalité*.'

480 BCE

300 (2007)

Director: Zack Snyder • Entertainment grade: E • History grade: Fail

Military: A Persian ambassador rocks up in Sparta, demanding submission. 'Rumour has it that the Athenians have already turned you down,' scoffs Leonidas. 'And if those philosophers and boy-lovers have found that kind of nerve…' It's odd to make a homophobic remark if you are in charge of the Spartan army, which insisted on homosexual contact between mature male warriors and young boys as part of social and martial training. Mind you, with their waxed chests and tight leather Speedos, the film's Spartans do at least look like they might be up for a bit of that.

Geography: Infuriated by the Spartan resistance, Xerxes sends armies 'from the darkest corner of his empire', including shouty Mongols, stampy Indian elephants, and some sub-Saharan Africans with a blinged-out battle rhino. Technically, it's still supposed to be 480 BC, but these warriors are taken from completely arbitrary points in history – except for the battle rhino, which is taken from no point in history, and can only have escaped from *The Lord of the Rings*. Moreover, none of these territories was part of the Achaemenid empire; though it was very large, stretching from modern-day Turkey to the Indus.

People: The solemn voiceover loses some of its impact because Dilios (David Wenham) seems to have learned his English accent from George, the camp pink hippo from 1980s children's programme *Rainbow*. 'I trust that scratch hasn't made you useless?' asks Leonidas, while Dilios ties a bandage around his own head. 'Hardly, my lord,' says Dilios. 'It's just an eye.' Dilios is based on the Spartan warrior Aristodemos, but he didn't get his eye slashed out in battle. All he had was a nasty infection. Real Spartans could withstand anything, except conjunctivitis.

Betrayal: In the film, a deformed Spartan called Ephialtes is tempted over to the Persian side when Xerxes shows him a tent full of naked ladies who just can't get enough of really ugly men. According to Herodotus, Ephialtes was a non-deformed non-Spartan, who showed the Persians a mountain trail around Thermopylae, leading them to victory. This makes a lot more sense than his betrayal in *300*, which consists of wearing a funny pointy hat.

Society: 'This day, we rescue a world from mysticism and tyranny,' brags Dilios. The real Spartans were not defenders of freedom and democracy. Spartan society maintained a permanent war footing to preserve its unequal structure, which was based on the exploitation of a large class of helots, or slaves. There was a nation in Greece that did have a democracy something like that associated with Sparta in the film: Athens. Run by the same Athenians that the film's Leonidas ridiculed earlier for thinking about stuff.

Verdict: Epic fail.

One of history's great heroes – whom filmmakers have repeatedly tried to turn into one of cinema's – is Alexander III, known as the Great, king of Macedon from 336–323 BC. Before the age of thirty, he conquered an enormous swathe of territory stretching from the Danube in the north-west to the Nile in the south and the Indus in the east, becoming pharaoh of Egypt, king of Persia and lord of Asia. He died aged just thirty-two. The famous quote: 'When Alexander saw the breadth of his domain, he wept for there were no more worlds to conquer' is often thought to be classical, but is in fact a Hollywood coinage. It was first said by Hans Gruber (Alan Rickman) in blockbuster action flick *Die Hard* (1988).*

Alexander has been played by Bollywood legend Prithviraj Kapoor in *Sikandar* (1941), by Richard Burton in *Alexander the Great* (1956), and even by *Star Trek*'s William Shatner in a TV movie also called *Alexander the Great* (1968), opposite Adam West of *Batman* fame as General Cleander of Macedon.

* Gruber's line is probably based on sixteenth-century theologian John Calvin's interpretation of Psalm 146: '... he censures the madness of princes in setting no bounds to their hopes and desires, and scaling the very heavens in their ambition, like the insane Alexander of Macedon, who, upon hearing that there are other worlds, wept that he had not yet conquered one, although soon after the funeral urn sufficed him.' (John Calvin, *On the Book of Psalms* (1557), translated by James Anderson.)

323 BCE

Alexander (2004)

Director: Oliver Stone • Entertainment grade: Fail • History grade: D+

Family: Pity poor Alexander. His mum, Olympias (Angelina Jolie), is in thrall to a Dionysian cult, sleeps with a bucket of snakes by her bed, and tends to overshare about how the god Zeus was hot stuff in the sack. His dad, Philip of Macedon (Val Kilmer), is a womanizing boozehound who spouts egregious platitudes in a baffling Irish accent. 'A king isn't born, Alexander, he is made,' he burbles. 'A king must know how to hurt those he loves. It's lonely. Ask anyone… Fate is cruel. No man or woman can be too powerful or too beautiful without disaster befalling. They laugh when you rise too high.' Despite what this speech might imply, there is no historical evidence that Philip of Macedon invented the fortune cookie. Still, some of the biographical details do have a basis in Plutarch's *Life of Alexander*.

War: The narrative jumps to Gaugamela in 331 BCE, with 40,000 Greeks facing down 250,000 Persians (an exaggeration: Persian numbers are generally estimated at closer to 100,000). Heading up the Greeks are Alexander (Colin Farrell), Hephaestion (Jared Leto) and Cassander (Jonathan Rhys Meyers), a mass of teased bouffants, sharp cheekbones and carefully applied mascara. They look like they've turned up for a walk-off. Instead, what follows is a battle, complete with charging horses, splatting faces, vomiting blood, scythe-bearing chariots and the occasional limb flying around in what is, regrettably, a slightly comic fashion. The sequence has been filmed and edited so bewilderingly that it's impossible to work out what's going on unless you already know (the historian Arrian has the full story in his *Anabasis Alexandri*). 'Avenge this betrayal!' howls someone at some point. What betrayal? Then some more heads get torn off. Darius looks extra cross, so you may surmise that things aren't going well for the Achaemenid Empire.

People: Alexander heads east to Bactria, then south through the Hindu Kush to India. The story feels compressed, though the film isn't entirely to blame for that: Alexander certainly kept himself busy. On the other hand, it is to blame for depicting one of the greatest military commanders in history as a tedious, highly strung sex tourist with a crippling addiction to Sun-In. By the time he gets to India, Farrell's Alexander has grown long bleach-blonde locks and is wearing billowing shirts, chunky jewellery and heavy eyeliner. All he needs to do is bite the head off a bat and he would be a perfect replica of Ozzy Osbourne circa 1985.

More war: At the Battle of the Hydaspes, Alexander takes an arrow to the chest and nearly dies. The real Alexander was not wounded at the Hydaspes. The scene has been borrowed from the later siege of what is now Multan in Pakistan, when an arrow that pierced Alexander's breastplate punctured his lung. This prompts Stone to film the rest of the battle in a crimson tint (it's like blood, do you see?), which is both nasty and confusing to look at, effectively throwing away what must have been a lot of expensive shots of charging elephants. You wouldn't necessarily know it from the movie, but Alexander won at the Hydaspes. It's hard to care. This is a masterclass in how to make one of the most interesting characters in history seem trivial and boring.

Verdict: The real Alexander conquered Turkey. Oliver Stone just made one.

About a century after Alexander came Asoka, who conquered a massive swathe of central and south Asia. He hasn't come in for the Hollywood treatment yet, but his story is tempting material for Indian filmmakers. In China, the third century BCE saw the end of the 'warring states' period and beginning of the Qin dynasty, which has been depicted in films like Zhang Yimou's gorgeous *Hero* (2004) and Chen Kaige's *The Emperor and the Assassin* (1998).

230 BCE

Asoka (2001)

Director: Santosh Sivan • Entertainment grade: C • History grade: B–

Asoka the Great was a Mauryan emperor, ruling from Magadha (modern-day Bihar, India) in the third century BCE. His territory stretched to the borders of modern Iran in the north-west, and to Tamil Nadu in the south. Following his victory in the Kalinga War, Asoka converted to Buddhism, and dedicated the rest of his reign to creating a tolerant, just and peaceful society.

Intrigue: Prince Asoka (Shah Rukh Khan) defeats a revolt in Taxila by rolling flaming logs down a hillside at the rebels. Afterwards, he is obliged to go into hiding, and hacks off his long, straggly hair with a rough dagger. This allows the third century BCE emperor to sport an immaculately gelled quiff, suspiciously similar to the look popularized by Shah Rukh Khan in 2001.

Romance: Disguised as Pawan, an ordinary soldier, Asoka spots the runaway Princess Kaurwaki of Kalinga (Kareena Kapoor) singing and gyrating on a nearby hillside. She skips girlishly into a waterfall. Their eyes meet shyly across a rock pool. Okay, this may all be a bit daft, but it's still nowhere near as inaccurate as *Braveheart*. The legendary Kaurwaki was a fisherman's daughter rather than an undercover warrior princess, but the screenplay does allude to that.

Dialogue: Leaving a tavern: 'You take over the bullock cart. It's dangerous to drink and ride.'

War: When his mother is murdered, Asoka turns into Chandasoka (Evil Asoka). He massacres his brothers, seizes the throne, and then brutally conquers most of south Asia, because he's in a really bad mood. In Kalinga – which the film bizarrely suggests is a 'democracy' – Kaurwaki is horrified. Not knowing that Chandasoka is her Pawan, she leads Kalinga's army into battle against him. By this time, Asoka is trying to cure his blackened heart with spa treatments, and spends most of the rest of the film getting in and out of hot tubs while flexing his pecs.

Religion: After the final battle, Asoka suddenly recognizes Kaurwaki's horse. Frantically searching for her on the battlefield amid sobbing widows and rotting corpses, the realization dawns on him that his behaviour has been rather a poor show. He spots an old Buddhist monk wading through the puddles of gore, and it is left to the end titles to inform us that at this point Asoka sorted his life out and did some things that weren't completely awful. Apart from the role of Kaurwaki and a gooey coating of melodrama, this moment of conversion is commendably faithful to the real Asoka's account.

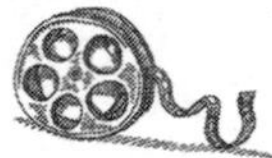

Cinema loves the Romans, who feature in many of the so-called 'swords and sandals' or 'peplum' films produced by their descendants, the Italians, in the 1950s and 1960s. This is where spaghetti western director Sergio Leone first made his name, directing *The Last Days of Pompeii* (1959), from a much-adapted novel by Edward Bulwer-Lytton, and the slightly pre-Roman *The Colossus of Rhodes* (1961), as well as assistant directing on Hollywood productions *Quo Vadis* (1951) and *Ben-Hur* (1959).

Popular themes in Roman movies, historical or fictional, were decadence, revolts and gladiators – providing excuses for well-muscled Hollywood stars to pose wearing only the aforementioned scanty peplum. Consequently, many of these films went on to become gay classics. Combining all three popular themes with ample opportunity for not-especially subtle homosexual subtext was the real-life story of Spartacus, a Thracian slave who led a revolt against the Roman Republic from 73–71 BC, known as the Third Servile War.

71 BCE

Spartacus (1960)

Director: Stanley Kubrick • Entertainment grade: A– • History grade: C+

People: Slaving away in a mine, Spartacus (Kirk Douglas) gets cross and bites a Roman on the ankle. He is sentenced to be tied to a rock until he dies. 'Oh, what a pity,' coos Peter Ustinov, swanning on as camp gladiator dealer Lentulus Batiatus. He gives Spartacus the once-over. 'You smell like a rhinoceros,' he adds. This must be an advantage: he buys him immediately. The real Spartacus was a soldier in the Roman army before being made a prisoner. He became a slave, and was sold as a gladiator. This is approximately the plot of *Gladiator*, which is not about Spartacus. Whereas this film *is* about Spartacus, but does not have that plot. Instead, it claims that Spartacus was born into slavery, and even at one point has him state that his father and grandfather were slaves. Nothing is known of Spartacus's family – nor of any love interest, though of course the film invents one.

Society: Spartacus is training as a gladiator in Capua when some rich kids turn up from Rome, led by Marcus Licinius Crassus (Laurence Olivier). Crassus offers 25,000 sestertii to watch something gnarly. Batiatus lets them select their gladiators. It's like one of those gimmicky fish restaurants where you choose your lobster, only with human beings. 'I want the most beautiful,' says Claudia. 'I'll take the big black one.' Helena obviously prefers hers coated in the Roman Republic's entire supply of bronzer, for she picks Spartacus. Batiatus looks irritated. 'Our choosings bore you?' Helena asks. 'No no, most exciting,' Batiatus replies caustically. 'I tingle.' By this point, Ustinov is well on course to steal the show. Poor Laurence Oliver, doing his best to project thinly iced evil as Crassus, doesn't stand a chance. The film's suggestion that Crassus engaged Spartacus as a gladiator is fiction – though ancient historian Plutarch agrees that Batiatus was a cruel master, and that the slave rebellion began in the gladiator school kitchen. In the next scene, it does begin exactly there, complete with Romans being pelted with pots, thrown into the impluvium, and drowned in vats of baked beans.

Politics: The escaped rebels have a fine old time looting on the escarpments of Vesuvius, but Spartacus wants to turn them into a guerrilla force and liberate Europe: 'We'll free every slave in every town and village!' It's true that Spartacus recruited huge numbers of slaves – conservative estimates suggest 90,000. And yet, though he has been seized upon by everyone from Karl Marx to, well, Kirk Douglas as an icon of freedom, there is no evidence that Spartacus planned a social revolution, nor even to end slavery. Meanwhile, Crassus attempts to seduce his own slave, Antoninus (Tony Curtis), with a creepy metaphor about whether he prefers eating oysters or eating snails. Antoninus is so grossed out that he joins the revolt. This scene – historically baseless, but cinematically remarkable – was cut from the original release. When it was restored in the 1990s the audio had been lost, so the lines had to be redubbed by an ageing Tony Curtis, and by Anthony Hopkins doing his best impression of the by-then-deceased Laurence Olivier.

War: The Third Servile War has been simplified, but the impression given of the politics behind it and of the campaign itself is reasonably accurate. The battles are outstanding. In victory, Crassus demands to know which of the captured slaves is Spartacus. They all stand up, shouting, 'I'm Spartacus!' Sadly, this is not true. Spartacus was never captured. He was killed in battle with a spear through his thigh, stranded in the middle of Roman forces by his fleeing comrades.

One of the most compelling stories of the ancient world is that of Egypt's Queen Cleopatra, lover of Julius Caesar and Marc Antony. Hollywood's interpretations owe much to William Shakespeare's *Julius Caesar* (1599) and *Antony and Cleopatra* (c. 1606–7), both of which draw on Plutarch's *Lives of the Noble Greeks and Romans.*

Though Cleopatra's African identity has often been asserted, hers is actually one of the few such cases where Hollywood may not be entirely wrong in casting actresses of European origin. Genetically, her father was entirely Greek: bred and indeed largely inbred (brother–sister marriages were the norm) down from one of Alexander the Great's Macedonian generals. Her mother is unknown to history.

Cleopatra has been played by international leading ladies such as Theda Bara (*Cleopatra*, 1917), Claudette Colbert (*Cleopatra*, 1934), Vivien Leigh (*Caesar and Cleopatra*, 1945), Amanda Barrie (*Carry On Cleo*, 1964) and Monica Bellucci (*Asterix and Obelix: Mission Cleopatra*, 2002). The most famous, of course, is...

30 BCE

Cleopatra (1963)

Director: Joseph L. Mankiewicz • Entertainment grade: C+ • History grade: A–

People: The film begins with Julius Caesar (Rex Harrison) defeating Pompey and travelling to Egypt. The boy pharaoh, Ptolemy XIII, gives Caesar Pompey's signet ring, together with a big jar containing the rest of Pompey. Caesar is totally squicked out. Ptolemy's estranged sister and co-regent, Cleopatra (Elizabeth Taylor), gives the Roman leader a better gift: herself, wrapped up in a rug. This story comes from Plutarch. Spying on Caesar afterwards, Cleopatra sees him suffer what the ancients called 'the falling sickness': an epileptic fit. This comes from Suetonius. These filmmakers have really done their research.

Grooming: In the same paragraph, Suetonius tells us that Caesar 'was so nice in the care of his person, that he not only kept the hair of his head closely cut and had his face smoothly shaved, but even caused the hair on other parts of the body to be plucked out by the roots, a practice for which some persons rallied him'.

Julius Caesar: fully waxed. Not enough is shown of Rex Harrison to verify whether the notoriously perfectionist director, Joseph L. Mankiewicz, splurged some of the film's $44 million budget (equivalent to well over $300 million today) on this historical detail.

Casting: Elizabeth Taylor is a knockout as Cleopatra. Admittedly, her styling owes as much to the 1960s as the first century BCE: the real Cleopatra is said to have drunk a pearl dissolved in vinegar, but pearlized eyeshadow was not invented until the twentieth century. Her arrival in Rome is sensationally staged, with dozens of horses, African dancers, the ceremonial opening of dove-filled pyramids, a burlesque performer with jewelled nipples, and Cleopatra herself bedecked in gold, nestled between the paws of a colossal sphinx. Some of the distinction is blurred between Caesar's palace in ancient Rome and Caesar's Palace in Las Vegas, but the message is clear. This was a lady who liked attention. Despite all her smouldering, there is a complete absence of sexual tension between Taylor and Harrison, which leaves the first half of the film feeling rather less passionate than it should be.

Style: By contrast, there is nothing but sexual tension between Taylor and Richard Burton, playing Mark Antony. Though they were both married to other people at the time, the two stars famously became a real-life couple. This produces an electric onscreen romance, despite Mark Antony's disturbing penchant for miniskirts (you'd be able to tell if he was the one obsessed with waxing). Undeterred, Cleopatra turns up to meet him in her 250 ft gold barge, complete with women strewing rose petals from the prow, a shoal of naked boys swimming in the wake, and

Twentieth Century Fox's money pouring out of the bilge pumps. Antony dons a special leopardskin miniskirt for the occasion. 'I find what you're wearing most becoming,' Cleopatra purrs. 'Greek, isn't it?' He replies: 'I have a fondness for almost all Greek things.' Which is a total set-up of a line, but it's worth it to let her say: 'As an almost all Greek thing, I am flattered.'

War: At the Battle of Actium, Antony sees Cleopatra sailing off. Blinded by love, he ditches the war and speeds off after her. It might seem too melodramatic to be true – but it is, according to Plutarch: 'For no sooner did he see her ship sailing off than he forgot everything else, betrayed and ran away from those who were fighting and dying in his cause, got into a five-oared galley… and hastened after the woman who had already ruined him and would make his ruin still more complete.' The film recreates this perfectly, right down to the five-oared galley. Unfortunately, in accurately portraying Antony's subsequent torpor, its pace slumps, and the four-hour-plus run-time starts to grate. If it had been an hour shorter and more consistently lively, this could have been a straight-A historical movie.

Another handy thing about the Romans, as far as filmmakers are concerned, is that they overlap with Jesus of Nazareth. Most Christian denominations encourage, rather than disapprove of, images of the man they consider to have been the son of God. The movie industry has obliged, with depictions of Jesus on film dating back to the nineteenth century. Many of these are extremely respectful and clearly aimed at a Christian audience.

A few are less orthodox and have proved controversial, notably Monty Python's *The Life of Brian* (1979) and Martin Scorsese's *The Last Temptation of Christ* (1988). When the latter opened in Paris, terrorists aligned to Christian fundamentalism and the far-right Front National firebombed a cinema. Thirteen people were injured.

29 CE

The Greatest Story Ever Told (1965)

Director: George Stevens • Entertainment grade: E • History grade: C

Violence: Told by three magi that a new king has been born in Bethlehem, King Herod the Great orders a massacre of local children. This massacre appears only in Matthew's gospel and is not mentioned in any non-biblical sources, such as Josephus's *Antiquities of the Jews*, which details Herod's murderous record at some length. Even if the massacre did happen, the staging in this movie – black-clad horsemen charging with drawn spears on a playground full of wide-eyed infants – owes a lot more to Russian director Sergei Eisenstein than to the Bible.

Temptation: Jesus (Max von Sydow) survives the purge, and we rejoin him at the age of about thirty. Judging by the film's beautiful but distinctive locations, Jesus was by this point living in the southwestern United States. In Death Valley or, as traditionalists would have it, a desert somewhere in the Levant, Jesus is tempted by a mean old hermit (Donald Pleasence). 'How'd you like to be the ruler of all this, hmm?' the hermit asks, indicating the Californian landscape.

Miracles: Jesus heals a few of the sick, but the supernatural side of the miracles is played down. They're depicted as if they could be the result of his charisma. Lazarus is raised from the dead in long shot, so you can't really see what's going on. The feeding of the 5,000 and turning water into wine are mentioned, but not seen. 'The next thing we know, they'll be calling him the Messiah,' complains a Jewish leader. 'And that's not all.' 'What else?' asks Pontius Pilate. 'He walked on water.' 'Get out!' Historically speaking, there's no independent evidence for the miracles, so fair enough. Still, if the director was concerned about excluding the sceptical audience, you've got to wonder why he bothered at all. Because, if you don't go in for God, this is just three hours of the musings of a first-century Middle Eastern hippie. A few whizz-bangs might have livened things up.

Casting: When *The Greatest Story Ever Told* was released, there was criticism of its parade of intrusive cameos by famous actors. These days, only obsessive film buffs will be gasping, 'Isn't that Joseph Schildkraut playing Nicodemus?' Some appearances still raise a giggle, including Charlton Heston as a shouty and bouffanted John the Baptist, Telly Savalas as Pontius Pilate (he was cast as Kojak years after making this film, but it's nonetheless difficult to watch without expecting him to drawl to Barabbas: 'Who loves ya, baby?'), and, infamously, John Wayne as the centurion at the crucifixion. Grimly clutching a wooden sword, Wayne deadpans: 'Truly, he was the Saaahn of Gaaaahd.' It's not an ideal moment to have the audience hooting with laughter. But, truly, only the Son of God could keep a straight face.

29 CE

Ben-Hur: A Tale of the Christ (1959)

Director: William Wyler • Entertainment grade: B– • History grade: C

Religion: American Civil War general Lew Wallace wrote his epic *Ben-Hur* in 1880. To the modern reader its appeal may be difficult to unlock, but this pious, turgid and contrived novel was a massive bestseller. Despite the subtitle, *A Tale of the Christ*, Jesus of Nazareth is an incidental character. The film's director, William Wyler, avoids showing his face. 'The Christian world would not tolerate a novel with Jesus Christ its hero, and I knew it,' Lew Wallace wrote in his 1906 autobiography. 'He should not be present as an actor in any scene of my creation.' Wyler obeyed.

Politics: Judah Ben-Hur (Charlton Heston) is a fictional Jewish prince living in Jerusalem. He was a childhood friend of Messala (Stephen Boyd), the new Roman tribune. It all goes wrong when Messala tries to persuade Ben-Hur to inform on anti-Roman Jews. 'I would do anything for you except betray my own people,'

Ben-Hur replies. Historically, it's true that there were tensions between Romans and Jews, but the two most interesting things going on in this scene (which doesn't appear in the novel) are about the 1950s, not the first century. First, the talk of informing is a swipe at McCarthyism, which had menaced Hollywood through much of the decade. Second, it's kind of gay. Gore Vidal, who wrote a draft of the screenplay, claimed to have envisaged a backstory in which Ben-Hur and Messala were lovers. This, then, is their breakup. 'You're either for me or against me,' Messala tells Ben-Hur. 'Then I am against you,' says Ben-Hur. Messala just about resists the urge to press himself literally against him. According to Vidal, Boyd faithfully acted this as a love scene. Heston, less cosmopolitan, was not told what was going on.

Slavery: When Ben-Hur is falsely accused of throwing a roof tile at Valerius Gratus, he is sentenced to slavery in the galleys. This is one of the film's (and the book's) biggest blunders. Galley slavery was hardly known in the Roman Empire, and there are no records of it being used as a punishment. Not least, this was because most Roman galleys – including the *triremes* shown here – required skilled rowers. The only substantial Roman use of galley slaves was recorded in the Second Punic War, over 200 years before this movie is set. During that war, the Romans used the *quinquereme*, which had five men to an oar. Only one had to be a professional. The rest merely added muscle. During the first century BCE, Roman general Sextus Pompey and Emperor Augustus did recruit slaves to their ships – but these men were freed first, then took the job by choice. Chained convicts enslaved as rowers are a modern phenomenon, first reliably recorded in 1443 when King Charles VII of France licensed a shipping magnate to press gang vagabonds into his private fleet.

Sport: More than half a century after it was made, *Ben-Hur*'s chariot race remains one of the most stunning action sequences ever shot. Legend has it that a stuntman was killed on set. Legend is wrong. Charlton Heston's stunt double, Joe Canutt, was accidentally thrown during a chariot crash. The extent of his injuries was a cut on his chin. Chariot racing is Ben-Hur's route back to riches, and at least this is plausible. Recent research claims that charioteers were the highest-paid sportsmen in the whole of history, making Tiger Woods and David Beckham look like paupers. One charioteer in the second century won almost 36 million sestertii during his career – which the research playfully (and tenuously) suggests is equivalent to US $15 billion today.

29 CE

The Passion of the Christ (2004)

Director: Mel Gibson • Entertainment grade: Fail • History grade: D–

Technology: Jesus (Jim Caviezel) is with his mother Mary (Maia Morgenstern). Being a carpenter, he is building a dining table. Mary comments that it is too tall, and people will have to eat standing up. He replies that he is going to make chairs. 'This will never catch on,' she mutters. Right, so Jesus isn't just *building* a dining table; he has *invented* the dining table. Not generally counted among his achievements: brought good news to the world, died for our sins, innovated in the field of home furnishings. Also, there is quite a lot of evidence for dining tables existing before Jesus.

Justice: Jesus is taken before the Sanhedrin, the Jewish court. *The Passion of the Christ* depicts the Jews as bloodthirsty savages. They bay for Jesus's execution, crying: 'His blood be on us and our children!' Following complaints that this was anti-Semitic, Gibson cut the line. 'I wanted it in,' he was reported as saying. 'But, man, if I included that in there, they'd be coming after me at my house. They'd come to kill me.' The ambiguous use of 'they' in this context did little to reassure his critics. Moreover, according to the late Geza Vermes, professor of Jewish studies at Oxford, the line persists in the final cut in spoken Aramaic. It is only the English subtitle that has been removed.

More justice: Pontius Pilate, the Roman leader, is portrayed here as a decent man trying to restrain the Jews. Philo and Josephus, two non-biblical historians of the first century, both condemn Pilate as an intolerant and arbitrary tyrant. From a historical perspective, the moderation ascribed to Pilate in the gospels – much enlarged upon by this film – was probably related to the fact it suited the Christian movement at the time of their writing to butter up the Romans. The Catholic Church is among those that have publicly denounced the interpretation that the Jews were responsible for Jesus's death.

Violence: Cackling Romans reveal an array of torture implements. What follows is filmed with unflinching – it's tempting to say psychotic – focus. There is no evidence for Jesus's torture by the Romans other than that in the gospels. Matthew, Mark and John all say simply that he was 'flogged'; Luke says that Pilate offered to punish him and release him, but ended up handing him over to the priests instead. The gospels mainly relate Jesus's teaching, and make only a fleeting mention of Jesus's torture. In this film, the proportions are reversed. It is not a historian's job to interpret scriptures except as historical documents; but, in this one's opinion, two hours of watching imaginative and grotesque mutilations being inflicted on a human being in flesh-ripping, blood-spraying close-up is not spiritually uplifting. Hey, whatever floats your boat. Though, if this does, maybe you should see a psychiatrist.

Family: Afterwards, the bleeding Jesus carries his cross to Calvary, complete with a whole load more tortures. His mother, Mary, sees him fall, and has a flashback to her life with him as a child. The child falls. She runs to pick him up. Back in the now, she runs similarly to her adult son. 'See, Mother, I make all things new,' he says (a line from the Book of Revelation). Corny, perhaps, but it's the one part of the film that this viewer found moving rather than horrendous. Not coincidentally, it's also the only moment in which Jesus is shown as a person with meaningful human relationships, and the only moment in which any sense is made of his sacrifice.

The Roman Empire reached its greatest extent in around 117 CE, under the Emperor Trajan. It became Christian under the Emperor Constantine in the fourth century CE. Filmmakers have found a few stories to tell in the imperial period, including, notoriously, *Caligula* (1979). This drama about the first-century emperor Gaius Julius Caesar Augustus Germanicus, better known as Caligula, had a split personality. Writer Gore Vidal and a highbrow cast (including Malcolm McDowell, Helen Mirren, Sir John Gielgud and Peter O'Toole) pitched it as a serious film; producer Bob Guccione, the owner of *Penthouse* magazine, insisted that hardcore pornographic scenes be added in. Various cuts of the film have been released and banned ever since.

This was also the period of Roman rule in Britain. Iceni queen Boudicca (also known by several alternative spellings, including Boadicea) has prompted a couple of British films – *Boadicea* (1928), written by Anthony Asquith and starring Phyllis Neilson-Terry, and *Boudica: Warrior Queen* (2003), made originally for television and starring Alex Kingston. Michael Fassbender starred in *Centurion* (2010), a thoroughly silly account of the disappearance of the Roman army's Legio IX Hispana in Britain in the second century CE, complete with Picts restyled as gothic-ninja babes.

The Roman Empire's gradual decline, combined with its military overextension into the grittier and less welcoming parts of Europe (like Britain), has also been the inspiration for various soldier films. The greatest among them in recent years was this winner of five Oscars (out of twelve nominations), including Best Picture:

180 CE

Gladiator (2000)

Director: Ridley Scott • Entertainment grade: A • History grade: C

War: It's 180 CE in Germania, and the nearly dead Emperor Marcus Aurelius is watching his army lay waste to the barbarians. His fictional general, Maximus (Crowe), clunks on to the screen in armour and wolfskins, growling: 'On my signal, unleash hell.' A moderately credible battle follows.

Politics: After the victory, Marcus Aurelius takes Maximus aside and offers to leave him the empire, disinheriting his nasty son, Commodus (Joaquin Phoenix). Some sources do suggest that Marcus Aurelius had doubts about his successor, but the film's claim that he wanted instead to revive the republic and make Rome democratic is more twenty-first century than second century.

People: Aside from various plot-facilitating errors (his reign of twelve years is elided into what seems like a couple of weeks), the main problem with *Gladiator*'s Commodus is that he's nowhere near bad enough. The real Commodus's pastimes included herding women, snogging men, killing rare animals, cross-dressing, boozing, coprophagy, being afraid of hairdressers, feeding his guards poisoned figs, and forcing people to beat themselves to death with pine cones. Despite, or perhaps because of, all this, he was popular with the people and the army alike. Phoenix's Commodus is a lightweight, indulging in little more than mild incest and the occasional bout of sneering. And patricide. Historian Cassius Dio, who knew Commodus personally, recorded that Marcus Aurelius was murdered by his doctors so that Commodus could become emperor.

Slavery: Following Commodus's coup, his guards bungle an attempt to bump Maximus off. Maximus escapes and rides back to his home in Hispania to find his family crucified by Commodus's agents. Exhausted and wounded, he collapses in the dust, whence he is abducted by slave traders. Considering that around a quarter of the empire's population was enslaved at this point, why would Mauritanian slavers be wandering around rural Hispania looking for half-dead men who need to be nursed gently back to health? Oh, these must be the *nice* slave traders.

Violence: Maximus is sold to a gladiatorial impresario, and director Ridley Scott doesn't flinch from spilling the guts of life in the arena. He allows the audience to retain its superiority about how sick the Romans must have been to watch people being stabbed with a trident, sliced in half by a scythed chariot, or socked in the face with a spiked ball flail for entertainment, while simultaneously watching exactly that for entertainment.

Death: Finally, Commodus and Maximus come face to face in the Flavian Amphitheatre. The real Commodus fought in gladiatorial events several hundred times, but was strangled in his bath by a hired wrestler called Narcissus. Apparently that name, which appeared in early drafts of the script, seemed a tad too fey for Crowe's character.

Verdict: Combining the stories of Spartacus and Commodus makes for an atmospheric film, so long as its implicit claims of authenticity don't lull you into, say, basing a piece of coursework on it. If you do, the examination board might beat you to death with a pine cone. Or just fail you.

2

Middle Ages Spread

The millennium between the fall of the Roman Empire in the fourth to fifth centuries and the beginning of the Italian Renaissance in the fourteenth century has been roundly dissed in European history. It is sometimes called the Dark Ages, implying its lack of intellectual distinction and general grimness, and more commonly as the Middle Ages, implying it fell between two more worthwhile things.

Cinema tends to have followed suit: there aren't many films about the Dark Ages. One character who does crop up occasionally is Attila, the ruler of the Huns from 434–435. There were two Attila the Hun movies in 1954: he was played by Anthony Quinn in the Italian-French co-production *Attila*, opposite Sophia Loren as the Emperor Valentinian's sister Honoria, and by Jack Palance in Hollywood's *Sign of the Pagan*.

Circa 430

Attila (2001)

Director: Dick Lowry • Entertainment grade: C– • History grade: C

Culture: Little is known of the Huns, but it's a pleasant surprise to find that the filmmakers have cast their eyes over what information exists. In an early scene, the young Attila correctly identifies the Huns' sacred animals as the wolverine, the she-bear and the horse. Later, his court is depicted in line with the description by the historian Priscus, who saw it with his own eyes.

Technology: Attila (Gerard Butler) falls for a comely ginger slave-girl, and she for him. But his jealous elder brother, Bleda, takes her for his concubine. An irritating witch covered in mud and sticks offers the slave-girl a solution: 'These seeds. Swallow one every day. They will keep little Bledas out of your womb.' Now, just hold on a minute. The ginger slave-girl isn't real, but lots of historical films invent romances. The irritating witch isn't real, but Huns did have prophetic priests. But you can't just go around inventing birth control pills in the fifth century to fill a hole in your plot. Had easy, safe, reliable contraception existed for the last 1600 years, the entire history of the world might have been different.

Romance: Attila strops off to Rome, which is full of hot babes stripping off at imaginatively depicted orgies. Enter Honoria, sister of the third Emperor Valentinian, clad in an improbable iridescent turquoise corset and matching skirt split from ankle to bikini line. She shows Attila her bath. He's totally freaked out. Later, he complains to an aide: 'We conquer cities, we rule the world, and yet we can't even build a bath.' Honoria is too polite to point out that this was no doubt obvious the minute he walked in the door, and – after a quick wash – seduces him. In real life, Attila never visited Rome, nor met Honoria. And he did have a bath.

War: Honoria is discovered in bed with her chamberlain, Eugenius, with whom she is plotting to kill her brother. The emperor exiles her to a convent in Constantinople. To escape, Honoria secretly sends a ring to Attila, proposing marriage. He accepts, and promptly invades the Roman Empire, half of which he claims as a dowry. Amazingly, this is pretty much what really happened. The chronology was different in real life, and the film misses out a few twists, including Honoria's forced betrothal to a senator. Still, it is basically justified in portraying fifth-century European history as a kind of high-velocity mash-up of *Sunset Beach* and *Rambo*. The truth is cracking stuff.

Battle: Finally, we get the Battle of the Catalaunian Fields – sometimes described as one of the most significant in history, despite its unclear outcome. It's even more of a muddle in the film, unless you already know your Visigoths from your Ostrogoths, and your Huns from your Alans. It was famously violent. The great historian Edward Gibbon quotes a death toll of between 162,000 and 300,000. The Roman writer Jordanes says a stream was swollen with the blood of the fallen, and 'those whose wounds drove them to slake their parching thirst drank water mixed with gore'. The film's budget isn't up to this, so we get some cheapo fireballs and two dozen extras lying around on a hillside, vaguely pretending to be dead.

Verdict: *Attila* gets a bit silly in places, but the research behind it is actually quite credible. Which is more than can be said for Gerard Butler's wig.

The Huns, or some version of them, also crop up in Disney's animated film *Mulan*, set in fifth-century China.

Circa 450

Mulan (1998)

Director: Tony Bancroft and Barry Cook • Entertainment grade: B+ • History grade: E

People: Young Mulan is too clumsy to qualify as a decent potential bride, even after a makeover song. But her father stops obsessing about that when he is called up to serve in the Chinese army against an invasion. Mulan disguises herself as a man to go in her father's place. So far, so accurate to the *Ballad of Mulan*, a poem first recorded in the sixth century, that is the only real evidence for Mulan's existence. Researchers have tended to identify Mulan with the Northern Wei dynasty, probably during the fifth or sixth century, when its territory was frequently invaded.

War: Speaking of frequent invasions, a whole load of foreigners swarm over the Great Wall of China. These are identified as the Huns. Attila may have been contemporary with Mulan, if she existed. But the eastern limit of his territory was around the Caucasus, 3000 miles from Northern Wei territory, and the thrust of his military efforts was westwards into Europe, not eastwards to China. So this isn't Attila. Some scholars think the Huns were linked with the Xiongnu, a central Asian tribal confederacy that did go to war frequently with the Han dynasty of China in the third century. But that was at least a couple of hundred years before Mulan's time, and in any case the link between the Xiongnu and the Huns is disputed.

Race: Disney's Huns are a bunch of evil-looking semi-monsters with handlebar moustaches. Their leader, Shan Yu, has sunken yellow eyes, vampire teeth and massive claws. And to think they wasted the makeover song on Mulan. The movie's Shan Yu is more or less fictional. There was a famous Chinese warrior called Xiang Yu who went to war with the Han emperor in the third century, but he wasn't a Hun. Or a Xiongnu. This is a right mess.

Violence: Meanwhile, Mulan herself gets made over again as a soldier, and with the other troops goes to face the Hun army. This puts the film in a quandary, for war notoriously involves violence and death. Disney princesses sing nice songs to woodland creatures and tidy up cottages for dwarves. Disney princesses do not whip out swords and hack people to death in a frenzied bloodlust, leaving severed limbs and straggly entrails all over the place. Gingerly, the film attempts to tread a middle path, implying that Mulan annihilates most of the Hun army by causing an avalanche, and having her despatch Shan Yu with a load of fireworks. Pretty. But still technically killing. 'My little baby, off to destroy people,' sighs her talking dragon happily. The *Ballad of Mulan* doesn't go in for visceral descriptions, but it does mention that Mulan travelled 10,000 miles in the service of war, that she was away for ten years, and that 100 battles were fought. It's a stretch to imagine she pulled this off without hacking at least a few people to death. There were no talking dragons, either.

Verdict: There is little historical evidence on Mulan and her time, but this film has managed to make a complete hash of it anyway. Still, as Disney princesses go, Mulan herself is great. If a dwarf asked her to tidy his cottage, she'd probably burn it down.

The most popular figure of the Dark Ages as far as cinema is concerned is King Arthur. Arthur is thought to have been king of the Britons in the fifth or sixth century, if he existed. Some historians think he was a real king (or composite of kings) whose exploits were embroidered with supernatural folklore. Others argue that there is no real evidence for his existence at all. He first came to prominence in the history of Geoffrey of Monmouth, written in the twelfth century. Arthurian movies often focus on the love triangle between Arthur, his queen Guinevere and his knight Lancelot.

Screen versions have included *First Knight* (1995), with Sean Connery as Arthur, Richard Gere as Lancelot and Julia Ormond as Guinevere; *Excalibur* (1981), with Nigel Terry as Arthur and Helen Mirren as the witch Morgan le Fay; and *Knights of the Round Table* (1953), with Mel Ferrer as Arthur and Robert Taylor as Lancelot fighting it out over Ava Gardner as Guinevere. A 2004 version titled *King Arthur*, with Clive Owen as Arthur and Keira Knightley as Guinevere, claimed puffily to be based on historical consensus and 'recently discovered archaeological evidence'. This was nonsense, and seemed to mean the filmmakers had just removed all the fun bits. There is no point making an audience slog through the purported true story behind the Arthurian legend when there may be no true story behind the Arthurian legend.

Medieval historians, like most people, are generally far more delighted by *Monty Python and the Holy Grail* (1975), which is full of well-researched Arthurian in-jokes and is a total riot. Or, if you want something even sillier...

Circa 500

Camelot (1967)

Director: Joshua Logan • Entertainment grade: Fail • History grade: E

People: The early Middle Ages didn't leave many written sources, and those that mention Arthur vary from the reasonably credible to the flagrantly weird. He is supposed to have defeated the Anglo-Saxons at the Battle of Mons Badonicus in around 500; to have gone to Jerusalem to find relics, or in later stories the Holy Grail itself; and to have battled giants, witches and the Cath Palug, a knight-eating cat-monster that lived on the Isle of Anglesey. Camelot opts for having Arthur (Richard Harris) skip through an icy forest on a soundstage, clinging to fairylit boughs and singing about being scared of girls. Guinevere (Vanessa Redgrave) rolls up in the Snow Queen's carriage, trilling about the simple joys of maidenhood. Arthur falls out of his sparkly tree on to her. He blanches at her forthright suggestion that he give her a good ravishing, and instead burbles something about a pink castle and the nice weather. Is this supposed to be valiant King Arthur, slayer of cat-monsters, defender of the Holy Grail, vanquisher of the hairy Anglo-Saxon hordes? Perhaps he embarrassed them to death.

Society: For reasons unaccountable, Guinevere falls in love with Arthur. Developing a sudden passion for justice, he sets up a Round Table, and advertises for knights. Thousands of written manuscripts are scattered out of towers and from horseback, all across the land. Yes, thousands. The printing press did not arrive in Britain for another millennium, so Arthur's monks must have been slaving round the clock to illuminate all those. As they are strewn, the toiling peasants of the fields pick them up and give them a good read. So very literate, these sixth-century farmhands. It's amazing they didn't leave more written sources. Over in France, Lancelot (Franco Nero) catches one manuscript. This prompts him to take a short break from striding around his battlements showing everyone how great he is, in order to sing a song telling everyone how great he is. He's French, so it's called 'C'est Moi'.

Scandal: Nobody likes Lancelot, because he's a tool. Guinevere even sings about how much she hates him. Then she notices his strong jaw and blue eyes, and decides that no, actually, she's in love with him. Thanks to the conniving of Arthur's illegitimate son Mordred (David Hemmings, clad inexplicably in head-to-toe burgundy motorcycle leathers), the lovers are caught mid-tryst. Gallantly, Lancelot escapes, leaving Guinevere to be burned at the stake for adultery. Arthur can't pardon her, because he has spent the entire film wittering on about the sanctity of what he calls 'legal laws'. Silly man.

Mysticism: Camelot ditches most of the goblin and wizard stuff from the Arthurian legend, but keeps Merlin. In the absence of any magical element in the film, he functions instead as a sort of possibly imaginary confidant that no one else can see. The Mr Snuffleupagus to Arthur's Big Bird. Merlin exhorts Arthur to deal with his marital strife by imagining himself in the body of a creature. 'Think yourself a fish! Feel yourself a fish! Breathe with your gills! Now *be* a fish!' Honestly, this is no less daft than if they'd just gone with the cat-monster. At least being attacked by one of those would have forced this invertebrate Arthur to shape up. Or, if he didn't, he'd have been mauled to death by a cat-monster – and, a couple of hours into the run-time, historians might settle for that.

Vikings, Hollywood's next big obsession after King Arthur, were seafaring Norse traders and raiders who rampaged across Europe, north Africa and even into Asia between the eighth and eleventh centuries. In 1960, a Viking site dating back to around 1000 was discovered at L'Anse aux Meadows in Canada. This was one of the most remarkable archaeological discoveries in history, proving that the Vikings had travelled all the way to the Americas five hundred years before Christopher Columbus. In tribute, Hollywood offered *The Norseman* (1978), a pile of garbage starring Lee Majors, which was filmed rather unconvincingly 2,600 miles south of L'Anse aux Meadows in Florida's Hillsborough River State Park. Since it is hopelessly inaccurate and quite dull, anyone who manages to struggle through *The Norseman* may wish the director had just gone the whole hog and let a Viking wrestle an alligator. Or visit Disney World and get a princess makeover.

The film industry has often seemed like it couldn't care less whether its Vikings are realistic or not, chucking out such bizarre offerings as 1957's *The Saga of the Viking Women and Their Voyage to the Waters of the Great Sea Serpent* ('See the dance of desire, prelude to orgiastic revelries that only ancient civilizations knew!' gasped the trailer), and 2008's *Outlander*, in which a spaceship carrying an alien crashes in eighth-century Norway. The serious efforts aren't much better – though they are sometimes hilarious.

Circa 850

The Vikings (1958)

Director: Richard Fleischer • Entertainment grade: C+ • History grade: C–

Though Vikings are famous for rape, fire and pillage, carried out while wearing horned helmets and drinking mead out of skulls, revisionist historians insist that in reality the Vikings were neatly groomed economic opportunists and seafaring innovators. With no horny hats. Or skull mugs.

People: The film opens on an animated Bayeux tapestry (not strictly about the Vikings), followed by an immediate, full-blooded depiction of rape, fire and pillage. The characters and plot are extensively fictionalized, though they are based on a Norse saga about the possibly real eighth- or ninth-century Viking lord Ragnar Lodbrok and the probably real Northumbrian king Aella (died 867). The film centres around two fictional sons of Ragnar, the long-lost Eric (Tony Curtis) and the party-hearty Einar (Kirk Douglas). Einar sets the scene by romping around a Viking village, making out with a Scandinavian babe atop a heap of pelts while wenches brew ale in barrels the size of skips, hairy old men hurl axes at their wives, and small children run around wearing reindeer-skin nappies. It may be deduced that director Richard Fleischer's interest in revisionist history is minimal.

Details: One of the film's big surprises is that it actually looks quite good. Production design gets points for the fact that neither horned helmets nor drinking out of skulls is in evidence, though

Kirk Douglas does sport a fetching hat with a bronze hawk on it, and there is quite a lot of hardcore boozing from non-cranial vessels. The locations – including some lovely fjords – are spectacular, even if a pedant might point out that medieval castles weren't built in a ruined state. The longships look terrific, and there's a very authentic funeral to look forward to. Amid all the reasonably convincing costumes, though, Tony Curtis debuts wearing nothing but a buttock-skimming leather jerkin. Daring attire indeed for location shoots in the forests of the frozen north. Perhaps the costume department hated him. Historical research indicates that Vikings wore trousers.

Technology: Ninth-century navigation comes in for a lot of criticism in the film, for being based on astronomy. Fearless brutes they may be, but, as the Daleks were at first defeated by stairs, so the Vikings are defeated by fog. Fortunately, Eric has a deaf mute black friend (the film doesn't try too hard to explain his origins, but the Vikings did raid parts of north Africa), who turns up with what looks like a shark-shaped bottle opener on a string. It's supposed to be a compass, even though the existence of those in Europe is not recorded until 1190. Nor in the Arab world till the thirteenth century.

Violence: The famous scene in which Ragnar gets thrown into a pit of wolves is underwhelming for a modern audience: all you get is some offscreen growling and chomping. (The saga of Ragnar says he was thrown into a pit of vipers, not wolves – which might have been easier to stage, given a few bits of old hosepipe.) Far better is the sentencing of Tony Curtis to be eaten by crabs in a rock pool. You think they're joking, but no: there he is, still without his trousers, tethered to a post and being advanced upon by man-eating crustacea. Sadly, at the last minute, the film misses an opportunity to deal out an accurate demise to Aella, shoving him, too, into the wolf pit. In the saga – and those of a delicate constitution may want to skip the rest of this paragraph – Aella was killed by Ragnar's son in the style called the 'blood eagle'. This meant his ribs were broken away from his spine at the back and his lungs pulled out to resemble wings. Revisionist historians dispute the existence of this practice. On this point, at least, let's hope they're right.

An eleventh-century Spanish mercenary and military leader who flip-flopped between Christian and Muslim allegiances might not seem like made-for-Hollywood material. Yet Rodrigo Díaz, known as 'El Cid' from the Arabic sidi or sayyid, meaning 'The Lord', became one of the great epic heroes of cinema.

1080

El Cid (1961)

Director: Anthony Mann • Entertainment grade: A • History grade: D

War: In 1080, when this film begins, the territory that is now Spain and Portugal was split between Christian and Muslim kingdoms. Emir Ben Yussuf (Herbert Lom) rouses the Muslim princes of the southern part, known as al-Andalus, to conquer the Christian north, some of which is known as Leon-Castile. The film's Ben Yussuf is the historical Yusuf ibn Tashfin, commander of the Almoravid Empire. At his summons, Emir Yusuf al-Mutamin of Zaragoza (Douglas Wilmer) has a go at conquering part of Leon-Castile, but is captured by Rodrigo Díaz (Charlton Heston). When Díaz offers him freedom rather than death, al-Mutamin honours him with the name El Cid. According to the historical sources, al-Mutamin was not attempting to conquer Leon-Castile. His war was with his own brother and rival emir, Mundhir. Díaz and al-Mutamin are said to have become close when the former joined the latter's army as a mercenary in the early 1080s.

Love: Díaz's girlfriend, Jimena (Sophia Loren), is upset with him for killing her father. When he fights an Aragonese knight in an astonishingly good jousting scene (which took *El Cid*'s enormous cast and crew five weeks to film), Jimena gives her colours to his rival. The bubbling hatred between Díaz and Jimena onscreen is the stuff of historical fantasy, but it was real enough on set. At the beginning of filming, Heston heard a rumour that Loren was getting a $1 million paycheque – substantially larger than his. He was so angry that he refused even to look at her in most of their scenes. This soon becomes amusing for the viewer.

Politics: King Ferdinand the Great of Leon-Castile dies, and divides his lands between his children Sancho, Alfonso and Urraca. This really happened 15 years earlier in 1065, but the film has bodged around the timeline to heighten the drama. At the king's funeral, Sancho tries to kill Alfonso. Alfonso teams up with his sister Urraca, the two blonde siblings conspiring to reunite and rule the several kingdoms. They want gruff warrior Díaz on their side – but he won't do their bidding, for above all else he believes in honour. All Alfonso and Urraca would need to do is indulge in a spot of incest and we'd be in *Game of Thrones*, perhaps because medieval history is George R. R. Martin's source material. *El Cid*'s version of the warring heirs has elements of accuracy, though in real life Ferdinand made it even more complicated by having five children, all of whom variously went into battle against each other, allied with Muslim princes, had affairs with runaway Muslim princesses, hatched world-domination conspiracies, and assassinated each other. If a couple of dragons and some ice zombies turned up, they could hardly make the eleventh century more dramatic than it really was.

More war: Alfonso is defeated by Ben Yussuf at the battle of Sagrajas. Díaz saves the day for the Christians by taking Valencia – but Ben Yussuf turns his forces and besieges him there. The battle sequences along the beach to the castle of Valencia (represented on film by the thirteenth century castle of Peñíscola) are some of the most spectacular in Hollywood history. Spain's military dictator Francisco Franco, who flattered himself that he might be compared to the Cid when this movie came out, loaned the filmmakers 3,000 soldiers and 1,100 mounted police, plus their horses, to make up the eleventh-century armies.

Even more war: The result was sublime cinema and awful history. Díaz did not, as in the film, take Valencia by giving bread to its people. According to the *Historia Roderici*, written probably around the middle of the twelfth century, he ransacked surrounding villages, starved the city, 'took it by assault', and seized all its riches. Díaz did not offer Valencia's crown to Alfonso, but ruled there himself. He did not die in agony from an arrow wound sustained in the defence of the city, but in 1099 during peacetime from an unknown cause. Also, Yusuf ibn Tashfin was not defeated. He led the Almoravids to victory at Valencia in 1102, when he was a sprightly ninety-six years old.

In England, the later half of the twelfth century and beginning of the thirteenth was preposterously exciting, ruled as it was by the Plantagenets – a historical dynasty so dramatic, so obsessed with sex and violence, and so essentially human as to be far more compelling than anything Hollywood makes up. There was the conquering King Henry II and his brilliant, powerful wife Eleanor of Aquitaine, the murder of Thomas Becket, the crusades and kidnapping of Henry and Eleanor's son King Richard the Lionheart, the troubled reign of Richard's brother King John and the signing of Magna Carta – and, if you like your legends, Robin Hood.

British and American filmmakers have marauded around the period, creating some great dramas and comedies as well as quite a few awful ones. In 1964, Peter O'Toole played Henry II in *Becket* – and he was so good at it that he reprised the role four years later in one of the finest historical comedies and the greatest historical Christmas movie ever made, *The Lion in Winter*.

1170

Becket (1964)

Director: Peter Glenville • Entertainment grade: B– • History grade: D

Thomas Becket became chancellor to Henry II of England in 1155, and Archbishop of Canterbury in 1162. He fought bitterly with Henry over various legal issues. In 1170, he was murdered in Canterbury Cathedral.

People: Life at the court of King Henry is a circus of boozing and wenching, with Henry occasionally tearing himself away from the bedchamber to belch, shout at archbishops, complain about his sore bottom, and patronize Thomas Becket, whom he calls 'my little Saxon'. Henry and Becket go hunting, and stumble across a comely Saxon peasant girl. 'She stinks a bit, but we could wash her,' observes Henry. 'I fancy her,' says Becket. 'That's very tiresome of you,' replies Henry. 'I fancy her myself.' Grudgingly, he lets Becket take the girl; and, demonstrating his Saxon solidarity, Becket quietly lets her go without molestation. Which would be fine, only Thomas Becket was a Norman, just like Henry II. Writer Jean Anouilh knew this, but he thought Norman-Saxon tensions made a good story. They do, but so do cowboys in space or monkeys versus robots, either of which would be approximately as accurate here as making Thomas Becket a Saxon.

Technology: Becket mentions to Henry an exciting new invention: the fork. 'It's for pronging meat and carrying it to the mouth.' Henry's amazement is justified, for the fork did not actually arrive in England for over 400 years after his death. The only people using forks in the twelfth century were the Byzantines and a few Italians, and they were teased mercilessly for it. In the Middle Ages, real men ate with spoons.

Casting: Richard Burton, as Becket, delivers a performance that is subtle and restrained to the point of lulling the viewer into a gentle snooze. By contrast, Peter O'Toole as Henry II seems to have escaped from a pantomime, and leaps around the screen throwing tantrums and howling. 'I am the law!' he bellows, like a camp, medieval Judge Dredd. He is ridiculous, and brilliant. Moreover, the act is no less bizarre than historical descriptions of Henry, a colossal, passionate monster who was reported to get so angry that he would froth at the mouth, drop to the ground and start chomping furiously at bits of straw. In the middle of all this, John Gielgud wafts on as Louis VII of France, is arch, and wafts off again.

Family: Henry walks in on his children playing. 'Which one are you?' he asks the biggest, who replies, 'Henry III.' In fact, Henry III was Henry II's grandson, and also wasn't called Henry III until he actually became king. Henry II's home life with Eleanor of Aquitaine was dysfunctional: she led a rebellion against him, and he had her locked up. But one would think the real Eleanor could have zinged back snappier retorts than the wishy-washy ones in this film. 'You have never given me anything except your carping mediocrity!' Henry screams at her. 'I gave you my youth!' she cries, somewhat inaccurately, seeing as she married him at the grand old age of thirty, which in the twelfth century was virtually dead. 'I gave you your children!' He explodes with rage. 'I don't *like* my children!'

Violence: Fed up with his meddlesome priest, Henry expresses his frustration in front of four knights. They go to Canterbury Cathedral and do Becket to death in the middle of vespers. Edward Grim, one real-life witness, lived up to his name by describing at great length the precise appearance of bits of brain and blood all over the cathedral floor. The film's budget obviously didn't stretch to cutting Becket's head in half, and instead there are lots of unconvincing sideways shots of rubber swords being jabbed between arm and body.

1183

The Lion in Winter (1968)

Director: Anthony Harvey • Entertainment grade: A– • History grade: B

The Lion in Winter takes place at Chinon, a French residence of English king Henry II, over Christmas 1183. Henry's heir, Henry the Young King, had died just months before. His wife, Eleanor of Aquitaine, was his prisoner. Relations with his three remaining sons, Richard the Lionheart, John and Geoffrey, were on a knife edge.

People: The events shown did not actually take place at Chinon over Christmas 1183. The film elides a meeting of Henry with his sons at Angers earlier that year, with a summit between him and Philip II of France at Gisors on 6 December. Still, the prickly family Christmas is an event with which many in the audience will identify, though most families only plot each other's grisly demises as a whimsical fantasy. Not so the Plantagenets, who are ready and waiting with actual armies to take each other out if the division of the turkey (or the kingdom) goes the wrong way. Peter O'Toole gives the same performance as Henry II he gave in *Becket*, with the same delicious result. This time, though, an Eleanor of Aquitaine has been found to match him in the form of Katharine Hepburn. 'I haven't kept the great bitch in the keep for ten years out of passionate attachment,' growls Henry. 'I could peel you like a pear and God himself would call it justice!' bellows Eleanor.

Romance: Henry has decided to marry his young mistress, Alys Capet, to his drippiest son, John. Petulantly, Alys objects: 'I don't like your Johnny. He's got pimples and he smells of compost.' Goodness, you couldn't be that picky in the twelfth century. Everyone had pimples and smelled of compost.

Dialogue: James Goldman's screenplay, based on his own stage play, is rich with quotable lines. 'Henry's bed is his province,' Eleanor tells Alys. 'He can people it with sheep for all I care. Which, on occasion, he has done.' There is no strict documentary evidence for that assertion, but Henry was notoriously promiscuous. 'What shall we hang?' retorts Henry. 'The holly, or each other?'

More Romance: A plotting scene between the young Richard the Lionheart (Anthony Hopkins) and the young Philip II (Timothy Dalton) veers into heavy flirtation. 'I never wrote because I thought you'd never answer,' says Richard. 'You got married.'

'Does that make a difference?' asks Philip. 'Doesn't it?' replies Richard, and they clasp hands. The question of whether Richard and Philip really did have a sexual relationship is a good one to ask if you want to watch medieval historians fight to the death. Roger of Hoveden, a chronicler who crusaded with Richard and Philip, wrote of a love between the two so intense that 'at night their beds did not separate them'. Traditionalists argue that two princes sleeping in the same bed was merely a demonstration of diplomatic trust. Revisionists argue that the traditionalists are in denial, and that their argument is a historical version of 'This isn't what it looks like, darling – I can explain.'

Verdict: *The Lion in Winter* is laugh-out-loud funny, and credible enough in its history that all but the staunchest defenders of the Lionheart's alleged heterosexuality will be chuckling along.

A few crusader movies made it to the screen in the mid twentieth century. There was Cecil B. DeMille's *The Crusades* (1935), with Henry Wilcoxon as Richard the Lionheart and Loretta Young as Berengaria, and *King Richard and the Crusaders* (1954), with George Sanders. Just as British and American films tended to cast white actors as ancient Egyptians, the great Saracen hero Saladin was almost inevitably played by a white man: Ian Keith in *The Crusades*, and Rex Harrison in *King Richard and the Crusaders.*

1187

Kingdom of Heaven (2005)

Director: Ridley Scott • Entertainment grade: E • History grade: C–

Jerusalem fell to Saladin in 1187, the climax of the Saracen sultan's dramatic reconquest of the Holy Land from the Crusaders. Saladin's victory triggered the Third Crusade, led by Richard the Lionheart.

People: The film's hero, Balian (a disastrously miscast Orlando Bloom), is a composite of two real-life brothers, Balian and Baldwin of Ibelin. In 1184, he sails for the Holy Land, but a storm wrecks his ship. Washed up on a Syrian beach, he makes for a watering hole. Two Arabs ride up, and there's a macho standoff. This plotline has nothing to do with the Crusades, but it is stolen shamelessly from *Lawrence of Arabia*. Almost seven and a half centuries out.

Politics: In Jerusalem, King Baldwin IV (Edward Norton) is busy dying of leprosy. He's wearing a silver mask that makes him look a bit like the Green Goblin, but he can be forgiven that, because he reminisces correctly about his victory as a sixteen-year-old lad over Saladin's forces at the Battle of Montgisard.

War: Hawkish fundies Reynald de Châtillon and Guy de Lusignan try to start a war with the Saracens at Kerak. But it becomes a bit of a washout when the Green Goblin has a friendly chat with Saladin, and everyone decides to calm down and go home. If only more of the Crusades could have been settled with a friendly chat. The real Saladin backed down from a fight at Kerak because his armies were called away to defend Egypt. By this point, the movie is far too busy trying to draw tiresome parallels between Reynald de Châtillon and Donald Rumsfeld to show anything so interesting as an actual battle.

Dialogue: 'I once fought for two days with an arrow through my testicle.' A proud boast, but implausible. However badass twelfth-century warriors may have been, an arrow lodged in one's testicle from any angle makes it extremely difficult to walk.

Violence: Following the king's death, Guy accedes to the throne of Jerusalem. He meets Saladin to negotiate. Saladin offers him a cup of water filled with precious ice, which Guy dismissively hands to Reynald. 'I did not give you the cup,' snarls Saladin. He whips out a curved dagger and slashes Reynald's throat, spraying blood all over the tent. Factually, this scene is spot on. But the brief moment of genuine historical thrill does little to quicken the pulse. Even the actors look bored.

More war: As Saladin's forces assemble digitally outside Jerusalem, Balian rallies the inhabitants for a last stand. What isn't shown is that the real Balian of Ibelin only ended up in Jerusalem by mistake, while he was in the process of doing a runner. Far from being a hero, he tried to weasel out of defending the city. In the film, Balian and Saladin sort things out with another friendly chat. In reality, Balian's behaviour was disgraceful, threatening that he would murder 5,000 Muslim slaves and torch the Dome of the Rock and the Mosque al-Aqsa unless Saladin let him surrender.

Religion: Saladin enters Jerusalem and, walking through a church, picks up a fallen crucifix and reverently replaces it. Some western audiences scoffed, but this scene is justified. Saladin's victory is renowned as one of the most honourable in history.

Verdict: The Crusades were never this dull.

Along with the Third Crusade in movie tradition goes Robin Hood, Anglo-Saxon freedom fighter and merry outlaw who took from the rich to give to the poor. Though there are a number of candidates for a possibly real historical Robin Hood, and ballads about him existed at least since Tudor times, his Hollywood image owes much to Sir Walter Scott. Scott's novel *Ivanhoe*, published in 1820, created the image of Robin as a hearty patriot and associated him with Richard the Lionheart.

The first big Hollywood Robin was *Douglas Fairbanks is Robin Hood* (1922). This big-budget silent feature was the first film to have a Hollywood premiere (at Grauman's Egyptian Theater, built on Hollywood Boulevard that same year in a style popularized by the rediscovery of Tutankhamun's tomb). There followed *The Adventures of Robin Hood* (1938), with Errol Flynn swashbuckling in a bright-green tunic and tights; Walt Disney's *Robin Hood* (1973), in which our hero is depicted as a fox and Peter Ustinov voiced the lions representing Richard the Lionheart and Prince John; *Robin and Marian* (1976), with Sean Connery and Audrey Hepburn; and, of course, *Robin Hood: Prince of Thieves*, a movie inexplicably beloved by many people who were kids in the 1990s, which is actually unbelievably bad. Apart from Alan Rickman, obviously.

1194

Robin Hood: Prince of Thieves (1991)

Director: Kevin Reynolds • Entertainment grade: D+ • History grade: Fail

Geography: The gaffes start with the very first title card, which states that Richard the Lionheart led the Third Crusade to reclaim the Holy Land from the Turks. He'd have been a bit late. The Turks left a whole century earlier. By 1194 – when this film is set – the Holy Land was under the control of the Saracens. Before you know it, Robin of Loxley has escaped a Turkish (or possibly Saracen) jail, along with improbable Moorish sidekick Azeem. They arrive back at Dover, where Robin cheerfully proclaims that it will only take them until nightfall to walk to his father's castle. Even if you had a car, from Dover to Loxley would take you five hours. Robin and Azeem only have feet. Worse still, Robin takes the scenic route, via Hadrian's Wall – a diversion of another 300 miles.

Technology: Scanning the horizon, Azeem notices one of the evil Sheriff of Nottingham's men in the distance, and whips out his telescope to have a closer look. Though the Islamic world was far ahead of Christian civilization in many aspects of science and technology, it wasn't ahead in telescopes, which were invented in the Netherlands in 1608.

Dialogue: Robin biffs off to the forest to lead the outlaws, a bunch of merry men (and the occasional woman) who keep shouting words like 'bollocks' and 'tosspot'. These expressions were not in recorded use until the eighteenth and sixteenth century respectively, but the screenplay is in modern rather than Middle English, so fair enough.

Details: Having bonded over anachronistic swearing, Robin and his band build a sort of Ewok village in a bosky glade, complete with rope ladders, engineered lifts, mood lighting, canopy-level walkways, and a mosque for Azeem. If medieval peasants, with nothing but the natural resources of the forest around them, could build this sort of thing, why did they mostly live in filthy huts made of sticks and manure?

Economics: The Sheriff's scribe frets about the cost of Robin's larceny: 'We reckon he's nicked three to four million in the last five months, sire.' Bearing in mind that the exchequer receipts for all of England in 1194 came to £25,000, this is impressive thievery. Even if the scribe is counting in pennies, Robin has managed to steal more than the entire crown revenue for five months, notionally equivalent to around £250 billion today. Admittedly, with that sort of cash, Robin probably could have had as many canopy-level walkways as he wanted. Still, you'd think people would stop driving money carts through Sherwood Forest after the first billion or so.

Warfare: The Sheriff calls in the Scottish Celts to fight Robin. A load of big, hairy, dirty, woady savages turn up, looking like they've just arrived from the second century, and setting bits of themselves on fire for kicks. You wouldn't find this lot among the refined society of twelfth-century Franco-Gaelic Scotland, unless they were going to a fancy dress party.

Romance: The Sheriff believes that marrying Lady Marian, the Lionheart's cousin, will give him a claim to the throne. In reality, the Lionheart didn't have any cousins on his English side. Even if he did, the Sheriff would have had to contend with the King of Castile, the Duke of Saxony, the Duke of Brittany and the Lionheart's own brother, John, all of whom had a much stronger claim, as well as proper armies not made up of blatantly fake Celts a millennium past their unleash-by date.

Verdict: Alan Rickman, playing the Sheriff, seems to be the only person in *Robin Hood: Prince of Thieves* who has realized it's a pantomime. Consequently, he is hilarious, and everything else in the film is terrible. Cancel the kitchen scraps for lepers and orphans, no more merciful beheadings, and call off Christmas.

The twelfth and thirteenth centuries were thrilling across much of the world. One of cinema's favourite tyrants was

Genghis Khan, a Mongol warlord who fought his way up from obscurity to conquer most of Asia by his death in 1227. He has been played by Omar Sharif in 1965's *Genghis Khan*, and by Japanese superstar Tadanobu Asano in 2007's *Mongol*.

The most infamous version is 1956's *The Conqueror*. It was written for Marlon Brando, but he dodged the bullet. John Wayne was then at the peak of his career, and producer Howard Hughes was inclined to let him do whatever he wanted. What he wanted – and really, who doesn't? – was to be a twelfth-century Mongol warlord. Writer Oscar Millard wanted to give the screenplay an 'archaic' flourish. 'Mindful of the fact that my story was nothing more than a tarted-up Western, I thought this would give it a certain cachet and I left no lily unpainted,' he said in 1981. 'It was a mistake I have never repeated.' Genghis Khan prances about saying things like 'I feel this Tartar woman is for me. My blood says, take her.' Few actors could make such lines sound good, and John Wayne wasn't one of them. He looks desperately miserable in every scene. 'You gotta do something about these lines,' he told Millard during filming. 'I can't read 'em.' It was too late.

In Russia, the big hero of the Middle Ages (and ally of the Mongols) was Alexander Nevsky, a prince of Novgorod and later ruler of the medieval state of Rus. When crusading Catholic Teutonic knights invaded, he led Russian forces to repel them at the Battle of the Ice on 5 April 1242. He is now remembered as a saint in the Russian Orthodox Church. His story was brilliantly filmed by Sergei Eisenstein in *Alexander Nevsky* (1938), but without the Mongol alliance. The script doctors from the NKVD, the Soviet communist law enforcement agency, got involved – both Eisenstein and the film's composer, Sergei Prokofiev, were in Stalin's bad books at the time. The scenes were considered politically, though not historically, incorrect, and were cut before they could be filmed.

At the end of the thirteenth century, there comes one of the biggest and most notoriously baddest historical films in Hollywood history: Mel Gibson's *Braveheart* (1995). Tremendously lauded at the time of its release and showered with five Oscars – including Best Picture – it is, historically speaking, one of the daftest films ever made.

1305

Braveheart (1995)

Director: Mel Gibson • Entertainment grade: C– • History grade: Fail

Sir William Wallace (*c.* 1270–1305) was a Scottish patriot who rebelled against the king of England, Edward I.

Politics: We begin in 1280 when, a voiceover informs us, the Scottish king has died with no sons. In fact, King Alexander III of Scotland didn't die until 1286, and in 1280 both of his sons were still alive. Meanwhile, outside a grubby West Highland hut, young Wallace is wandering around in the mud. The real Wallace came from Renfrewshire and was the privileged son of a noble landowner. This isn't going at all well, and we're only three minutes in.

Laws: Edward I expresses a desire to enforce high taxes on the rich. Apparently, in Gibson's world, this makes him evil. In case you need even more evidence, on a whim he reinstates *ius primae noctis*, allowing English nobles to interrupt Scottish weddings and shag the bride. No, obviously this isn't true.

Society: Cut to a jolly wedding party in Scotland, complete with dancing peasants and a fun competition where they throw rocks at each other's heads. Everyone looks like they're at a *Mad Max: Beyond Thunderdome* convention, except, oddly, for Mel Gibson, who has turned up dressed as Fabio. The English arrive to spoil the party, with the local lord (seemingly played by John Cleese being Sir Lancelot the Brave, except you're not supposed to laugh) claiming his freebie with the wife.

Romance: Wallace falls for a local girl from a neighbouring hut. She has the perfect teeth so typical of Scottish peasants in the thirteenth century. He is surprised to find out that she can't read. The audience is not so surprised, because she is supposed to be a thirteenth-century peasant and lives in a hut. And then the big ponce starts trying to talk to her in French.

Violence: After his lady love is murdered by the English, Wallace pretends to surrender. At the last minute, he whips out a concealed nunchaku. Wait, what? Glossing over its implication that medieval Scotland imported arms from China, Wallace's rebellion gathers pace at the Battle of Stirling Bridge, which the film has inexplicably set in a field. Rather than, you know, on a bridge. For pity's sake. The clue's in the name.

More sex: Meanwhile, the king's daughter-in-law Isabella of France is finding stories of Wallace a lot sexier than her gay husband, who prances around the palace in a baby-blue crushed-velvet tunic while a pageboy carries a mirror in front of him (Gibson denies that his film is homophobic). Bizarrely, the king sends her to negotiate with Wallace. So irresistible are the Scotsman's hairy charms that she allows him to impregnate her. This scene is set in 1304 or 1305, when the real Isabella would have been nine years old. She was also still living in France, and wouldn't marry the Prince of Wales until three years after Wallace's death.

More war: At the Battle of Falkirk, Edward I attacks with Irish troops, who are gamely waving a big green banner with harp (which became an Irish symbol in 1642). The very loosely accurate portrayal of Robert the Bruce as a flip-flopper torn between England and Scotland provides the only passable historical contention in the entire movie. Wallace loses, but goes on to invade England and sack York. No, he didn't do that, either.

Verdict: 'Historians from England will say I am a liar,' intones the voiceover, 'but history is written by those who have hanged heroes.' Well, that's me told: but, regardless of whether you read English or Scottish historians on the matter, *Braveheart* still serves up a great big steaming haggis of lies.

1356

A Knight's Tale (2001)

Director: Brian Helgeland • Entertainment grade: C+ • History grade: C–

Set in the fourteenth-century world of jousting tournaments, *A Knight's Tale* follows the story of William Thatcher, a peasant, who disguises himself as Sir Ulrich von Lichtenstein, a noble knight and jousting champion.

Sports: The film lays its historical cards on the table straight away, showing a cheering crowd at a tournament clapping and stamping in time to Queen's 'We Will Rock You', then doing a Mexican wave. Amazingly, a search of the JSTOR academic journal catalogue yields no results for the history of the Mexican wave. It is probably safe to assume that it was a late twentieth-century invention. As was Freddie Mercury. The scene is pretty funny, though.

People: William/Ulrich is a fictional character, though there was a real Ulrich von Lichtenstein (*c.* 1200–1275). The real one wrote about jousting in his 1255 work *Frauendienst (Service of the Lady).* It is true that cash-strapped knights could earn their livings in tournaments. Examples include Ralph the Red, Giles of Argentine and William the Marshal. The screen William's herald, Geoffrey Chaucer, was certainly a real person, though it is not recorded that this most distinguished of Middle English writers had a gambling problem that left him wandering around the French countryside completely naked as he does here. 'You've probably read my book,' he brags to William and his peasant squires. '*The Book of the Duchess*.' They look blank. 'Fine, well, it *was* allegorical.' Despite its title, the film is not an adaptation of *The Knight's Tale*. Literary geeks will instead have to relish the in-joke when Chaucer's creditors, the Summoner and the Pardoner, make an appearance.

War: William's jousting career takes off when two of his key opponents, the villainous Adhemar, Count of Anjou and the heroic Edward the Black Prince, head off to fight at the Battle of Poitiers in 1356. Not much is shown of the actual battle, but it was one of the greatest victories of the Hundred Years War, and it was won by the Black Prince. However, it was lost by King John II of France, who also happened to be... Count of Anjou.

Romance: Like all the best knights in medieval chivalry, William pursues the love of a lady alongside his victories in the field. Unfortunately, the lady in question – known oddly as Jocelyn, which historically was a man's name – is a supremely irritating character. When Jocelyn isn't demanding that William perform ridiculous feats to impress her, she's wearing punk hairstyles and face paint, as if she's wandered on to set from a 1981 Adam Ant video shoot. The medieval concept of courtly love, told in the songs of troubadours, in which a poor knight romanced an aloof noble lady, did indeed involve various stages of rejection and challenges. *A Knight's Tale* is aiming at this sort of thing, but the form doesn't translate easily to modern romantic comedy. As for the Hoxtonista styling, darling, so passé – in the fourteenth century, kirtles, poulaines and wimples were the new black.

Violence: Aside from great performances by Paul Bettany as Chaucer and Heath Ledger as William, the film's main highlight is the tilting. Tilting was a jolly medieval pastime in which two armoured horsemen rode straight at each other as fast as possible while holding massive solid oak lances, resulting in frequent injury and death. In the days before Mario Kart Wii, people had to make their own entertainment. Contrary to what the film suggests, it was common for royalty to compete. The real William the Marshal killed the future Richard I's horse with a single lance blow in one famous tilt. Eagle-eyed viewers might also notice some people in crowd scenes flicking V-signs – but, seeing as the legend these were invented by archers at the Battle of Agincourt in 1415 is untrue, the movie gets away with that.

Verdict: It's wildly speculative about the facts, but many of the anachronisms are clearly deliberate in this funked-up medieval romp. Good fun, as long as you don't pay too much attention.

Plenty of historical movies are based on historical plays or novels – quite often, the historical plays of William Shakespeare. This results in interpretations of history with multiple layers: for instance, Kenneth Branagh's *Henry V* is Branagh's take on Shakespeare's play, probably written in 1599. Shakespeare's play was largely based on Raphael Holinshed's 1577 *Chronicles*, which took as their major source on Henry V the *Vita Henrici Quinti*, written in about 1438 by the historian Tito Livio dei Frulovisi of Ferrara. Tito Livio based his account partially on Latin and vernacular *Bruts*, prose writings compiled by unknown authors, which were circulated in around 1436. These told the story of Henry V and the Battle of Agincourt in 1415 – perhaps accurately, perhaps not. By the time any fact has been through that many authors' hands, it may have been Chinese-whispered quite a long way from the truth: especially when all these authors, whether they set out to produce fiction or non-fiction, were determined to tell a really good story.

1415

Henry V (1989)

Director: Kenneth Branagh • Entertainment grade: A • History grade: C+

Henry V became king of England in 1413. Though he reigned for just nine years before dying of dysentery aged thirty-five, he is remembered as a great warrior king for his victory over the French at the Battle of Agincourt in 1415. His military career was depicted by William Shakespeare across three plays: *Henry IV* Parts 1 and 2, and *Henry V*.

Casting: Kenneth Branagh directed this production as well as taking the lead role as Henry V. He was exactly the right age to play the king – twenty-nine – but too fresh-faced. The real Henry V had been wounded at the Battle of Shrewsbury in 1403, when he was the teenaged Prince Hal. He briefly lifted his helmet's visor, and an arrow pierced just below his eye and to the left of his nose. Despite the arrow being lodged in his face to a depth of six inches, he stayed on the battlefield until the day was won.

The arrowhead was later removed by surgeon John Bradmore with something like a corkscrew, and the wound treated with an ointment of flour, barley, honey and turpentine. The future Henry V survived – but with a striking facial scar which is nowhere to be seen in this movie.

War: The film's centrepiece is the Battle of Agincourt itself. Famously, it was won by English archers, whose longbows wiped out huge numbers of the French. Shakespeare's play is inaccurate, focusing on hand-to-hand fighting. The movie is able to redress this balance by showing lines of archers firing deadly hails of arrows into the air – along with the looting of the dead, the trampling of horses and pools of muddy rainwater turned pink with the blood of the wounded. All of which would have been quite challenging to stage at The Globe in 1599, but make terrific material for cinema.

Violence: In the real Battle of Agincourt, just after England appeared to have won, Henry V notoriously ordered the mass slaughter of French prisoners – perhaps thousands of them. In the movie, this doesn't happen. It does, however, in the play. At the end of Act IV, Scene 6, Henry says to the Duke of Exeter: 'The French have reinforced their scatter'd men:/Then every soldier kill his prisoners:/Give the word through.' Shakespeare played up the violence, bloodshed and destruction of the French campaign, in contrast to his main historical source, Holinshed's *Chronicles*, which did not. Neither Branagh's version nor Laurence Olivier's 1944 production included the murder of the French prisoners. Branagh's film is far closer to the gritty Shakespearean version than Olivier's, though, and does include some of the nasty bits, which Olivier cut. For instance, he delivers with venom the speech in Act III, Scene 3 in which Henry announces to the citizens of Harfleur that, if they don't surrender, his soldiers will defile their daughters, murder their fathers and impale their babies on pikes. Still, unlike the murder of the prisoners, these lines are from Shakespeare's imagination rather than the historical record – so Olivier's film was not necessarily historically inaccurate in leaving it out, and Branagh's no more accurate for keeping it in.

Romance: Having finished the fighting, the film shifts genres abruptly and becomes a romance. The Treaty of Troyes, by which Henry became heir to the French throne and married Catherine de Valois (Emma Thompson), actually took place five years after Agincourt. Shakespeare elided these events, and used dramatic licence in suggesting Henry and Catherine were unable to speak the same language. In real life, Henry certainly would have spoken French. It's easy to forgive: the Franglais courtship in Act V, Scene 2 may be inaccurate, but it is one of Shakespeare's most charming love scenes.

Verdict: The play ends with an epilogue from the Chorus: 'Thus far, with rough and all-unable pen,/Our bending author hath pursued the story,/In little room confining mighty men,/ Mangling by starts the full course of their glory.' There are plenty of historical movies of which that could be said, but not this one.

3

Renaissance Men (and Women)

As Hollywood history and actual history have established, the first Europeans in the Americas were Vikings. Even so, Christopher Columbus's 'discovery' of the Americas – never mind that millions of people already lived there and had been 'discovering' it on a daily basis for at least 20,000 years – and similar stories of the conquest have remained popular themes. Tyrone Power played a Spanish conquistador opposite Cesar Romero (the Joker from the 1960s TV version of *Batman*) as Hernan Cortés in *Captain from Castile* (1947); Robert Shaw played Francisco Pizarro against Christopher Plummer as the Inca king Atahualpa in *The Royal Hunt of the Sun* (1969); Marlon Brando played the inquisitor Torquemada with Tom Selleck as King Ferdinand of Castile in *Christopher Columbus: The Discovery* (1992); Julian Clary, Alexei Sayle and Rik Mayall cavorted around telling scatological jokes in the less serious *Carry on Columbus* (1992). But the biggest pomposity of the 500th anniversary releases was this flop, which took only around $7 million at the US box office against a reported $47 million budget:

1492

Conquest of Paradise (1992)

Director: Ridley Scott • Entertainment grade: D • History grade: D–

Geography: Columbus (played by Gerard Depardieu, lazily) is sure that the world is round, but the court rejects his proposal for an expedition. His dignified response consists of shouting 'Raaaargh!', throwing his papers around and falling over a table. After half an hour of this sort of thing, Queen Isabella (Sigourney Weaver) finally stumps up the cash, maybe just to get rid of him. Off he sails, pointedly using his quadrant to demonstrate that the screenwriter has read a book. 'A mistake of one degree, and we'll be out 600 leagues!' he exclaims. The real Columbus was a poor navigator, missing the 28th parallel by three whole degrees and falsifying the ship's log to con the crew into thinking they hadn't gone too far. (His estimates were usually wrong anyway, and the fake log is often more accurate than the real one he kept for himself.)

International relations: Some clouds roll back theatrically to reveal a palm-fringed Bahamian shore. Columbus sinks to his knees on the sand and renames the island San Salvador. He meets some of the locals. 'We come in peace and with honour,' he intones. 'They are not savages, and neither will we be.' Then he biffs off to Hispaniola to turn them all into slaves and steal their gold.

Location: On another trip – the film conflates Columbus's second and third voyages – he settles at La Isabela. It appears to be the Caribbean's first luxury spa resort, complete with billowing white linen curtains, ironwork chandeliers, sisal matting and thick clusters of church candles. Recent archaeology and history suggest that women and Africans were present on Columbus's early voyages, but no one has yet proven that he brought an interior designer. And it's tricky to square this with the real accounts of La Isabela as a filthy, poorly situated camp with appalling sanitation, in which large numbers of Spaniards were ailing with tropical diseases, as well as with their own specially imported syphilis.

Violence: The film portrays Columbus as a heroic protector of the Tainos, the indigenous people of Hispaniola. In real life, he did have a sense of religious duty towards the Tainos' souls, and said they should be kept well enough 'that they do not rebel', but displayed no humanitarian feeling. During a famine, he ramped up the tribute of gold the Tainos were supposed to pay him. The colonist Miguel de Cuneo, an old friend of Columbus's, wrote a graphic account of his violent rape of a Caribbean woman 'whom the Admiral [Columbus] gave to me', and cheerfully recorded his exploits murdering Taino men – none of which seems to have earned him so much as a slap on the wrist from the boss.

People: The film invents a bad guy, gloating aristo slime Adrian de Moxica – possibly based on Adrian de Mújica, who was involved in a revolt on Hispaniola. But the evidence doesn't suggest Mújica was evil. Nor was he known for dressing up as the dark-haired twin of Lucius Malfoy, though watching the big goth stagger around Caribbean beaches in his sweaty black and silver doublet is quite amusing. It was Columbus who enslaved the Tainos (against Queen Isabella's judgement), and Columbus who instituted the harsh punishments Moxica doles out in the film. So *1492: Conquest of Paradise* works best if you view it as fifteenth-century *Fight Club*, with Moxica as Columbus's Tyler Durden. Since some historians argue Columbus was mentally unstable – for instance, he convinced himself that Cuba was full of griffins – this interpretation is justifiable, though clearly not what the director intended.

Verdict: 'The New World is a disaster,' moans Queen Isabella. Yes, that's about right.

Films about the pre-conquest Americas are unusual, though as a curio some might remember 1963's *Kings of the Sun*, with Yul Brynner (from Vladivostok, then USSR) and George Chakiris (of Greek origin) pretending to be medieval Meso-Americans. But then there's one of the weirdest historical films ever made. After the enormous box-office success of *The Passion of the Christ* (2004), Mel Gibson could get the money to make pretty much anything he wanted. He wanted to make this:

Circa 1511

Apocalypto (2006)

Director: Mel Gibson • Entertainment grade: C– • History grade: Fail

The Maya dominated Mexico's Yucatán Peninsula. Their sophisticated political systems, extraordinary visual culture, advanced science and development of the only written language in the Americas have long endeared them to historians. In the 1520s, Spanish conquistadors arrived in Yucatán, signalling the beginning of the end for Mayan civilization.

Conquest: The film opens with a quote about the Roman empire from Will Durant: 'A great civilization is not conquered from without until it has destroyed itself from within.' In other words, *Apocalypto* blames the Mayan people for being conquered. Actually, the Mayans put up a good fight – partly because their civilization was integrated and coherent, not destroyed, by the time the Spanish arrived. The real reason the Spanish were able to conquer the Americas was that they had guns and syphilis, against which the indigenous peoples had sticks and no antibodies.

Culture: A bunch of Mayan villagers are hanging out in the jungle, improbably hunting big game with a zany Indiana Jones-style contraption that looks like a giant sideways meat tenderizer. They use this to swat a tapir to death, and divide its flesh up between them. Someone cons the big lunk of the gang into eating its testicles, at which they all fall about laughing. The big lunk reacts by telling a mother-in-law joke. Then someone else tricks him into rubbing hot chilli sauce on his own private parts. Admittedly, not much is known about Mayan humour, but there is no reason to assume it would have been exactly like that of spoilt American frat boys.

Violence: Another lot of Mayans roll up. You can tell these ones are evil, because they are scowling, have weirder facial piercings, and wear epaulettes made of human jawbones. The bad Mayans take the good Mayans prisoner, and march them off to the big city. It is full of drugged-up dancers with bones through their noses, terrifying masks and jade-inlaid teeth, blood-drenched high priests making towers of skulls, and ghostly underlings caked in white mud. Remarkably similar to the scene if you get off at Camden tube station at 11.30 on a Saturday night, but not much like anything from Mayan history.

Religion: Bad news for our plucky heroes: it's human sacrifice day in Maya Town. The ceremony shown here is very faithful to the most lurid sources on the Aztec ritual. The victims are splayed on a column at the top of a pyramid, and a priest cracks their ribcage open with an obsidian knife to pluck out their still-beating hearts. Just one problem: Mayans weren't Aztecs. They did go in for a bit of human sacrifice, but it was more a case of throwing the occasional child down a well for the water god to eat. Which admittedly wasn't super nice, either.

Timing: The sets, costumes, references to plague-like diseases and social context of the film seem to set *Apocalypto* firmly in the ninth century, when the classic Mayan collapse took place.

And yet, all of a sudden, a boatload of Spaniards turn up waving great big Christian crosses, like they did in 1511. *Apocalypto* seems to have been made to argue that Mayan civilization at its height was evil and revolting, and that it was a jolly good thing the Spanish turned up to conquer everyone. To make this historically questionable point, it is obliged to set itself in completely the wrong century.

Verdict: Mostly about the wrong people and six hundred years out of date.

The Renaissance was a flowering of art, literature, science and learning, which began in around the fifteenth century in Italy. There aren't many movies about Renaissance artists, aside from *The Agony and the Ecstasy* (1965), starring Charlton Heston as a tormented, inaccurately heterosexual Michelangelo. Since the 1990s, the names Leonardo, Michelangelo, Donatello and Raphael have been more closely associated by Hollywood with the Teenage Mutant Ninja Turtles.

At the same time, the Reformation saw a clutch of breakaway movements from the Catholic Church after what many felt to be decades of increasing corruption and loss of spiritual authority. The most famous reformer was radical Catholic priest Martin Luther (1483–1546), whose ideas led to what became known as Protestantism. Though he was a hugely influential figure in European, and ultimately, world history, Luther personally was a severe and spiky character.

1522

Luther (2003)

Director: Eric Till • Entertainment grade: D • History grade: B–

Religion: Martin Luther (Joseph Fiennes) is a monk, but not a happy one. He spills communion wine, hurls himself into the mud, and shouts things like 'I wish there were no God!' His superior, Johann von Staupitz (Bruno Ganz), sends him to Rome to cheer him up. There, he finds stalls selling religious nick-nacks, priests canoodling with strumpets, and Pope Julius II blinging around town in shiny gold armour. All of this would doubtless cheer most people up – but not Luther. It makes him even grumpier. Julius II, known as the 'Warrior Pope', did wear full armour (though gold armour is too soft for a battlefield, unless you're hoping to impress your enemies into submission). The depiction of him here is influenced by one of the real Luther's favourite pamphlets, *Julius Excluded from Heaven*, probably written by Erasmus. Among other things, it mocked the Pope for his belching – but mostly for his warmongering, corruption and enormous wealth.

Science: Next, Staupitz sends Luther to university in Wittenberg. He's bored in class. Instead of making notes on his vellum, he doodles a picture of a dinosaur. Wait, what? Luther was a radical, but not that radical. And dinosaur remains were first identified as such in the early nineteenth century. Rewinding the film for another look… okay, it might be a dragon. In Luther's German New Testament of 1522, he published a highly controversial woodcut of a dragon wearing a papal tiara, which was supposed to represent the beast from the Book of Revelation. All right, then. The film can have a dragon.

Controversy: Luther preaches fiery sermons against church practices. 'For a silver florin I freed my grandfather from purgatory,' he says. 'For twice that, I could have sprung grandma and uncle Marcus too.' His audience is in hysterics. Hey, it's the sixteenth century. Life expectancy is roughly thirty, everyone's covered in boils, and no one has told a joke for about a millennium. They must be desperate for a laugh. The Catholic Church doesn't find him funny, though. The local prince, Elector Frederick of Saxony, is ordered to arrest him. 'No, I'm not going to send my monk to Rome,' says Frederick (Peter Ustinov, who camps it up to the max). 'They'll only kill him. It's so irritating.'

Trials: Instead, Luther is subjected to the Diet of Worms, which wasn't as disgusting as it sounds (a diet was an imperial assembly, and Worms is a place). Presiding is the Holy Roman Emperor, Charles V, looking like a lost contestant from *RuPaul's Drag Race* in his flamboyant silks, velvets and jewels, his hair cut in a sharp Vidal Sassoon bob. Glam, yes, but a dead ringer for the real thing. The bizarre incident afterwards, in which Luther is fake-kidnapped by agents of his protector Frederick, is also real.

Health: As the film shows, Luther spent his subsequent exile translating the New Testament into German and having visions of the devil. The film shows him ranting rhetorically at thin air.

In real life, it was weirder than that: Luther believed poltergeists were attacking his ceiling with walnuts, and once threw a dog out of a window because he thought it was Satan. He also suffered physically. 'The Lord has struck me in the rear end with terrible pain,' he complained to a friend. To another, more prosaically: 'My arse has gone bad.' This does at least explain why he was so grumpy.

As far as British and American filmmakers are concerned, the sixteenth century really gets into its swing when lusty King Henry VIII meets hot young vixen Anne Boleyn. The two first met in the 1520s and, gradually, Henry became enraptured. His desire to annul his existing marriage to Catherine of Aragon and marry Anne instead led to a split with the Roman Catholic Church, a series of events known as the 'King's Great Matter'. There have been dozens of screen treatments of the story of Henry and Anne, though fewer of his other five wives. An exception is Alexander Korda's *The Private Life of Henry VIII* (1933), a heartily enjoyable romp with Charles Laughton setting the mould for how Henry VIII would ever after be imagined. It focuses on his relationships with Jane Seymour, Anne of Cleves, Katherine Howard and Katherine Parr.

1536

Anne of the Thousand Days (1969)

Director: Charles Jarrott • Entertainment grade: C • History grade: C+

Family: Having seen Anne (Geneviève Bujold) dancing at court, Henry (Richard Burton) visits her father, Thomas Boleyn, and demands sex with his younger daughter. This is nothing new: the king has already done Sir Thomas's elder daughter, Mary. Abandoned, pregnant and miserable, Mary throws herself on her father's mercy. It's not a soft landing. 'What his majesty is denied, he goes half mad to obtain,' rasps Sir Thomas to his distraught girl. 'What he gets freely, he despises. You have lost him. I can't help you. Go now and cause no trouble.' In real life, Mary was no wide-eyed ingénue, and her affair with Henry probably began after she was married. The film's firm conviction that one or both of Mary's children were Henry's is disputed.

Sex: There's just one problem with the king's plan: Anne won't put out. Henry is furious, and also really turned on. Some historians, such as G. W. Bernard, have suggested that any no-sex rule may have been Henry's decision. He was still trying to make nice with the Pope, and he would have lost piety points if his girlfriend started popping out his bastards. Others, like Alison Weir, argue that Henry's 'seventeen surviving love letters to Anne strongly suggest that the more traditional assumption is likely correct, and that it was she who kept him at arm's length for all that time, only to yield when marriage was within her sights'. Those letters demonstrate that the two were intimate, even if they didn't go all the way. In one, Henry wrote that he was 'wishing myself specially an evening in my sweetheart's arms whose pretty dukkys I trust shortly to kiss'. There, you've just learned a sixteenth-century word for breasts.

Reformation: While Henry's long wait for a payoff only increased his passion, this film fails to recreate that effect for the audience. For all its gorgeous sets and costumes, and despite a spirited effort by Bujold in the title role, *Anne of the Thousand Days* is so longwinded and ploddingly paced that it feels like it might actually go on for a thousand days. The stories of Thomas Wolsey, Thomas Cromwell and Sir Thomas More could be engrossing, but the prosy screenplay leaves barely a scratch on any of their surfaces.

Foresight: Henry's and Anne's eventual marriage falls apart over Anne's inability to bear a live son – only a 'useless daughter', Elizabeth. Soon, she is in the Tower, awaiting execution. Henry turns up for a last visit. 'Agree to annul the marriage and give up all rights,' he beseeches her. 'You shall go abroad and take Elizabeth with you.' Anne flies into a not very sixteenth-century-sounding feminist rage. 'Elizabeth shall be a greater queen than any king of yours!' she yells. 'She shall rule a greater England than you could ever have built!' It's a super scene – sparking up some of the fire the rest of the movie has failed to light – but fictional. Henry did not visit Anne in the Tower. He did not offer her exile with their daughter. If he had, she would surely have taken it.

Succession: The film tries to paper over the gaping hole it has just torn in the plot by suggesting that Anne chose death to keep Elizabeth in the line of succession. This is daft. In May 1536, you wouldn't have had to be a witch – and, these days, we can probably assume Anne wasn't – to predict that Elizabeth would be removed from the succession swiftly after her mother's execution. Few then could have imagined that Elizabeth would ever end up queen.

1536

A Man for All Seasons (1966)

Director: Fred Zinnemann • Entertainment grade: B • History grade: A–

Marriage: Luck and Tudor obstetrics have failed to provide Henry with a son. He blames the queen, and wants to dump her. Sir Thomas More (Paul Scofield) is summoned to Hampton Court to see the chancellor, Cardinal Wolsey (Orson Welles). 'England needs an heir!' bellows the spherical cardinal, resembling, in his bright scarlet robes and pointy hat, the *Attack of the Killer Tomato*. Contemporary portraits reveal that this was indeed the look Wolsey rocked. More replies that private conscience is more important than public duty. His wife, Alice, doesn't agree, commenting that he could be chancellor of England if Wolsey fell. 'If Wolsey fell, the splash would swallow a few small boats like ours,' murmurs More. A vivid image. Anyway, the cardinal bungles the divorce, then dies (no splash, just a bit of a gurgle). The Duke of Norfolk turns up to swipe the chain of office from his deathbed. This is a slight elision of events – Wolsey actually died a year *after* being stripped of his position. But the politics are accurate.

Royalty: The chancellor's chain finds its way on to More's shoulders. Henry VIII (Robert Shaw) comes visiting. He turns up with an entourage of toffs in pastel cloaks, whose job it seems to be to guffaw at everything he says; then tries to chat up More's daughter, Margaret Roper, by talking to her in Latin and showing her his shapely legs. The real Henry was proud of his legs, once bragging about them to the French ambassador. Until one of them turned into a mass of ulcers after a nasty jousting accident and, allegedly, the other was eaten away by syphilis. Still, this scene is set in around 1530. The accident did not happen until 1536, and many historians dispute that Henry ever had syphilis. (The film claims that he did.)

Dialogue: The screenplay, based by Robert Bolt on his own stage play, is elegant and subtly witty. 'Will you forfeit all you have,' asks Norfolk, 'for a belief?' 'Because what matters is that I believe it – or rather, no, not that I believe it, but that *I* believe,' says More. 'I trust I make myself obscure.' Readers of More's own writing, notably his *Response to Luther* (1523), may detect a more hard-boiled turn of phrase. He may have been a saint, but he talked like a gangster (if gangsters spoke Latin). More disses Luther as a 'pimp' and an 'arse', claims his mouth is 'the shit-pool of all shit', alleges that he celebrated Mass on the lavatory, and lists four types of ordure with which he was apparently filled (merda, stercus, lutum and coenum). Now, I'm not suggesting that the story of the Henrician Reformation be written in the language of *The Wire*, but… actually, yes, I am. That would be excellent. And, it seems, historically justifiable.

Treason: The film's most significant invention is its portrayal of Richard Rich (John Hurt), the Solicitor-General. Rich's onscreen backstory, showing a lengthy association with More, is speculative. But the depiction of Rich's probable perjury during More's trial does fit with the record, and with the judgement of most historians. In the film, he has done it all to be made Attorney-General of Wales. 'Why, Richard, it profits a man nothing to give his soul for the whole world,' sighs More, 'but for *Wales*?'

The brief reign of Henry's son with Jane Seymour, Edward VI, doesn't seem to appeal to filmmakers. But the very, very brief reign after his death of his cousin Lady Jane Grey – a teenage girl bundled on to the throne on 10 July 1553, then bundled off it nine days later and beheaded – has more cinematic potential. In 1936, John Mills starred as Guilford Dudley and Nova Pilbeam as Lady Jane in *Nine Days a Queen*, also known as *Tudor Rose*.

1553

Lady Jane (1986)

Director: Trevor Nunn • Entertainment grade: C+ • History grade: D+

Family: The scheming Duke of Northumberland wants to marry his youngest son Guilford Dudley (Cary Elwes) to Jane. 'He's a quiet, studious boy,' says Northumberland. 'I imagine even now, in fact, among his books, or else at prayer.' Cut to Guilford staggering around a pub, howling, 'More wine!' before passing out on a nearby prostitute. Amazingly, Jane doesn't want to marry him. So her horrible mother, the Duchess of Suffolk, drags her off to a gallery, and flogs her unconscious with a birch. Though not particularly graphic, this scene is, well, a bit weird. But it is based on historical sources, though some say it was her father who beat her until she agreed to marry. Either way: grim. In the film, she is reluctant because she has the hots for the young king, Edward VI. In real life, she considered herself betrothed to another Edward – Edward Seymour, Earl of Hertford.

Marriage: At the wedding, Guilford is monosyllabic, sinking flagon after flagon of mead and making kissy faces at nearby wenches. Afterwards, Jane is ushered into his chamber to submit to a consummation, but finds her husband passed out on the bed. In fact, according to the recollections of the Spanish ambassador, many of those at the party (including Guilford himself) came down with a hideous bout of food poisoning, after the cook 'plucked one leaf for another'. So, in real life, Guilford probably spent his wedding night in the privy.

Politics: Guilford and Jane retreat to a country estate, where to Jane's horror they observe some poor people. Out of the blue, Guilford launches into a rant about the social damage caused by the dissolution of the monasteries: 'I want a world where men are not branded or sent into slavery because they can't grow the food they need to eat!' Jane glows with desire. Historically, not only is there no evidence that Lady Jane had a thing for sanctimonious toffs who moan on about how much life sucks for poor people while lazing around in massive castles swigging fine wine from Venetian goblets, but there's very little evidence that Lady Jane had a thing for Guilford Dudley. The two did not spend the months after their marriage rolling around in sunny meadows, discovering a shared love of land redistribution. Jane was obliged to live with Guilford's parents, and became convinced they were trying to murder her.

Treason: It's a shame the film has made Jane and Guilford such a couple of prigs, because you should be really upset when it comes to the whole beheading thing. The execution scene is recreated with impressive accuracy, then spoiled by bungling Jane's last words. In the film, she whimpers: 'Guilford!' In real life, she said loudly and with great dignity: 'Lord, into thy hands I commend my spirit.'

The reign of Henry VIII's eldest daughter, Mary I, and the Catholic restoration has been largely ignored by filmmakers. Instead, they tend to skip straight to Mary's younger half-sister: Elizabeth I, the redheaded daughter of Henry VIII and Anne Boleyn; the queen whose reign brought some stability after the Anglican schism and brief Catholic restoration; the queen who loved her loyal pirates and oversaw the beginning of the British Empire; the queen who defeated the Spanish Armada; the Virgin Queen, who never married.

There have been scores of screen Elizabeths. These are some of the best – and worst.

1558

Elizabeth (1998)

Director: Shekhar Kapur • Entertainment grade: A– • History grade: E

Religion: Young Princess Elizabeth (Cate Blanchett) is dragged away from a sunny afternoon at Hatfield, dancing around in fields and snogging hunky Robert Dudley (Joseph Fiennes), and sent to the Tower of London. She is accused of involvement in Thomas Wyatt's Protestant rebellion against the Catholic Mary. 'I ask you why must we tear ourselves apart over this small question of religion,' she says to her interrogators. 'You think it small?' bellows Bishop Gardiner. 'Though it killed your mother?' Elizabeth looks shocked. It would have been more realistic if she looked confused. The question of religion did not kill Elizabeth's mother, Anne Boleyn. Correct answers to 'what killed Anne Boleyn?' include (a) being convicted of adultery, incest and high treason, (b) Henry VIII's changeable passions, and (c) a French swordsman.

Sex: Elizabeth escapes death, but is put under house arrest. Instead, Mary dies – leaving Elizabeth to be crowned queen. Robert Dudley soon becomes a fixture at court, dancing with her majesty, molesting her in public, and strolling openly into the royal bedchamber. It is made clear that this Virgin Queen… isn't.

Much though readers of romantic historical fiction might like to think that Elizabeth boinked Dudley, there's scant evidence she ever boinked anyone. In the film, Sir William Cecil (played by a 75-year-old Richard Attenborough, which is strange considering the real Cecil was only 37 at the time) spoils her fun. 'You cannot marry Lord Robert!' he cries. 'He's already married!' Again, Elizabeth looks shocked. Again, wrong expression. Elizabeth had attended Dudley's marriage to Amy Robsart in 1550, so she probably would have noticed that he had a wife.

Betrayal: The film amalgamates various plots against Elizabeth. The Duke of Norfolk (Christopher Eccleston) conspires with the Pope (John Gielgud) to put Mary, Queen of Scots on the throne. In real life, Norfolk tried to marry Mary of Scots in 1569 but escaped execution till 1572, following a second bungled attempt at treason. The film also drags Robert Dudley into the plot. Though the Spanish ambassador suggested in 1559 that he could cultivate Dudley as a possible influence on Elizabeth, the real Dudley never joined any conspiracy against her. Instead, they were at some points estranged by scandals – including the mysterious death of Dudley's aforementioned wife in 1560, and his secret remarriage to Lettice Knollys in 1578.

Verdict: Elizabeth is a skilfully made, brilliantly acted, smartly structured and intelligently written movie, which could hardly be more beautiful to look at. Historically, though, it's a hot mess.

1587

Mary, Queen of Scots (1971)

Director: Charles Jarrott • Entertainment grade: C+ • History grade: C+

Mary, Queen of Scots was the heir to James V of Scotland, crowned before her first birthday in 1542. She also claimed the English throne, and became involved in a power struggle with Elizabeth I.

Romance: In France, the young Mary (Vanessa Redgrave) is skipping through the sunny fields with her beloved husband, the Dauphin. They're just taking a boat trip down a picturesque stream when – 'Waaargh! My head!' – the Dauphin collapses. These 'fevers of the brain' were the result of an ear infection. As in the film, they killed him. Meanwhile, in England, Elizabeth (Glenda Jackson) is rolling around in the royal barge with Robert Dudley. Both remain fully clad, so the film stays just on the right side of propriety: this Virgin Queen stays virginal.

Plot: Critic Roger Ebert slighted the film for taking 'a soap-opera approach to history'. True, it's full of plot devices that the *EastEnders* writing team would dismiss as being too far-fetched. Dudley's wife dies in a mysterious fall down the stairs at the exact point he wants to be free to marry Elizabeth. Instead, she tries to marry him to the widowed Mary. But Mary moves to Scotland and marries dimwitted hunk Lord Darnley (Timothy Dalton), who becomes convinced that she is having an affair with her Italian music teacher David Rizzio (Ian Holm), who may also be a papal spy. When she is seven months pregnant, Scottish rebels supported by Darnley storm her palace, drag Rizzio away and stab him fifty-six times. Then Darnley is done to death in the night at his house, Kirk o'Field – which is destroyed by a massive explosion. Crazy, right? The thing is, all of this is true. The filmmakers do add twists of their own – bigging up a gay affair between Rizzio and Darnley, and suggesting that Darnley had set the explosion at Kirk o'Field to kill Mary. Why did they bother? There's far too much plot here anyway, as indeed there was in the sixteenth century.

People: Vanessa Redgrave plays Mary as a combination of sanctimonious and needy. It doesn't make her any more likeable when the screenplay implicates her in Lord Darnley's murder, a crime of which many heavyweight Tudor historians consider her innocent. Meanwhile, Glenda Jackson makes Elizabeth fierce, clever and hard as nails. Too hard. When Dudley returns from failing to woo Mary, she asks him to describe her. Dudley waxes lyrical, and she attacks him. 'I went only at your command! I love only you!' he bleats. Unimpressed, she delivers a vicious punch straight to the codpiece. This seems to calm her down. 'I am no longer angry,' she tells him sweetly (the poor man is, at this point, bent double and wheezing). 'Is she really as beautiful as they say?' 'Well, she is quite beautiful,' he replies, stupidly. This earns him a right hook to the jaw. In real life, Elizabeth's relationship with Dudley was tempestuous and fascinating in terms of its power balance, but as far as is known not abusive.

Virtue: The film squashes thirty years into its two-hour run-time. At first, events flow into each other plausibly. In the final act, there's an abrupt jump of almost two decades, and suddenly everyone's old, dead or about to be beheaded. Perhaps this is unavoidable. It's certainly better than showing at great length Mary's tedious years of imprisonment. But it means that her transformation from sanctimonious and needy girl into a strong, dignified woman in the last ten minutes comes as something of a surprise. This undercuts a (mostly) historically accurate execution scene, which could have been quite moving, complete with a sexed-up, wasp-waisted version of the red chemise that the real Mary wore under her black gown – red being the colour of martyrdom.

1596

The Private Lives of Elizabeth and Essex (1939)

Director: Michael Curtiz • Entertainment grade: D+ • History grade: B–

Robert Devereux, 2nd Earl of Essex, was the stepson of Elizabeth I's favourite, Robert Dudley, the Earl of Leicester. By the time of Dudley's death in 1588, Essex had taken over as her main man. Though he was thirty-three years her junior, there was a charge to their relationship, which historians have variously interpreted as a mother–son relationship, a grand romance, or both.

People: It's 1596, and Essex (Errol Flynn) has just returned from Cadiz, where he has pilfered Spanish treasure but failed to deliver it to Elizabeth (Bette Davis, who would play Elizabeth again sixteen years later in 1955's *The Virgin Queen*). She is furious. He tries to flirt his way out of punishment. Unbeguiled, she smacks him one in front of the entire council. 'I would not have taken that from the king, your father,' he growls. 'Much less will I take it from a king in petticoats.' The king, her father, Henry VIII, died nineteen years before Essex was born – but this is a very nearly accurate scene and quote. It happened when they had a fight about who should be sent to represent her in Ireland, so it's in the wrong place, but the style is spot on.

Casting: Bette Davis shaved her hairline and uglied herself up to play Elizabeth, but her constant twitching – seemingly an attempt to convey age – almost tips the performance over into pantomime. She evokes vividly Elizabeth's quick political wit and the trials of a life torn between public duty and private desire, even though the real Elizabeth probably spent a little less time sitting in front of a mirror, drinking herself into a stupor, eating bonbons and moaning about being old. Meanwhile, Errol Flynn can barely be bothered to lift an eyebrow as Essex, though something of the real character's arrogance does come through as a result.

Details: This is old-school historical filmmaking. The past is a bright, shiny place full of clean people with colourful costumes who start sentences with the words 'Rumour hath it', and Tudor England enjoys blazing sunshine just like southern California. Elizabeth's pillarbox-red lipstick and neon-green ostrich feather fans were not high fashion in the 1590s, and it is surprising when Essex emerges from his grimy cell in the Tower of London wearing a dazzlingly starched white shirt. More surprising still is the fact that he emerges from a concealed solid granite staircase, which flips up at the touch of one flunky from the flagstones in Elizabeth's floor. Elizabethans did not have superhuman strength, and it would have been a lot easier to escape from the Tower of London if it really had been built out of foam rubber.

Politics: Essex arrives at Whitehall Palace with an army and tries to take the throne from Elizabeth. 'The throne's yours by descent and by possession,' he tells her. 'If this had been a freer time – if the people could elect – I'd have swept the country before me!' Though he was popular, the Earl of Essex did not have an American dream, and nor did he aim to promote freedom and democracy. He did not turn up with an army, either: just on his own, covered in mud (Flynn, of course, looks like he's just stepped out of a salon). This so-called rebellion was really more of a tantrum, but the film has smooshed it together with a later plan of his to lead a coup. In real life, Elizabeth was a lot keener to see Essex beheaded than she is in the film; but still not quite so keen as the audience.

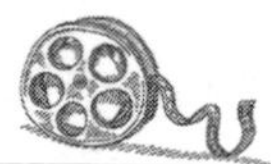

Unwittingly, William Shakespeare has had a hand in a lot of historical films. Not only are his plays still constantly adapted; he also set the standard interpretation for several key historical characters, including Cleopatra, Henry V and Richard III. He is, to a considerable extent, responsible for the modern concept of historical drama. He has also featured as a character in a few movies, though – considering the huge debt their industry owes him – historical filmmakers aren't always respectful.

1593

Shakespeare in Love (1998)

Director: John Madden • Entertainment grade: A– • History grade: B–

People: It's 1593, and Will Shakespeare (Joseph Fiennes) is scribbling away at his desk, working out how to spell his name. He crumples his efforts up into a ball and throws them at a novelty mug bearing the words: 'A Present from Stratford-upon-Avon'. You may get the idea that this movie isn't going to take its history too seriously. It does care a bit, though. The characters surrounding Will – including teenage proto-Gothic playwright John Webster, full-of-themselves actors Richard Burbage (Martin Clunes) and Ned Alleyn (Ben Affleck), and oddball theatre manager Philip Henslowe (Geoffrey Rush) – are all real and well-researched characters. For instance, both Alleyn and Henslowe left diaries: Henslowe's tends to support the movie's image of him as an eccentric. Alongside accounts for the seasons at his theatre, the Rose, it ventures into astrology and witchcraft – including a recipe for curing earache with fried earthworms.

Authorship: Will is trying to write his new play, *Romeo and Ethel the Pirate's Daughter*, but has lost his muse. He ends up in a pub with fellow playwright Christopher Marlowe (Rupert Everett). 'Romeo,' says Marlowe, thinking. 'Romeo is Italian. Always in and out of love. Ethel. The daughter of his enemy. His best friend is killed in a duel by Ethel's brother. Or something. His name is Mercutio.' It's a glancing reference to the much-trumpeted idea that Shakespeare may not have written his own plays: Marlowe is among those proposed as the 'real' author. This is a conspiracy theory bandied around by the sort of people who can't accept that an ordinary bloke from the Midlands wrote the best poetry ever without even going to Oxbridge first. Clearly, they've never heard of Noddy Holder.

Controversy: The film goes further after Marlowe's murder: 'My *Henry VI* was a house built on his foundations,' Will says. Some scholars have argued that Shakespeare effectively rewrote two plays by Marlowe or another dramatist to shape *Henry VI*, others claim that it was written by committee, and others yet passionately defend Shakespeare's authorship. It is true, though, that some phrasings in *Henry VI* echo lines in Marlowe's plays.

Marriage: In the movie, Will gets his muse back in the form of Viola de Lesseps (Gwyneth Paltrow), a fictional lady who dresses as a boy to perform in the theatre. The film plays up the theory that Shakespeare's marriage to Anne Hathaway may not have been a happy one. When they married in 1582, he was eighteen; she was twenty-six, and three months pregnant. It cannot really be called a shotgun wedding in the age of the arquebus, but that may have been what it was.

Sexuality: The movie's Will ditches Ethel the Pirate's Daughter along with his wife and other girlfriends. In her place, he writes Juliet as inspired by Viola. He also writes *Twelfth Night* and Sonnet 18 (Shall I compare thee to a summer's day?) for her. Sonnet 18 is one of those addressed to 'Fair Youth', an unidentified man. The fact that the movie's Viola is a cross-dresser gives this a witty twist – though not one with any historical validity.

1600

Anonymous (2011)

Director: Roland Emmerich • Entertainment grade: E • History grade: Fail

William Shakespeare's plays were written by William Shakespeare, a well-documented historical figure who lived between 1564 and 1616. In 1920, a schoolmaster with the apt name of John Thomas Looney invented a conspiracy theory suggesting that Shakespeare's plays were written by Edward de Vere, 17th Earl of Oxford.

Class: Director Roland Emmerich (who made *2012*, *Godzilla* and *Independence Day*, all more realistic than this movie) is an Oxfordian. This is the designation preferred by supporters of the Looney theory, who think Shakespeare's plays were secretly penned by Oxford. The reason they think that is simple. They're snobs. Their root belief is that Shakespeare was just not posh enough to be a good writer. Shakespeare, the screenplay sneers, was the mere 'son of a glove maker... armed only with a grammar school education'. Derek Jacobi speaks these lines on an empty stage at the beginning of the film, in a shameful pastiche of his own role in the opening of Kenneth Branagh's production of *Henry V*. Who thinks Shakespeare couldn't have been a good writer because his father was a tradesman? Snobs, that's who. And who thinks he couldn't have had the breadth of cultural knowledge his plays reveal with 'only' a grammar school education? Ignorant snobs. A grammar school education in sixteenth-century England would have equipped Shakespeare with Latin, some Greek, classical history, mythology, rhetoric and drama – a fine start for a playwright.

Romance: Not only does *Anonymous* credit Shakespeare's plays to the Earl of Oxford (an aged-up Rhys Ifans, wearing so much powder and eyeshadow that you might start wondering whatever happened to Baby Jane). It must also fabricate a reason for Oxford to hide his real identity. The film goes for broke on this, claiming that he had a passionate affair with Elizabeth I (played young by Joely Richardson, and old by Vanessa Redgrave). The real Elizabeth was probably a virgin, and certainly one of the most intellectually distinguished women of her age. The Elizabeth of *Anonymous* is a dimwitted nymphomaniac who has been wandering around since the age of sixteen getting herself up the duff by various boyfriends.

People: William Cecil (David Thewlis) hides Elizabeth's resulting stream of babies in well-to-do households, with the apparent result that her majesty has spawned the entire English aristocracy. *Anonymous* imagines a flotilla of bastards, specifying that the Earl of Southampton is her son by Oxford, and the Earl of Essex her son by some unnamed hook-up. In reality, Southampton may have been the 'Fair Youth' of Shakespeare's sonnets (which, again, were written by Shakespeare); Essex may have been a romantic figure in Elizabeth's later life. But they were not the queen's kids. Really not.

Arts: Oxford tries to bestow authorship of 'his' plays on Ben Jonson (Sebastian Armesto), but Jonson's a gibbering idiot. Instead, illiterate actor Will Shakespeare (Rafe Spall) gets them. Bearing in mind he went to grammar school, as the film itself points out, how come he's illiterate? Everybody good in *Anonymous* is a tall, fair-haired aristocrat, and everybody bad is a short, dark, greasy commoner, probably with a hunchback. At least that's vaguely Shakespearean. Shakespeare and Jonson, one incomparable and one great English writer, are played here as the Chuckle Brothers. Only way less funny.

Family: Wait! It gets worse! In a supposedly dramatic but actually farcical scene, it is revealed that Oxford is actually Elizabeth's secret *son* as well as her lover. With the addition of mother–son incest, the plot that was previously just deranged becomes actively repulsive. Also, that was a major spoiler. Now you've got no excuse for going to see it. Feel free to thank me.

Verdict: Historians and literary scholars must assemble themselves into a colossal Godzilla formation, rise towering from the Pacific Ocean, rampage around Hollywood breathing fire, and stomp the hell out of Roland Emmerich's production company.

During Elizabeth's reign, all sorts of interesting things were going on in the rest of the world. In Japan, this was the turbulent Sengoku period. One of that country's greatest filmmakers, Akira Kurosawa, made *Ran* (Discord), the definitive film about the period. It cleverly combines elements of the contemporary Shakespeare play *King Lear* with the real life of Mori Motonari, a famous daimyo (lord) in western Honshu.

1570

Ran (1985)

Director: Akira Kurosawa • Entertainment grade: A– • History grade: B+

Family: Hidetora (Tatsuya Nakadai), the film's version of Motonari, has decided to divide his kingdom between his three sons: the dutiful Taro and Jiro, and the rebellious Saburo. Saburo throws a strop. 'You are either senile or insane!' he shouts. Hidetora explains that the three brothers will have to ally in the face of a threat, and illustrates this by giving each of them an arrow. One arrow alone is easy to snap. But if you put three together, it is much harder to snap them as a bunch. Saburo strains, grimaces and petulantly snaps all three. Hidetora glowers. There's just no impressing some people with your picturesque paternal wisdom. The arrow proverb is indeed attributed to Motonari, so this scene gives a nod to history, even if it is written for dramatic effect.

Murder: Taro, the eldest brother, is installed in the most important castle, and with him goes his scheming wife Kaede (Mieko Harada). If you like your *King Lear* spiced up with plenty of Lady Macbeth and a hint of the woman who crawls out of the telly to kill people in *Ring*, Kaede is the real star of this movie. Years before, Hidetora killed her family, and now she plans an elaborate revenge. Kaede is a fictional character but, in a real-life parallel to her backstory, Motonari did murder most of the house of Amako.

Society: Cast out by his own son, Hidetora wanders around the countryside, accompanied by his loyal fool, a topknotted irritant who alternates between platitudinous observation and the striking of poses commonly seen in a Year 10 drama class. He's enough to drive anyone mad, and soon poor Hidetora is losing his marbles all over the place. Some kindly peasants take pity on him. 'Don't take charity from peasants!' cries a vassal. 'A samurai would rather starve than beg!' 'That's right!' exclaims Hidetora. 'The peasants are presumptuous. Burn their villages!' This is all *Ran* has to say about the lot of early modern Japanese peasants, but they did have rather a hard time.

Romance: There's a storming battle scene, and Taro is killed. The widowed Kaede immediately transfers her terrifying attentions to Jiro, who is already married to another woman whose entire family was killed by Hidetora back in the day. (Motonari, like Hidetora, made a habit of this sort of thing: in addition to his slaughter of the Amako family, he ravaged the house of Ouchi. A prequel to *Ran* would be thrilling stuff.) After seducing Jiro, Kaede bursts into tears, because she's so jealous of his wife. The bewildered Jiro offers to dump his wife, and at this Kaede sobs even more. 'That's not what I want!' she bawls. Ah, thinks the viewer: so she is morally honourable at some level. 'Such a woman should not remain alive!' Oh. Maybe not.

War: Everyone hates each other, most people are dead, and the deranged Hidetora is living rough. His long, white beard has gone all straggly, and in his red and white robes he looks like a sad, defeated Father Christmas. The fool makes him a pointy hat out of reeds with two daffodil horns. This cheers him up a bit. Finally, there is an epic battle sequence, which is the most beautifully and accurately recreated sequence of early modern Japanese warfare you're ever likely to see. Based meticulously on the stunning panel and scroll paintings of the era, it includes gorgeous reproductions of contemporary armour, hundreds of charging horses ripping up great clods of earth, and great blasts of pink gunpowder. Sensational.

Verdict: *Ran* expands the historical story of Mori Motonari into the realm of fiction, but as an evocation of Senguko Japan it is a knockout.

Ruling as an almost exact contemporary to Elizabeth I (1558–1603), the Mughal emperor Akbar the Great (1556–1605) was a military prodigy who consolidated and expanded his dynastic empire in south Asia. He promoted a tolerant society, oversaw a cultural boom, and created his own religion. Brought up a Muslim, he married a Hindu princess, sometimes known as Jodhaa. She became the mother of his heir, Jahangir. As one of the most interesting men in history anywhere, Akbar has proved irresistible to Bollywood. The greatest Mughal movie is probably K. Asif's 1960 masterpiece *Mughal-e-Azam*, with Dilip Kumar as Akbar's son, the future emperor Jahangir, and the sensational Madhubala as his lover Anarkali. But the most beautiful to watch may be...

1556

Jodhaa-Akbar (2008)

Director: Ashutosh Gowariker • Entertainment grade: B+ • History grade: C+

War: The film opens in 1556 at the second battle of Panipat, where the teenage Akbar is watching Hindus and Afghans under King Hemu being trounced by his own Mughal army. A Mughal archer gets Hemu in the eye. He is brought before Akbar for a ceremonial beheading. But Akbar, showing an unlikely early interest in non-violence, won't play along. The sources conflict on this one, but most historians find the version where Akbar does cut the king's head off more convincing. Still, a decent start.

Sport: Akbar has grown up into beefy model-turned-actor Hrithik Roshan, and is showing off his pumped-up arms to the best possible effect by using them to tame a wild elephant. It stomps around angrily while he waves them at it. The real Akbar's court chronicler, Abul Fazal, devoted an entire, slightly embarrassed chapter to his sovereign's enthusiasm for pachyderm-based extreme sports, and there is even a record of the emperor leaping aboard a raging elephant in 1561, just like in the movie. Spot on.

Romance: King Bharmal of Amer insists that Akbar marry his daughter Jodhaa (Aishwarya Rai), in order to protect their political alliance. Initially, she is reluctant, but gradually they fall in love. It's not surprising that most of the wooing has been made up: the records of the time aren't even conclusive about the princess's name before marriage. What is surprising is how marrying a Mughal emperor has been reinvented as a very modern boy-meets-girl love story. As one of his biographers noted, Akbar married 'early and often'. He had at least two wives before Jodhaa, and many more afterwards. In the film, they're nowhere to be seen. It was also alleged that he had several thousand concubines, though, bearing in mind all the elephant riding, religion inventing and nation invading, it's not obvious how he would have fitted them into his busy schedule.

Religion: Dressed as an ordinary bloke, Akbar goes for a wander around the bazaar. He isn't very good at it. 'Insolent fool!' he shouts when someone tries to overcharge him for rice. 'Do you know with whom you have an audience?' Somehow managing not to blow his own cover, he hears that Hindus are disgruntled on account of a tax he charges them to go on pilgrimages. Horrified, he revokes it. In response, his happy subjects stage the biggest dance sequence ever seen in a Bollywood movie (or possibly any movie), and give him the title of Akbar. The real Akbar did abolish the pilgrim tax in 1562, but he was named Akbar at birth. The history books don't say anything about dance routines, either, but we'll let that pass.

Politics: The revolt of Sharifuddin Hussain (a terrific performance by Nikitin Dheer) is creatively enhanced, though the payoff line on Akbar's victory feels like it could have done with some extra oomph. 'Sharifuddin!' Akbar shouts, towering over his prone foe. 'You will not be allowed to make any more administrative decisions from now on!' The real Akbar sentenced Sharifuddin to be placed under the feet of an elephant (yes, another one). This was not supposed to kill him, only freak him out.

Verdict: 'This is just one version of the historical events,' notes a title card at the beginning of the film. 'There could be other versions and viewpoints to it.' How honest. This version of Akbar's life is unquestionably one of the most gorgeous-looking historical films ever made, and scores respectably on sixteenth-century subcontinental politics.

Akbar's court hosted the first English traders in India. Though at that time the mighty Mughal Empire was far more powerful than scabby little England, this was the beginning of a relationship that would, a couple of centuries later, see Britain rule India.

Yet England had already started colonizing places. On the other side of the world, one woman was all too aware of that. Pocahontas is the name by which history remembers Matoaka, the daughter of a chief of the Powhatan Confederacy (based in what is now Virginia) in the early seventeenth century. In 1607, 104 Englishmen and boys established Jamestown in that territory. It would become the first permanent European settlement in what is now the United States.

An English settler, John Smith, claimed that as a child Pocahontas had saved his life. She later moved to England and became a celebrity of sorts. Her story has been made into several movies, notably Terrence Mallick's gorgeously filmed *The New World* (2005), starring Q'Orianka Kilcher, Colin Farrell and Christian Bale. It gives in to the historical myth that Captain Smith and Pocahontas had a very mad affair – but subtly sets Smith up as a fantasist, which he was. Furthermore, Pocahontas is now officially a Disney princess, an all-American achievement in a modern America that this Native American woman would hardly recognize.

1607

Pocahontas (1995)

Director: Mike Gabriel & Eric Goldberg • Entertainment grade: B • History grade: D+

Culture: In 1607, John Smith and his crew are setting sail from Jacobean England for the New World. The ship is flying the brand new Union flag (designed in 1606). Smith's commander, the evil Governor Ratcliffe, has a pet pug (brought to Europe from China by Dutch traders in the sixteenth century; fashionable from around 1600). Extremely impressive attention to detail, Disney.

International relations: The natives are milling happily around their villages, singing a lovely song about their peaceable ancient ways. Meanwhile, the English are gloating about how they want to find gold, steal land and murder Indians. They land and immediately get started on some heavy-duty environmental destruction. John Smith wanders off to a waterfall, where he meets Pocahontas and they fall instantly in love. The real Pocahontas was probably not friends with quite so many winsome forest creatures and magic talking trees, but that's Disney for you. She was also about ten years of age when she met the twenty-seven-year-old John

Smith. The real Smith was a mercenary and a fantasist, but not a paedophile: he and Pocahontas were not romantically involved.

War: Pocahontas sings to Smith about how he needs to start listening to nature until he can 'paint with all the colours of the wind'. Unfortunately, the other Englishmen aren't down with folk wisdom, and set out to slaughter the 'savages'. Meanwhile, the natives are shown as being not much better, preparing for war against the 'paleface demons'. So, apparently, when Europeans conquered the Americas, Disney thinks there was equal fault on both sides.

Colonization: Having seen the error of their ways, the English and the natives all make friends. No, that's not quite what happened, but the truth isn't exactly feelgood family movie territory. Waves of infectious disease and genocide wiped out up to 90 per cent of the indigenous population. The white colonizers' belief in 'manifest destiny' licensed a fifty-year transcontinental land-grab and brutal campaign of cultural and ethnic cleansing. Those native peoples who survived were confined to reservations where they were subjected to forcible assimilation policies until the 1970s and, even in the modern day, suffer significantly higher rates of poverty, alcoholism and suicide than the American average. On the bright side, they can paint with all the colours of the wind.

People: Pocahontas is torn between staying with her people and going to England with the man she loves, but in the end decides to stay with her father, her friends, her raccoon, her hummingbird and the governor's pug, which has gone native and started wearing tattoos and feathers. In real life, Pocahontas was kidnapped by the English and married off to a man called John Rolfe. They moved to Brentford in Middlesex, where she had a short career as an object of curiosity before dying, probably of tuberculosis, in her early twenties.

Verdict: Disney's *Pocahontas* attempts to give a generation of children the impression that the conquest of the Americas was a cheerful, cooperative effort between the enlightened Europeans and the accommodating natives. Not to mention the impression that a pug might marry a raccoon.

4

Darkness and Enlightenment

English Civil War political and military leader Oliver Cromwell is one of the least prepossessing figures in English history: ugly, grumpy, puritanical and murderous. Plus he actually did call off Christmas, as the Sheriff of Nottingham (Alan Rickman) threatens in *Robin Hood: Prince of Thieves*. Or, more accurately, Puritan radicals called it off – but, when Cromwell became Lord Protector of the Commonwealth of England in 1653, he allowed the ban to continue and observed it himself.

Cromwell has been played by Tim Roth in *To Kill a King* (2003) and John Le Mesurier in *The Moonrakers* (1958) – no, not the James Bond film. The 'moonrakers' were legendary gin smugglers who had hidden their contraband in Wiltshire ponds. When they were discovered by the authorities in the act of fishing it out, they pretended to be village idiots attempting to rake out a piece of the moon that they believed had fallen from space.

1640

Cromwell (1970)

Director: Ken Hughes • Entertainment grade: C– • History grade: D

People: It's 1640, and curmudgeonly Puritan Oliver Cromwell (Richard Harris) is packing up to move to America with the rest of the anti-fun lobby. He might not fit in with the Pilgrim Fathers, though: he starts out rabidly pro-king. When one fellow suggests taking up arms against the monarch, Cromwell bellows that it is treason, and throws him out of his house. Then he's in a church and, would you believe it, some royal twit has only gone and put gold things on the altar. Cromwell completely loses his rag, chucking plates and candlesticks hither and thither while yelling about graven images. 'God damn this king!' he howls. It's only twenty minutes in, and already the film's apparent hero, played by Harris as if suffering from acute constipation, has lost the audience's sympathy. Unless, of course, you just can't get enough of wild-eyed, pompous, middle-aged men shouting at you. It's like watching Fox News.

Politics: The hero void cannot be filled by languid fop-in-chief King Charles I (Alec Guinness). Inaccurately, Cromwell suggests that England become a democracy. 'Democracy, Mr Cromwell,' replies the king, 'was a Greek drollery based on the foolish notion that there are extraordinary possibilities in very ordinary people.' Cromwell goes on to suggest that everyone should have schools and universities as well as democracy, and someone even talks about votes for the poor and underprivileged. This is completely wrong. The groups that spoke for the rights of the common man during the English Civil War were the Levellers and the Diggers. Cromwell suppressed both. Some Levellers actually went on to ally with Royalists. Absent entirely from the movie, too, is his Irish campaign, which even in its most forgiving interpretation doesn't do much for Old Ironsides' supposed status as a hero of liberation.

War: At the Battle of Edgehill, Charles's dashing nephew Prince Rupert of the Rhine (Timothy Dalton) arrives with his big flashy sword and fluffy white poodle, the latter groomed to match his elaborately plumed hat. Rupert did have such a poodle, Boy, which was the envy of the Grand Turk. It was often seen on the battlefield, and ultimately joined the death toll at the Battle of Marston Moor. Prince and pooch are shown leading the Royalists to a resounding victory, despite Cromwell's brave frontline fighting. This isn't true at all. Edgehill was inconclusive, and Cromwell arrived a day too late to fight. Predictably, he reacts by shouting even more, and stomps off to form the New Model Army. Cue a training montage of recruits struggling over fences, clashing swords together and decapitating straw Royalists. Thereafter the film skips directly to the Battle of Naseby, at which it claims the Parliamentarians were outnumbered. That's exactly the wrong way round.

Regicide: The most accurate scenes are those of Charles's goodbyes to his children and execution, and even those aren't right. His marriage is portrayed as a half-hearted struggle against a scheming Catholic wife, Henrietta Maria, lazily characterized as Lady Macbeth. When king and queen kiss goodbye, the earth stays resolutely still. Finally, the axe falls, and the executioner holds up the king's severed head, crying, 'Behold the head of a traitor!' Famously, no words were spoken at Charles's execution, for the executioner wished to remain anonymous – a few not especially credible rumours said it was Cromwell himself.

1649

Winstanley (1975)

Director: Kevin Brownlow • Entertainment grade: C+ • History grade: A

Gerrard Winstanley began the True Levellers, a Christian group devoted to egalitarian and communal living, which formed in the wake of the English Civil War. They became known as the Diggers, and are often considered precursors of socialists or communists.

Society: In April 1649, the Diggers toil on common land at St George's Hill in Weybridge, Surrey. Scowly-faced local Presbyterian parson John Platt (David Bramley) disapproves. His wife (Alison Halliwell) has had quite enough of him moaning on and, what's more, he slurps his soup. She stomps off up the hill to join the hippies. Winstanley (who is played not by an actor but by a schoolteacher, the late Miles Halliwell) soon runs into trouble with the law, represented by Fairfax. 'Many local gentlemen and freeholders have complained to the council of state that you are tumultuous, and a danger to the county,' Fairfax says. To be fair, they are a bit tumultuous. One of them gets naked and capers around. No one seems to know whose children are whose. Shocking stuff.

Economics: 'Was the earth made to preserve a few covetous and proud men to live at ease,' says Winstanley, 'to bag and barn up the treasures of the earth from others, that these may beg and starve in a fruitful land?' This line is from the real Winstanley's 1649 pamphlet *The New Law of Righteousness*. Many of Winstanley's real words are used in the film, and the fidelity to seventeenth-century life is extremely impressive. 'We made the film to see if it is possible to make an absolutely authentic historical film,' said director Kevin Brownlow in 1997. 'Even the animals came from rare breeds, and the armour for the battle scene came from the Tower of London.'

Adversity: They may be right-on, but it isn't much fun hanging out with the Diggers. If you're a kid, your only toy is a muddy bank you can slide down (mind you, in the seventeenth century, that wasn't such a bad deal). For the grown-ups, it's a daily grind of hacking around unsprouting seeds in tough ground, contracting respiratory infections, and sleeping in straw huts huddled up to other stinky folk for warmth. Plus, the Diggers irritate the locals by rejecting property and propriety, so they keep getting beaten up by landowners, soldiers and assorted agents of privilege. Then the Ranters want to join in, and frankly they seem like rather hard work. (In a pleasingly credible touch, their leader is played by Sid Rawle – again, not an actor, but a peace campaigner and twentieth-century adherent to Digger ideas.)

Violence: The violence Winstanley and the Diggers face in the film is accurate, notably from the real-life Parson Platt. According to T. Wilson Hayes's *Winstanley the Digger*, Platt and a gang 'attacked a Digger family, beat the wife so that she miscarried, and destroyed their house'. He later summoned fifty men and torched the entire colony. Eventually, the Diggers have had enough. 'We have turned the cheek once too often,' says one. 'Soon we will be without a face.'

Verdict: *Winstanley* scores modestly for entertainment: it's a fine film but it moves slowly, and may confuse those who aren't familiar with the subject. As a piece of historical representation, though, it's exceptionally spot on.

One of the most intriguing monarchs of the seventeenth century was Sweden's Queen Christina, a highly educated and cultured woman who famously dressed as a man for considerable parts of her life. She was played by Liv Ullmann in *The Abdication* (1974), but the iconic Christina will surely always be Garbo.

1650

Queen Christina (1933)

Director: Rouben Mamoulian • Entertainment grade: A– • History grade: B+

Christina Vasa became king (technically not queen) of Sweden at the age of five in 1632. She was brought up as a boy and became a noted intellectual, debating with René Descartes and inspiring a resurgence in the arts. Her efforts as an administrator were less impressive. By 1654, she was fed up with her government, and it was fed up with her. She abdicated, converted to Catholicism, and spent the rest of her life travelling around Europe dressed as a man.

Sexuality: Queen Christina (Greta Garbo) strides around in britches, slaps her thigh and delivers hearty guffaws. Her fictional love interest is the Spanish ambassador, Don Antonio. Garbo had Laurence Olivier fired from this role and replaced with her boyfriend, John Gilbert. He does an acceptable job, even if he does look like Bert from *Sesame Street* with a goatee. The council hassles Christina to marry her cousin, war hero Charles Gustavus. It is true that Christina was deeply annoyed by the constant pressure to marry – not least because she was passionately in love with her lady-in-waiting, Ebba Sparre. Being pre-censorship, the film casts a glance that way. Garbo greets Ebba with a big kiss on the lips, and throws a strop when her lady-in-waiting wants to marry a man.

Politics: Christina ends the war in the face of opposition from her nobles, generals and bishops. 'But what of the peasants?' she asks, gesturing to a troupe of slouching yokels with unkempt beards cowering in the corner. Swedish government did indeed have peasant representation from 1527.

Marriage: Don Antonio enters to a chorus of castanets (he's Spanish, see?) and presents Christina with a portrait of his king and her suitor, Philip IV of Spain. Philip has boggly eyes, sticky-out ears and a gigantic chin. 'Oh! Does he look like that?' she asks, with another hearty guffaw. Sadly, yes: intensive inbreeding over many generations didn't exactly turn the Spanish royals into hotties. By now, her council is panicking. 'You cannot die an old maid!' gasps an accurately portrayed Axel Oxenstierna. 'I have no intention to, Chancellor,' she replies. 'I shall die a bachelor.'

Religion: Christina's conversion to Catholicism is glossed over. In the film, it's her affair with Antonio that stirs up public anger. She is accused of 'Spanish witchcraft', and starts to be followed around by a disgruntled mob brandishing flaming torches in an orderly fashion. Well, this is Sweden.

In France, the fabulous reigns of the Bourbon kings Louis XIII and Louis XIV are largely known on film through Alexandre Dumas's stories of *The Three Musketeers*. Vincent Price played Cardinal Richelieu in the 1948 version, starring Gene Kelly and Lana Turner; Charlton Heston played Richelieu in 1973 among an all-star cast, also featuring Oliver Reed, Christopher Lee and Spike Milligan; Tim Curry does a fine turn as the Cardinal in a 1993 version, alongside an improbably Brat Packy cast including Kiefer Sutherland and Charlie Sheen. There have also been many versions, in French and English, of the fanciful sequel Dumas based on a real-life mystery: *The Man in the Iron Mask*.

1700

The Man in the Iron Mask

(1998)

Director: Randall Wallace • Entertainment grade: B– • History grade: Fail

During the reign of Louis XIV, a mysterious masked man was kept prisoner for thirty-four years in the Bastille and other jails. His identity has never been established.

Identity: The film opens in a dungeon. 'Are you dead yet?' grunts a jailer through a hatch, and then we see him: the man in the iron mask. The writer Voltaire suggested that the prisoner's mask was iron, but it seems he made it up. The only piece of first-hand evidence available reports that the prisoner's mask was of black velvet. Identities suggested for the prisoner have included Richard Cromwell, the Duke of Beaufort and an Italian diplomat. While he was busy making things up, Voltaire suggested that it might have been the king's secret brother. Alexandre Dumas père's last Three Musketeers novel, *The Vicomte de Bragelonne*, made him Philippe, the king's secret *twin* brother. The film plumps for this, too. In real life, the masked prisoner was registered as Eustache Dauger.

Politics: Dumas's novel is steeped in the politics of Louis XIV's court, including the complex machinations of Jean-Baptiste Colbert, and the king's love affair with Louise de la Vallière. This film couldn't give a monkey's for any of that. In place of Colbert, there is a fleeting cameo by a massive wig, under which is concealed Hugh Laurie, playing 'King's Advisor'. Other than that, the French state appears to have no politicians at all. This will be news to the French. Instead, it is a musketeerist dictatorship, run by the petulant Louis XIV (Leonardo DiCaprio) under the watchful eye of the loyal, fictional D'Artagnan (Gabriel Byrne). The three ageing musketeers, Athos (John Malkovich), Porthos (Gerard Depardieu) and Aramis (Jeremy Irons), loiter around the edges, grumbling treasonously about replacing the king. If you're thinking this cast is too good for this film: yes, it is. DiCaprio, Malkovich and Byrne give conspicuously excellent performances, which really show the script up.

Royalty: Aramis springs Philippe from the Bastille and carries him off to the country, where the Three Musketeers embark on a three-week makeover to help the traumatized boy pass himself off as his cocky twin, Louis XIV. Which means… king training montage! Watch him learn to dance all formal! Whack about with swords! Prance on a horse! Flirt with passing shepherdesses! Wear high-heeled girly shoes without giggling every time he sees his own feet!

Plot: The musketeers have to switch the princes at a swanky masked ball, under the nose of D'Artagnan. This won't be easy, for it has already been established that D'Artagnan is the kind of badass dude who can slice an apple in half in mid-air, hurl a sword into the chest of a running man from twenty feet away, and stop an escaping helicopter by throwing a jeep at it so it blows up. One of these things doesn't actually happen in *The Man in the Iron Mask*, and instead comes from the 2009 Telugu movie *Magadheera*; but its inclusion would not have made this film much less accurate. In fact, it's a pity that writer-director

Randall Wallace didn't push the camp factor even further. The screenplay is one smart rewrite and a few Jerry Bruckheimer/ Michael Bay explosions away from producing a wildly enjoyable, though ridiculous, movie. Unfortunately, the madcap, contrived plot occasionally sags, and flashes only now and then with the wit it would need to make it an all-out guilty pleasure. A few lines hit the mark, such as when ninja priest Aramis growls, 'It's Judgement Day,' before punching the king in the face. Not sure that line is in *The Vicomte de Bragelonne*. Maybe *Terminator 2*.

In 1615, Japan was united under the Tokugawa shogunate, ushering in the Edo period, two and half centuries of peace and prosperity, after the chaos of the preceding years. The most famous film about Edo Japan is probably Akira Kurosawa's masterpiece *Seven Samurai* (1954), remade in Hollywood as *The Magnificent Seven* (1960). Hollywood has also had a go at one of Japan's most beloved historical stories of the Edo period: that of the Forty-Seven Ronin.

1701

47 Ronin (2013)

Director: Carl Rinsch • Entertainment grade: E • History grade: D–

In 1701, Japanese daimyo (lord) Asano Naganori attacked Kira Yoshinaka, a court official, in Edo Castle (now the site of Tokyo's imperial palace). Asano was ordered to commit ritual suicide. His samurai became ronin (masterless), a state of disgrace. Knowing Asano had been provoked into attacking Kira, forty-seven of them plotted to avenge his death and restore their honour.

Date: 'Ancient feudal Japan,' intones a voiceover. It's not ancient, though, is it? It's 1701 and they have firearms and mechanical clocks and printing presses and everything. 'A land shrouded in mystery. Forbidden to foreigners. A group of magical islands, home to witches and demons.' Righto, so that's: factual error, orientalism, more orientalism, heavy-handed magical realist orientalism. The voiceover perfectly sets the tone for the movie: a sludgy, pompous and witless mash-up of oriental fantasies with little care for the historical story. Our hero, or at least the closest we have to one, is Kai (Keanu Reeves), a fictional changeling who stumbles out of the demon forest and into the household of Lord Asano.

Fauna: A bunch of samurai are hunting a local computer-generated monster. It's a sort of big, angry marmoset with heaps of eyes and twigs for arms. Despite the film's often beautiful production design and a whopping great budget of $225 million, the compositing looks shonky; the easiest way to kill this thing might be control-alt-delete. But of course the only one who can stop it is Kai. The real story of the forty-seven ronin has spawned a whole genre of literature and art called chushingura, which is held very dear in the Japanese cultural canon. Wisely, Japanese viewers (and most other viewers) stayed away from this movie, making it one of the biggest flops of 2013.

More fauna: The film stumbles back towards the historical record when Asano organizes a reception for the shogun, Tokugawa Tsunayoshi. In real life, the fifth Tokugawa shogun is remembered mainly for being an animal rights fanatic, so obsessed with the welfare of dogs in particular that he made it illegal for people to harm them in any way – even if a dog attacked and a person was trying to fight it off. You just had to let it eat you if it wanted. He also banned the selling of live birds, shrimps and shellfish. He'd have been absolutely furious about Kai killing that twig-armed marmoset thing, but the film can't be bothered to give him any elements of his real character, so he doesn't even notice.

Magic: Asano hopes to impress the shogun. Evil Lord Kira (Tadanobu Asano) has other ideas, put into his mostly empty head by a Lady Macbeth-style sorceress whom the film rather unimaginatively calls Witch. She is played by Rinko Kikuchi, whose ultra-high-camp overacting produces the only genuinely enjoyable performance in this otherwise relentlessly dour movie. 'Rivers of blood and mountains of corpses will not stand in our way,' she hisses to Kira, like a sexy Enoch Powell. Quite a niche market, sexy Enoch Powells.

Romance: Witch tricks Asano into attacking Kira. The shogun orders him to commit seppuku – ritual suicide – and makes his samurai ronin. The film drags itself exhaustingly through a series of story points straight out of a screenwriting primer – the ronin have to band together, get magic swords, face a couple of increasingly big challenges, blah blah – while the audience fight desperately to stay awake. There's a tedious subplot whereby Kira intends to marry Kai's fictional love interest, Asano's daughter and heir Mika (Ko Shibasaki). In real life, Asano had no children and adopted his brother as his heir. The film puts Mika in a white wedding dress with veil. This was not even traditional in Europe until Queen Victoria wore one to marry Prince Albert, 139 years after the forty-seven ronin affair. In Edo Japan, a bride would have worn a brightly coloured uchikake kimono. Meanwhile, everybody's running around thwacking each other with swords and turning into dragons and whatnot. It's quite a feat to make this stuff boring, but somehow the filmmakers have really pulled it off.

In Scotland, the eighteenth century was a time for rebellion. The two big Jacobite risings – known as the Fifteen (1715) and the Forty-Five (1745) – aimed to restore the Scottish Stuart monarchy deposed by the so-called Glorious Revolution of 1688, and restore Scottish independence from Great Britain. The Scottish outlaw Rob Roy MacGregor, who fought in the Fifteen and afterwards, has been the subject of biopics including *Rob Roy: Highland Rogue* (1953), starring Richard Todd, and the dismal Highland soap-opera *Rob Roy* (1995), starring Liam Neeson. The Forty-Five and its hero, Charles Edward Stuart, known to supporters as Bonnie Prince Charlie and to detractors as the Young Pretender, have also had several treatments. These include *Bonnie Prince Charlie* (1923), with Ivor Novello; *The Master of Ballantrae* (1953), with Errol Flynn; and this:

1745

Bonnie Prince Charlie (1948)

Director: Anthony Kimmins • Entertainment grade: D– • History grade: C

Production: '*Bonnie Prince Charlie* was one of those huge florid extravaganzas that reek of disaster from the start,' star David Niven admitted. Halfway through the nine-month shoot, Niven cabled producer Sam Goldwyn: 'I HAVE NOW WORKED EVERY DAY FOR FIVE MONTHS ON THIS PICTURE AND NOBODY CAN TELL ME HOW THE STORY ENDS STOP ADVISE'. Goldwyn couldn't help: according to Niven's biographer Sheridan Morley, he thought the movie was called 'Charlie Bonnie', and was 'apparently under the mistaken impression that it was to be the story of a lovable Scots terrier'.

Claimants: In Rome, the Old Pretender, James Stuart, and his son Charlie (Niven) plot their return. The Old Pretender is wearing a massive grey wig and rhinestone-encrusted frock coat; his son is in a white wig and bedazzled jacket. If you remember how Sir Elton John and his husband dressed for Sir Elton's fiftieth birthday party, that's the look. The Young Pretender sails for Scotland ('Look! Look over there! Scotland!' he cries from the deck of his ship, in case you haven't been following). Ashore, he meets a shepherd, who is dressed less glitzily in some mud. 'I do ken it!' the shepherd burbles in the film's hammy attempt at Scots dialect. 'You're your father's son! I bid ye welcome!' He bursts into patriotic tears. Hooray for toffs.

Culture: The clan chiefs assemble, all competing for the most extravagant Scottish accent. The Marquess of Tullibardine wins, rolling his Rs so fiercely one fears his head might fall off. Charlie puts on the charm, and soon they're all up for a war. Another of the film's twee peasants appears. This one's kind of a wizard. 'Blind Jamie can see into the morrow as easy as a lass can look into a glass,' trills the shepherd. Blind Jamie turns to Charlie. 'Ye have yellow hair,' he intones, mystically. Uncanny. Then, just when you think things can't get worse, he starts to sing.

War: Charlie macks on Clementina Walkinshaw (Judy Campbell), who in real life would go on to bear him a daughter in the course of a relationship that was more abusive than romantic. Meanwhile, Lord George Murray (Jack Hawkins) keeps him away from the fighting. 'Am I to sleep through the campaign?' Charlie wails. 'Why not, sir?' snaps Murray. 'So long as you find the crown of Great Britain on your head when you awake.' By this point, the audience may also be considering sleeping through the campaign, and the film's dismal attempt to liven itself up with Charlie's victory at Prestonpans doesn't help. The Highlanders' surprise attack on the Hanoverian forces is filmed in the dark, which is historically accurate but makes things quite hard to see.

Escape: Worse yet, when it gets to Culloden, the film misses out the battle entirely – cutting straight to everyone already dead or half-dead, slumped on a battlefield set up in a very small studio. Someone just off-camera is ruffling the gorse with a hairdryer to make it look like windswept Culloden Moor. Perhaps Mr Goldwyn had stopped sending the cheques. Left with almost an hour of its bloated run-time to fill, the film stretches the story of Charlie's escape with Flora MacDonald (Margaret Leighton) beyond any possible interest. This could have been quite jolly – in real life, the Young Pretender dressed as a woman and called himself Betty Burke – but instead the film wheels Blind Jamie back on to do some more singing'n'soothsaying, and half-heartedly contrives a romance between Charlie and Flora. 'Dear Flora! I wish I could give you a kingdom,' Charlie says, before heroically scuttling off back to the continent to spend the rest of his life getting drunk and having affairs.

Verdict: Maybe they should just have made that movie about the lovable Scots terrier.

By the eighteenth century, South America was mostly divided into European colonies. During the seventeenth and eighteenth centuries, Jesuits travelled from Europe to bring Christianity to the newly colonized inhabitants. They set up missions, known as 'reductions', to preach to the indigenous people. The autonomy of these reductions came to be seen as a threat to Spanish and Portuguese imperial power. The indigenous Guaraní people of the reductions in part of what is now Argentina, Paraguay and Brazil fought a war against Spanish and Portuguese forces in 1756. This contributed to the expulsion of Jesuits from the Americas at the end of the 1750s. It doesn't sound like the kind of thing Hollywood would leap to make a movie about, but it did – and the result earned seven Oscar nominations (winning just one, for Best Cinematography).

1756

The Mission (1986)

Director: Roland Joffé • Entertainment grade: B • History grade: B

Crime: Everything goes wrong for slave trader Rodrigo Mendoza (Robert de Niro) when his girlfriend dumps him for his own brother at the town carnival. (Incidentally, the carnival troupe dressed in what appear to be twentieth-century Ku Klux Klan outfits are actually Nazarenos – Catholic penitents following a completely separate tradition from Seville.) Mendoza reacts pretty badly to this news, stomping into the couple's bedroom, calling his brother out, and stabbing him to death in the street. Afterwards, he mopes around in the local monastery, until Jesuit Father Gabriel (Jeremy Irons) helps him get over it by making him lug a massive bag of clunking armour twice the size of himself up the Iguazú Falls. This sort of works, if by 'works' you mean 'makes him have a nervous breakdown and turns him into a fire-breathing religious fanatic'.

Culture: Soon, Mendoza is helping to build a reduction in the jungle, and having tribal markings painted on his chest by nubile indigenous Guaraní women. But disaster is just around the corner in the shape of Cardinal Altamirano (Ray McAnally), who has been sent to bring the Jesuits to heel and make sure the slaveholding traders get their way. 'I had arrived in South America,' muses the cardinal in voiceover, while he watches a young Guaraní boy sing. 'But I soon began to understand for the first time what a strange world I had been sent to judge.' This is a bit rich coming from a grown man wearing a big white lace apron, coiffed horsehair wig and spiffy red cape. The boy looks way more normal in 1750s Argentina than he does.

Ideology: Father Gabriel takes the cardinal on a tour of the reductions, where profits are shared equally among the indigenous and European reduction inhabitants. 'There's a French radical group that teaches that doctrine,' says the cardinal, somewhat prophetically. The French radical Gabriel Bonnot de Mably started to write proto-communist works in the 1750s, but these made little impact before 1763. Within the context of this film, the Jesuits are presented entirely as lefty heroes. However, there is another opinion that suggests the reductions were repressive theocratic city-states with a high degree of coercion and imposition on the local population.

Violence: At this point, anyone familiar with South American history will start to feel vaguely sick at the prospect of inevitable onscreen genocide. Lo and behold, the Europeans team up to destroy the native culture, enslave and abuse indigenous people, and pile up babies to murder. All of this is horribly accurate. The battle sequences dramatizing the Guaraní war of 1756 are superbly recreated, but the exceptional technical achievement doesn't detract from the appalling reality.

Thousands of miles away in the northern extremes of the Americas, more wars were in progress between Americans of European origin and indigenous peoples. Movies about settlers versus Native Americans were quite fashionable in the first half of the twentieth century – but those conflicts now tend to be seen by historians in less glorious terms. It seems highly unlikely Hollywood would make such a straightforwardly pro-white-conquest film as this in the twenty-first century:

1759

Northwest Passage: Book I – Rogers' Rangers (1940)

Director: King Vidor • Entertainment grade: D • History grade: C

Rogers' Rangers were an independent company within the British Army during the Seven Years' War in North America.

Uniforms: Fictional mapmaker Langdon Towne (Robert Young) meets a fellow who appears to be dressed as Peter Pan. It's 1759, so Peter Pan won't be invented for another 143 years – which may be why this doesn't freak him out as much as it should. He accepts Peter Pan's offer of hot buttered rum, and awakes the next morning to find he has joined the British Army. Peter Pan turns out to be Major Robert Rogers of the Rangers (Spencer Tracy). The costume department got carried away with the Rangers' uniform, which in real life was a simple green jacket rather than something fit for a boy who refuses to grow up.

War: Rogers leads his men to the French-allied Abenaki village of St Francis, 180 miles north through a hostile wilderness. Their task is to wipe out the village, in revenge for what the real Rogers called the 'barbarities' that the Abenaki had inflicted on the British. The screenplay – drawing from the guts-and-glory novel on which it is based – gives one Lieutenant Crofton the lines about Abenaki warfare, which are supposed to justify this genocide. 'Phillips had a strip of skin torn upwards from his stomach. They hung him from a tree by it while he was still alive. ... They tore my brother's arms out of him. They chopped the ends of his ribs away from his backbone and pried them out through his skin, one by one.' Even spoken rather than shown, this is strong stuff for a big-budget MGM movie in 1940.

Race: The movie's presentation of the raid on St Francis as a heroic act is historically questionable, and it isn't helped by the unceasingly racist depiction of all Native Americans as degenerate subhumans. 'Them Mohawks had pelts half as good as a weasel, they'd be worth shooting,' snarls one British soldier, who is supposed to be a sympathetic character. The Mohawks were Britain's allies.

More war: It was 3 a.m. on 6 October 1759 when the real Rangers attacked St Francis. In the film, this has been shifted to a more Technicolor-friendly time of day. St Francis is shown to contain no Abenaki women and only one (male) child, who is saved and taken prisoner. In history books, and in the novel, the Rangers were less clear about sticking to General Jeffrey Amherst's order to spare women and children. In 1940, MGM likewise thought it was just fine for a hero to massacre native men, but the sight of Spencer Tracy gleefully plunging a bayonet into the chest of a five-year-old girl might have taken things too far.

Cannibalism: The Rangers stumble back through the wilderness, facing starvation. *Northwest Passage* is surprisingly disgusting on this point, and thereby true both to the novel and to history. Lieutenant Crofton hoards something in his knapsack, eating bits of it at intervals. Don't watch this film on a full stomach: it turns out to be the head of an Abenaki warrior. Real-life Rangers George Campbell and Robert Kirkwood said that human bodies were eaten on the raid, including an Abenaki woman who may have been killed for that purpose. Contemporary historian Thomas Mante, working from Campbell's first-hand account, wrote that some Rangers found the mutilated remains of their own comrades by a river: 'But this was not a season for distinctions. On them, accordingly, they fell like Cannibals, and devoured part of them raw; their impatience being too great to wait the kindling of a fire to dress it by.'

Exploration: The search for a northwest passage from the Atlantic to the Pacific has little to do with what's going on in this film. At the end, Rogers announces his intention to find one. This was supposed to be the sequel. Though *Northwest Passage: Book I* was a hit with audiences, it had cost too much to make. MGM canned Book II – and, just as in real life, no northwest passage was ever found.

The single most interesting woman of the eighteenth century as far as cinema is concerned is Catherine II of Russia, known as Catherine the Great. She was a German princess who became Empress of Russia in 1762 after the murder of her mentally infirm husband, Peter III. Over a reign of thirty-four years, she greatly expanded the Russian Empire and instituted a cultural renaissance. Despite this, she is most often remembered for a persistent myth that she died while indulging her carnal appetites with a horse. There are three really great screen Catherine movies. *The Rise of Catherine the Great* (1934) casts a somewhat limp Elisabeth Bergner as Catherine, but the incomparable Flora Robson as her mother-in-law Empress Elizabeth and an outstandingly camp Douglas Fairbanks Jr as her husband Peter III. *A Royal Scandal* (1945) is the wittiest, with Tallulah Bankhead as Catherine. But the most iconic may be:

1762

The Scarlet Empress (1934)

Director: Josef von Sternberg • Entertainment grade: B • History grade: D–

Society: The film opens with a montage depicting life in Russia in 1745, which largely seems to consist of elaborately fetishized torture. This film was released just as the Hays Code imposed heavy censorship on American films, and it doesn't abide by any of the rules. Heads are axed off, bodies are broken on a wheel, naked women are burned at the stake, and someone is peeled out of an iron maiden (not invented for another half century). This sequence tells you a lot more about the mind of director Josef von Sternberg than it does about the reign of the Empress Elizabeth, which was quite clement.

Casting: The S&M stuff dissolves to a pretty scene with the teenage Catherine in her German bower. Despite piling tiers of flouncy tulle and bows on the 33-year-old Marlene Dietrich, Sternberg has failed utterly to make her believable as a 16-year-old innocent. Enter the Count Alexei, a Russian envoy who is to take her away to be married to the tsar. He seems to be based on Empress Elizabeth's real-life lover, Alexei Razumovsky, and is played by future Republican Congressman John Lodge as a moody sexpot in tight black trousers, eye make-up and wild hair. In reality, Razumovsky looked a lot less like Russell Brand, and a lot more like what you might imagine if you picture a Republican Congressman, perhaps one that had just enjoyed a very long lunch. Also, wrong empress.

Romance: Catherine arrives in Russia to discover that her sole purpose is to incubate a son for Elizabeth's half-witted heir, Peter. Unfortunately, Peter is busy burbling malignities and playing with his toy soldiers. This is true: he was famously attached to his dolls. Meanwhile, his mistress Elizabeth Vorontsova's main occupation is to shoot death stares at Catherine. This bit is reasonably accurate. 'Your husband doesn't mean a thing to you,' Alexei says to Catherine. 'He does! I'll always be faithful to him,' Catherine replies. 'Don't be absurd,' says Alexei. 'Those ideas are old fashioned. This is the eighteenth century.'

Politics: After discovering her sexuality in the arms of a random guardsman, Catherine is transformed into a political sophisticate. Not historically supportable, but at least Dietrich is finally allowed to drop her painfully unconvincing ingénue act. Catherine's road to power is simplified down to an intertitle: 'And while His Imperial Majesty Peter III terrorized Russia, Catherine coolly added the army to her list of conquests.' What, *all* of them? The real Catherine plotted with lots of supporters but just one paramour, Grigory Orlov, depicted briefly and inaccurately here as a man with a moustache. Orlov does away with Peter (in reality, the murderer was probably his brother), leaving the way clear for Catherine to ride her white stallion all the way into the imperial throne room. It was probably too much to hope that Sternberg wouldn't mention the horse.

There are too many films about the American Revolution of 1776 to mention here, but film fans interested in a pretty accurate version of events might look up the director's cut of Hugh Hudson's *Revolution* (1985), with Al Pacino and Donald Sutherland. Panned by critics on its initial release, the restored version is greatly improved; its recreation of common soldiers' experiences is particularly impressive. Hollywood has also produced some much less serious revolutionary stories...

1776

1776 (1972)

Director: Peter H. Hunt • Entertainment grade: D • History grade: C

The Second Continental Congress was a meeting of delegates from the colonies of North America. It declared independence from Britain in 1776.

Entertainment: Most history flicks feature at least two of the following elements: swordfights, explosions, gladiators, spies, pirates, cowboys, Nazis, heaving bosoms, cavalry charges, sex, intrigue, murder, torture, ridiculously large guns and Henry VIII. Work out how to get all of those into one movie, and your fortune is made. The Second Continental Congress, landmark of world history though it was, featured none of them. It was a group of men sitting in a stuffy room in Philadelphia, arguing over details of policy. For six years. Not only have the makers of this film bravely attempted to turn this into popular entertainment; they have made it three hours long. And a musical.

Dialogue: 'I say vote yes! Vote yes! Vote for independency!' trills John Adams, while the rest of the Congress choruses: 'Sit down, John! Sit down, John! For God's sake, John, sit down!' Wonderful. All politicians should be forced to debate in song. There's a minuet about conservatism. There's a waltz about slavery. Benjamin Franklin, portrayed as Father Christmas moonlighting as a mad professor, declines to write the Declaration of Independence, singing: 'The things I write are only light extemporania/I won't put politics on paper; it's a mania/So I refuse to use the pen in Pennsylvania.'

Sex: The writing of the constitution is left to Thomas Jefferson. But there's a problem: he's sexually frustrated. Martha Jefferson is shipped in, and Franklin and Adams wait outside their digs for Jefferson to get his rocks off. 'Positively indecent!' spits Adams. 'Standing down here waiting for them to... er... well, what will people think?' 'Don't worry, John,' says Franklin, 'the history books will clean it up.' Certainly, some historians can be prudish to the point of actual censorship of their subjects' lives, but here the movie is just being silly. Martha Jefferson was perilously ill during the writing of the Declaration of Independence – and pregnant. This explains the real Thomas Jefferson's keenness to return to her side. To be fair, it was always going to be tricky to get gladiators or Nazis into the Second Continental Congress, so they've had to make do with one heaving bosom, and the implication that the future third president of the United States was a sex addict.

Politics: Abigail Adams beseeches her own husband to return to Boston: 'Just tell the Congress to declare independency/Then sign your name, get out of there and/Hurry home to me/Our children all have dysentery.' Magnificent. Meanwhile, Jefferson and Adams have a showdown with the southern delegates, who walk out of the Congress over the possible outlawing of slavery. In real life, according to Jefferson, the South Carolina and Georgia delegates did request that a line criticizing slavery be struck out of the Declaration. But they did not strop out of the Congress altogether. Moreover, some northerners agreed with them.

Free speech: In the song 'Cool, Cool, Considerate Men', Pennsylvania delegate John Dickinson and his chorus of pompadoured Brit-loving conservatives sing about how the poor majority can be conned into supporting the privileges of the extremely wealthy. 'Don't forget that most men with nothing would rather protect the possibility of becoming rich than face the reality of being poor,' Dickinson snarls. It's unexpectedly incisive, and by far the best moment of the movie (apart from the line about dysentery). When this film was released in 1972, President Richard Nixon himself asked his friend Jack L. Warner, the producer, to cut this song. Too close to the bone, apparently. Warner complied. It's a wonder that Mount Rushmore didn't patriotically launch itself into the stratosphere, and land with a splat on the pair of them. The song has been reinstated for the DVD version.

1780

The Patriot (2000)

Director: Roland Emmerich • Entertainment grade: C • History grade: Fail

People: South Carolina militia leader Benjamin Martin (Mel Gibson) is a humble single father whose hobbies include freeing slaves, being lovely to his seven angelic children, and whittling rocking chairs. Martin is based on a sanitized composite of several historical militiamen, most obviously the 'Swamp Fox', Francis Marion. In contrast to the virtuous Martin, the British Colonel Tavington (Jason Isaacs), based on the real Banastre Tarleton, is a sneering, sadistic monster. Tarleton was accused of various evils – including firing on surrendering troops at Waxhaw Creek – but the deeds attributed to Tavington here are wholly made up. Furthermore, for all Martin keeps banging on about Tavington breaking 'the rules of war', there were none in the 1780s. There was an expectation that officers and soldiers would respect certain customs, but nothing was formalized until the first Geneva Convention in 1864.

International relations: In one scene, Tavington herds noncombatant men, women and children into a church, locks the doors, and sets it on fire. At the time of the film's release, some historians noted the similarity between this and the notorious Nazi massacre of French villagers in Oradour-sur-Glane in 1944. It is, however, nothing like anything that happened in the American Revolution. 'This will be forgotten,' scoffs Tavington. It's a disgraceful attempt to sow the seed of a completely unfounded conspiracy theory, implying that the fact nobody has ever heard of the British Army burning a church full of innocents in South Carolina doesn't mean it didn't happen. Well, it didn't. As the American historian Richard F. Snow commented: 'Of course it never happened – if it had do you think Americans would have forgotten it? It could have kept us out of World War I.'

Politics: According to *The Patriot*, slavery was practically nonexistent in South Carolina and really not that bad, anyway. The few slaves shown are a cheerful lot, all of whom have been given their freedom to retire to a beachside cabaña. There's even a token slave in Martin's militia. 'We will have a chance to make a new world,' Martin's son Gabriel (Heath Ledger) tells him earnestly, 'where all men are equal in the sight of God.' 'Equal,' intones the slave. 'That sounds good.' Don't get your hopes up, old chap. It took the Civil War to end slavery in the US, almost a century after *The Patriot* is set. Even then, South Carolina was on the wrong side, being so attached to its slaveholding that it was the first state to secede from the Union after Abraham Lincoln's election.

War: The film's final set piece looks vaguely like the Battle of Cowpens in 1781, with elements of the Battle of Guilford Courthouse. Martin grabs the Stars and Stripes and leads the charge towards General Cornwallis's troops. The Brits are taken by surprise, and defeated. It would have taken the real Cornwallis by surprise, too, for he was never defeated in South Carolina, and he wasn't even at the Battle of Cowpens. He won Guilford Courthouse. Tarleton lost Cowpens, though, unlike Tavington in the film, he survived and lived till a ripe old age. The real general whose victory against Cornwallis won the war, following the siege of Yorktown, was some bloke called George Washington. Here, all he gets is a passing mention.

Verdict: Truth is the first casualty of Mel Gibson.

1785

Jefferson in Paris (1995)

Director: James Ivory • Entertainment grade: D • History grade: C–

Thomas Jefferson was one of the Founding Fathers of the United States. He served as ambassador to France between 1785 and 1789.

Family: The film begins with the story of Madison Hemings (James Earl Jones). He was the son of Sally Hemings, a slave belonging to Thomas Jefferson. Hemings claimed his father, and that of his siblings, was Jefferson himself. For two centuries, historians pooh-poohed this, arguing that Jefferson was a moral puritan, that he disapproved of miscegenation, and that the whole story was a far-fetched smear campaign. Then along came DNA testing, and whoops: it looks like Madison Hemings was probably right all along. So don't listen to historians. Anyway, the film was released three years before the consensus swung behind Madison Hemings' story, but treats it as fact – making it not only accurate, but more accurate than most historians in 1995.

Society: Back in 1785, the widowed Jefferson (Nick Nolte) arrives in Paris with his uptight daughter Martha. She is supposed to be 12, but for some reason is played by a 23-year-old Gwyneth Paltrow. He bungs her into a convent school, which is a weird thing to do with a grown woman. Then she meets Marie-Antoinette, but is too shy to speak, and has to hide behind her dad. Understandable for a twelve-year-old; from a woman in her twenties, worrying behaviour. Jefferson meets William and Maria Cosway, a pair of English painters, and falls madly in love with Mrs Cosway (Greta Scacchi). This is basically true. After their first meeting, Jefferson cancelled all his arrangements for the next few days, so he could follow her around the Louvre like a big ginger puppy.

Romance: The film repurposes Jefferson's famous letter to Mrs Cosway, 'The Heart and the Head', as a garden party game. It's a neat idea, but ruined – as the entire Mrs Cosway plot is – by the fact Scacchi and Nolte have the sexual chemistry of a pair of recalcitrant pandas. Nonetheless, Jefferson insists she should move to Virginia, and he will break the vow he made to his dying wife never to marry again by marrying her. In real life, Jefferson invited both Cosways to Virginia. There is no record of him offering to marry Mrs Cosway.

Slavery: The French are reading the declaration of independence, and picking nits. 'Are all men created equal, Mr Jefferson, or should this read "all *white* men are created equal"?' one asks. Jefferson looks as if he has never thought of this, and burbles some sort of half-baked biological determinist nonsense. Another Frenchman concludes smugly: 'Your revolution appears to be incomplete.' And yours, monsieur. The scene is set in 1786. The Declaration of the Rights of Man, proclaimed by the French national assembly in 1789, was applied only to white men. Which is why there was a massive slave revolt in the French colony of Saint-Domingue in 1791, leading eventually to the establishment of Haiti as the first black republic. The film's repeated implication that France during the 1780s was racially equal is plain wrong. Slavery was not outlawed by the French until 1794 – five years after Jefferson left – and was reintroduced by Napoleon in 1802.

More romance: Jefferson's younger daughter turns up with a chaperone, Sally Hemings (Thandie Newton). The real Hemings was fourteen at this point; Newton, like Paltrow, was twenty-three. Presumably, watching Nolte (fifty-four when he made this film, to Jefferson's forty-four) cop off with a genuine fourteen-year-old would be a shade too authentic for modern audiences. In any case, there's even less sexual chemistry between Nolte and Newton than there was between Nolte and Scacchi. Picture the recalcitrant pandas wearing 1960s space suits to protect their chastity. Actually, that movie sounds a lot more fun than this one.

Britain's two great military heroes of the period were Horatio Nelson and the Duke of Wellington. On film, both of them have tended to be portrayed in terms of their romantic relationships with women. Wellington was played by George Arliss in the 1934 British movie *The Iron Duke*. Nelson is usually played opposite his lady love, Emma Hamilton. There have been several screen versions of their love affair.

1786

That Hamilton Woman! (1941)

Director: Alexander Korda • Entertainment grade: C+ • History grade: C

People: 'My life began, really began when I was eighteen,' says Emma Hamilton (Vivien Leigh), 'and one day I arrived in Naples.' In reality, Emma was twenty-one when she arrived in Naples. She had started out as a sort of spokesmodel for the Temple of Health, a dodgy London clinic which sold infertile couples sessions on an electrified Celestial Bed. The shocks, it claimed, aided conception. She became mistress to Sir Harry Featherstonhaugh and had a child before moving on to the MP

Charles Greville. This all happened before she went to Naples, and it is not the backstory of a woman whose life had yet to begin. The film is approximately right in suggesting that Greville ungallantly passed Emma on to his uncle, Sir William Hamilton. To everyone's surprise, the two married.

Heroes: Explosions out in the bay announce the arrival of Horatio Nelson (Laurence Olivier). Correctly, he and Emma do not fall in love immediately. There follows a gap of several years. By then, Nelson was the hero of the Battle of the Nile, and during his campaigns had lost the sight in his right eye as well as most of his right arm. Emma goes to meet him in his cabin, and starts with shock at his eyepatch and empty sleeve. The stories of Nelson's exploits and his portraits were all over Europe, so it's unlikely she would have been surprised by his war wounds. Furthermore… oh dear, this is one of those times when it's just no fun to be a historian, like when you have to tell people the Vikings didn't really wear horny helmets. So I'm sorry about this, but: Nelson didn't wear an eyepatch. He may have worn a less glamorous eye shade on his hat when it was sunny on deck. In fact, this film is largely responsible for spreading the myth that he wore a pirate-style patch.

Morality: Some biographers claim *That Hamilton Woman!* was Winston Churchill's favourite film, and that he may have watched it as many as a hundred times. Perhaps he always fell asleep in the middle. The pace slackens in the second half, owing to the film's discomfort with its own subject. The story of Nelson and Emma Hamilton is, after all, about adultery. The lovers travelled back to

Britain together, and during that time Emma became pregnant. In the film, Emma's historically inaccurate waist-cinching gowns reveal no pregnancy (though she is later shown registering the birth of her daughter Horatia, as if the child had been left under a mulberry bush by pixies). In real life, Nelson and the Hamiltons all lived together in a ménage-à-trois. In the film, Nelson has to wait for Sir William to die before he can shack up with the lady. Worst of all, Emma's performance career is almost entirely ripped out and replaced with dreary domesticity. Not only is watching Vivien Leigh play goody-goody wifelet a lot less fun than watching her play crazy freewheeling nympho, it's also wrong. The real Emma's devotion to Nelson was notoriously flamboyant.

Propaganda: Churchill wasn't big on romance, so perhaps his enthusiasm for the film was sparked by its not-very-subtle repurposing of Britain's fight against Napoleon to reflect Britain's fight against Hitler for a wartime audience. 'You cannot make peace with dictators!' barks Nelson. 'You have to destroy them, wipe them out!' A few of the parallels the film draws are clunky, but it does at least reward its audience with a spirited and technically impressive recreation of the Battle of Trafalgar.

The four Georges were Hanoverian kings of England 1714–1830. They are not generally remembered fondly. The first two were German; the third one mad; the fourth debauched. There is an extremely good film about the mad one. The story that the title of Alan Bennett's play *The Madness of George*

III was changed to *The Madness of King George* because American audiences would otherwise think it was a sequel to two other films called *The Madness of George* is 'not totally untrue', according to director Nicholas Hytner. But it was not the whole story: he added that 'it was felt necessary to get the word "king" into the title'.

1788

The Madness of King George (1994)

Director: Nicholas Hytner • Entertainment grade: A– • History grade: A–

Politics: King George III (Nigel Hawthorne) is opening parliament, and prime minister, William Pitt the Younger is sparring with Whig leader Charles James Fox. 'Do you enjoy all this flummery, Mr Pitt?' 'No, Mr Fox.' 'Do you enjoy *anything*, Mr Pitt?' 'A balance-sheet, Mr Fox.' Pitt did make himself somewhat unpopular by raising taxes to pay the national debt, but since everyone's doing that these days we may judge him less harshly now than they did back in 1994. In addition to balance-sheets, a thing Pitt enjoyed was a bottle of port (sometimes two) a day, which may have contributed to his death, possibly from cirrhosis, aged forty-six.

Health: The king crashes children's cricket matches, pretends a shrubbery is the Americans and wallops it with his stick, runs around in his pyjamas, and launches himself bodily upon ladies-in-waiting. These seem like the sorts of things a lot of otherwise sensible people might do were they king for a day. But in the film, and in real life, they were taken to indicate that George III was going mad. The famous story that he mistook an oak tree for the King of Prussia does not make it to the screen: correctly, because it was almost certainly not true. The film doesn't mention porphyria as a likely cause of the king's condition until the closing title cards. This, too, is quite correct. The diagnosis is a modern one, suggested by some historians, but not provable. It does, however, lay into George's doctors, depicting them as a bunch of wackos obsessed with scrutinising his effluvia and inflicting blistering, cupping and purgatives. Unfortunately, this is accurate.

Scandal: The Prince of Wales (Rupert Everett) prances around in a shantung dressing-gown and conspires to have his father declared mad, so he can become Prince Regent. But he has compromised himself by his secret marriage to Maria Fitzherbert. This was illegal because he didn't have his father's consent, and because she was a Catholic. 'You performed an illegal marriage!' says the king's agent to the guilty curate. 'And he only gave me £10,' moans the curate. Robert Burt, the curate who really married the pair, got £500 and a never-fulfilled promise of appointment as a royal chaplain.

Medicine: The mean Dr Willis turns up to torture the king. (In fact, there were two Doctors Willis – father and son.) 'Get away from me, you scabby bumsucker!' bellows his majesty. But Willis won't go away. Instead, he straps the king into a restraint chair, while the king struggles and howls. In a stroke of cinematic genius, while George III is being forced on to this horrible parody of a throne, the soundtrack fires up Handel's 'Zadok the Priest' – the music usually played at the anointing of a British monarch. 'I hate all the physicians, but most the Willises,' complained the king in real life.

Regency: Parliament is having a ding-dong over the regency, and it looks like the Prince of Wales ('The fat one?' exclaims the king, crossly) may get his way. But the king regains his senses and, in a frantic carriage-ride, just manages to get himself there in time to scupper his son's ploy. There's a touch of dramatic licence here – the king didn't actually have to race to parliament at the eleventh hour – but it is true that his recovery sank the bill. It was temporary, and the Prince of Wales would become regent in 1811.

Verdict: A triumph. Shockingly, Nigel Hawthorne lost the Oscar to Tom Hanks for *Forrest Gump*. Since that makes even less sense than mistaking an oak tree for the King of Prussia, perhaps it was a final act of revenge by what the film calls those 'ramshackle colonists in America' on their last and unlamented king.

The Battle of Waterloo in 1815 was a crucial event in European history, but is crazily expensive to stage – which is perhaps why it hasn't been filmed all that often. Stanley Kubrick's *Napoleon*, exhaustively planned during the 1970s but never made, was expected to run at ten or twelve hours, though it was scripted at a modest three and a half. We can only imagine it would have cost an absolute fortune. A rare attempt at capturing the scale of Waterloo was made in 1970 – with a little help from the Red Army.

1815

Waterloo (1970)

Director: Sergei Bondarchuk • Entertainment grade: C– • History grade: A–

With his catastrophic attempt to invade Russia in 1812, Napoleon Bonaparte began to fall from glory. In 1814, he was forced into exile on the Mediterranean isle of Elba. He escaped, and returned to France in triumph. But his second reign, known as the Hundred Days, was nipped in the bud by defeat at Waterloo.

Casting: Napoleon (Rod Steiger) must abdicate. Cue a massive tantrum from the little lad. 'I will not, I will not, I will not, not, not!' he bellows, though two minutes later he has calmed down and done it. Steiger is inescapably dreadful in the role, serving up high camp in place of charisma. He does at least look approximately like Napoleon, though much more like Ricky Gervais. Director Sergei Bondarchuk goes in for long scenes of nothing happening, so there's plenty of time to imagine your way through a prequel in which David Brent conquers Europe but overreaches himself and has to eat Gareth on the road back from Moscow. Napoleon is replaced on the throne by King Louis XVIII, played by Orson Welles. Welles looks like Jabba the Hutt, but so did Louis XVIII, so that's fine.

Power: Napoleon escapes from exile on Elba and is on his way back to Paris. The king does a bunk. 'Perhaps the people will let me go as they let him come,' says Welles, clambering into a gilded carriage. Meanwhile, in the south, Napoleon strides out alone in front of the bayonets of the 5th regiment, crying: 'If you want to kill your emperor, here I am!' They defect to him immediately. Save a certain dramatic flourish and the amalgamation of a couple of different events, this is accurate.

Society: Soon afterwards, the Duchess of Richmond's ball in Brussels is interrupted by news that Napoleon is on his way. Fighting would begin the next day at Quatre Bras. Some of the officers at the party had no time to change, and were obliged to go to war in evening dress. The film does a superb job of recreating that night, right down to the Duchess's daughter finding herself 'quite provoked' by handsome young ADC Lord Hay dashing off to his death (which he is supposed to meet at Quatre Bras, though the film lets him live till Waterloo). Watching her daughter and Hay dance, the Duchess remarks to the Duke of Wellington that 'I don't want her to wear black before she wears white.' She's getting ahead of herself: it's 1815, and white only became a popular colour for wedding dresses after Queen Victoria wore it to marry Prince Albert in 1840. Still, overall, this is good stuff.

War: Bondarchuk made the film with 15,000 infantrymen and 2,000 cavalry on loan from the Soviet army. Trained up to fight in nineteenth-century style, and given time to grow proper moustaches, these men do an outstanding job as French, British and Prussian soldiers. It was said at the time that this put Bondarchuk in command of the seventh largest army in the world. As a result, the scenes of battle at Waterloo are visually and technically sublime, and must be seen to be believed. Moreover, the mostly hokey screenplay has its finest hour when the immutably deadpan Lord Uxbridge falls foul of a grapeshot. Uxbridge: 'By God, Sir, I've lost my leg.' Wellington: 'By God, Sir, so you have.' It is a joy to confirm that those lines are accurate. The leg was buried in a nearby garden, and became a tourist attraction.

5

The Empires Strike Back

The Industrial Revolution – generally dated from around 1760–1840 – brought huge social, political, military and technological changes that would gradually seep out from the revolution's origin in Britain to affect the whole world. With machine manufacture and steam power, railways and steamships allowed people – and empires – to move across the globe. It was an age of extraordinary drama, with great progressions and great oppressions.

It was also an age of culture. Milos Forman's extraordinarily successful *Amadeus* (1984) was based on the idea that Wolfgang Amadeus Mozart (Tom Hulce) was killed or hounded to death by fellow composer Antonio Salieri (F. Murray Abraham). In real life, though Mozart and Salieri were in competition for some of the same work, there is little evidence they were rivals. They seem to have been supportive friends. The idea that Salieri had murdered Mozart was based on a piece of gossip (which cannot be traced or verified) that Salieri once confessed to killing his friend in the course of a nervous breakdown. The rumour was whipped up into drama by the Russian writer Alexander Pushkin, whose short play *Mozart and Salieri* (1830) depicted the latter murdering the former onstage. Peter Shaffer, who originally wrote *Amadeus* as a stageplay, took the story from that.

As far as historians are concerned, there is no truth in the story at all – though this didn't stop *Amadeus* from winning eight Oscars. Even thirty years after the movie's release, so widely believed was the myth about Salieri killing Mozart that the Mozarthaus museum in Vienna held an exhibition specifically to try to rehabilitate his reputation. 'We wanted simply to enlighten people and show the authentic Salieri, getting away from a very strongly fictionalized version,' the museum's director told the press.

Mozart and Salieri aren't the only two great composers poorly served by cinema…

1820

Immortal Beloved (1994)

Director: Bernard Rose • Entertainment grade: C • History grade: Fail

Among Ludwig van Beethoven's papers was found a love letter to an 'Immortal Beloved', who has never been conclusively identified.

Premise: What would be the most clangingly obvious way to open a Beethoven biopic? If you guessed a shot of the grumpy, aged Ludwig (Gary Oldman), illuminated by a stage lightning flash, and accompanied by the 'duh-duh-duh-DUUUUUH' opening notes of the Fifth Symphony, give yourself a gold star and a pat on the frightwig. He dies, and his executor, Anton Schindler (Jeroen Krabbé), finds that his will bequeaths everything to an unnamed 'immortal beloved'. Stop right there, movie! Beethoven's will did not mention the immortal beloved. So basically the film's entire premise – that Schindler was obliged to turn detective and interview all of Beethoven's old conquests, looking for the anonymous true love mentioned in his will – is wrong. In real life, the immortal beloved letter is thought to have been written in 1812. Beethoven had quite a lot of romances in his life. There is no evidence that he was still hung up on this particular beloved by his death in 1827.

People: Through Schindler, the audience meets a couple of immortal beloved candidates – including Giulietta Guicciardi and Anne-Marie Erdödy. More are left out, including Antonie and Bettina Brentano, two sisters-in-law, the latter of whom also seduced Johann Wolfgang von Goethe. The film soon veers off into an emotionally unsatisfying tangent about Beethoven's tumultuous relationship with his brother's widow, Johanna van Beethoven, and their five-year custody battle over her son and his nephew, Karl.

Politics: Beethoven seeks an audience with Austria's arch-conservative minister of foreign affairs, Klemens von Metternich. In the role of Metternich, who dominated European politics for much of the first half of the nineteenth century, is Barry Humphries. He's actually not that bad. When casting Dame Edna Everage as Prince Metternich is the least camp and silly thing in your movie, though, you've probably gone a bit over the top with everything else. The film gains a point for suggesting that Metternich had his secret police spy on Beethoven, which is true. It loses the point again for suggesting that Beethoven and Metternich met in person, for which there is no evidence, and that Beethoven offered to write an oratorio praising Metternich in return for the minister intervening in his custody dispute, which is absurd and borderline slanderous.

Mystery: Finally, Schindler realizes the truth (or, rather, the massive lie): Beethoven's own sister-in-law, Johanna, is the immortal beloved! And Karl is actually his son, not his nephew! And it's, like, OMG, the whole reason he's abusive and horrible to Johanna is because he's really secretly crazy in love with her. What is this, *Twilight*? It is wildly unlikely that Johanna was the immortal beloved. In real life, Schindler alleged that Guicciardi was the most likely candidate.

Style: The film's climax is the Ninth Symphony, accompanied with dreamlike footage of a young Beethoven floating in a pond, then a starry sky. The *New York Times* described this movie as 'an extremely ambitious classical music video'. Seeing as it came out soon after the video for Meat Loaf's 'I'd Do Anything For Love (But I Won't Do That)', to which it bears a striking visual and thematic similarity, it's not nearly ambitious enough. Where are the explosions? Where are the motorbikes? Where are the bootylicious Rhinemaidens in pleather corsets? Okay, so Rhinemaidens are technically Wagner rather than Beethoven –

but the rest of this film is made up anyway, and a few misattributed nineteenth-century German music babes would scarcely have made things any worse.

Sometimes, writers and filmmakers seize an obscure point of history and turn it into an iconic event. This is certainly the case with *Les Misérables*, a film of a musical of a book about the June Rebellion of 1832 in France, against the rule of King Louis-Philippe. The rebellion only lasted a couple of days and failed comprehensively. It would probably not be remembered at all, except for the fact that the writer Victor Hugo was caught up in it and later made it the key event in his epic 1862 novel *Les Misérables*.

On the 150th anniversary of its publication, the movie industry commemorated *Les Misérables* with a blockbuster movie, which received eight Oscar nominations (winning three) and setting records for the highest-grossing musical film opening of all time in the US and UK.

1832

Les Misérables (2012)

Director: Tom Hooper • Entertainment grade: C • History grade: C

People: The film begins with Jean Valjean (Hugh Jackman) completing nineteen years of hard labour: the penalty for stealing bread and repeatedly trying to escape. His overseer is the unrelenting Javert (Russell Crowe). Victor Hugo's novel was inspired in part by the true story of Eugène-François Vidocq, who turned a criminal career into an anti-crime industry. He created the Bureau des Renseignements, said to be the world's first detective agency, in 1833, though he himself continued to be pursued by police. Vidocq was friends with several authors, including Hugo, Honoré de Balzac and Alexandre Dumas père. In *Les Misérables,* Hugo split him into two characters, Valjean and Javert, at odds with each other. So this is an eighteenth-century *Fight Club*. With singing.

Grime: The reformed Valjean becomes mayor of Montreuil-sur-Mer. Young Fantine (Anne Hathaway) is fired from one of his factories. On the streets, she sells her hair, then her molars, then her body. Cue the standout solo, 'I Dreamed A Dream'. Like many of the big numbers in this film, it's shot in blistering, uncut close-up. With each actor you get a chance to see the smears of stage blood, the sweat, the tears caught in the eyelashes, the veins throbbing in the forehead on the high notes, the dirt, the spots, the drool, the snot and the poverty stains on whatever remains of their teeth. In a movie already determined to cover all its characters in filth, vomit and human excrement, this is a bit relentless. A historian can't complain about the past being shown to be dirty – it was – but it seems contrary to insist on gritty realism if you're going to have your cast express themselves exclusively in show tunes.

Justice: Hathaway's performance veers between fragile sobbing and Susan Boyle-style operatics. It's so nakedly an Oscar clip that they might as well have flashed up the words 'OSCAR CLIP' on the screen, as they do in *Wayne's World* when Wayne splashes water over his eyes and bawls, 'I never learned to read!' Fantine hits back at a would-be customer. Javert arrests her; Valjean performs a rescue. But why is the saintly Valjean hanging around in the red-light district? This is a lot easier to get away with on stage. Melodramatic though it may be, Fantine's story is apparently based on a real event. In 1841, Hugo himself saved a woman falsely accused. The story is described in his *Things Seen* (1887).

Politics: There is no historical context provided for the June Rebellion of 1832 beyond a general sense that students are annoyed and ordinary working folk are hard done by, which they have been throughout history. 'Lamarque is dead!' trills Enjolras (Aaron Tveit). 'The people's man!' That would be General Jean-Maximilien Lamarque, a political opponent of Louis-Philippe, whose death during a cholera epidemic provided the trigger for the rebellion. The film does little to correct the popular misconception that *Les Misérables* is set in the more famous French Revolution of 1789: Enjolras even claims at one point that it is 'the French Revolution'. No, it isn't.

Love: Fantine's daughter Cosette (Amanda Seyfried), who has been adopted by Valjean, and her childhood rival Éponine (Samantha Barks) both fall for revolutionary Marius (Eddie Redmayne). Why? He's soppy and inadequately committed to the cause of whatever it is they're fighting for. Everyone else is singing the song of angry men; he's warbling on about Cosette, having rather frivolously fallen in love with her on the strength of a single glimpse. The film grinds on through the rebels' last stand on the barricades, and chucks in several more one-take close-up solos – including poor old Éponine bravely belting out her swansong with a musket ball in her chest. It's exhausting in its sincerity. Of course, this is what many people love about it. Still, when in the finale Valjean declares himself ready for death, some in the audience may empathize.

Verdict: A hulking, merciless adaptation, which will delight many of the musical's fans.

The Battle of the Alamo was a crucial event in the Texas revolution, fought between American settlers and the government of Mexico. It was in its time compared to the Battle of Thermopylae, and became a romantic and rousing trope in American political and military culture. There have been dozens of film versions of the battle and its hero, Davy Crockett, beginning in 1911 with ten-minute silent film *The Immortal Alamo*. It starred real military cadets and Francis Ford, the brother of Hollywood legend John Ford, who directed *Stagecoach*, *The Searchers*, *How Green Was My Valley*, *The Man Who Shot Liberty Valance* and *The Grapes of Wrath*.

Walt Disney got hold of the story in the 1950s and made a miniseries and movie about Davy Crockett; you can still stay at the Davy Crockett Ranch at Disneyland Paris. John Wayne, who loved the story, fought to make it for years before he finally appeared as Crockett in 1960's *The Alamo.* This film was considered so bad from a historical point of view that two historical advisers, J. Frank Dobie and Lon Tinkle, asked for their names to be removed from the credits. It was banned in Mexico. A more recent and more credible attempt was...

1836

The Alamo (2004)

Director: John Lee Hancock • Entertainment grade: C– • History grade: B+

In 1836, Mexican forces took the Alamo mission, near what is now San Antonio, Texas, from a small band of Texian defenders. (Texians were American settlers in Texas. They did not start to be called Texans until after the state's declaration of independence later that year.)

People: Washed-up alcoholic Sam Houston (Dennis Quaid) is selling investment in Texas. Washed-up politician Davy Crockett (Billy Bob Thornton), rejected by the electors of Tennessee, is interested. 'I told them, "You can go to hell. I'm going to Texas,"' he says defiantly. They're joined by washed-up knife-fighter and committed slave owner Jim Bowie (Jason Patric), who is ailing with tuberculosis, and washed-up lawyer William Travis (Patrick Wilson), who cruelly abandons his family. Usually, these men are represented as all-American heroes, so many historians will welcome corrective portrayals. When it comes to making a watchable film, though *The Alamo*'s tone of unrelieved gloom isn't a great start, and nor is its ponderous pace. This may explain why it was one of the biggest flops of cinema history, making only $25 million back at the box office against a $145 million budget.

Enemies: Mexican general Antonio López de Santa Anna (Emilio Echevarría) approaches the Alamo mission with his troops. You're left in no doubt that Santa Anna is the baddie. He executes prisoners with cannonfire, puffs around in gold braid, and eats bonbons non-stop off fancy silverware while everyone else starves. 'What are the lives of soldiers but so many chickens?' he says airily, when aides urge him not to send his infantry forward. The real Santa Anna was indeed a hard case. His hobbies included gambling on cockfights, consuming opium and dishonouring women. Even so, he would have made a more interesting character onscreen if the film had included a hint of his real-life charm alongside his real-life brutality.

Celebrity: The Texians are surrounded. Bowie coughs violently. He has to do this in every scene, to remind you that he has tuberculosis. He stops for long enough to note that Crockett is without his raccoonskin hat. 'What happened to your cap?' he asks. 'Crawl away?' 'The truth is, I only started wearing that thing because of that feller in the play they did about me,' says Crockett. 'People expect things.' It has been argued that Davy Crockett was the first modern American celebrity, thanks to his portrayal as 'Nimrod Wildfire' in the 1831 theatrical sensation *Lion of the West*. According to this film, he was also the first modern American celebrity to bore everyone silly moaning about it. In real life, he courted fame. The film is right about the hat, though – that was invented for the play. And it was originally wildcat fur.

Death: Bowie is on his sickbed when the Mexicans make their final assault. Soldiers burst into the room. Summoning his remaining strength, he fires off his pistols with both hands. He reaches for his famous knife, but the soldiers stab him to death with bayonets. Historically, there are various accounts of Bowie's death. Some suggest that he was comatose during the siege, that he died shortly before it, or even that he shot himself. Everyone likes the one in the movie, where he gets to be a hero.

More death: Popular legend says Davy Crockett died fighting. This film opts for the version preferred by some historians, based on the controversial but credible diary of Mexican officer José Enrique de la Peña, which has him being taken alive. It can't resist adding a bit of Hollywood dialogue, though. 'If you wish to beg for your life,' gloats Santa Anna, 'this would be the proper time.' 'Are you Santa Anna?' replies Crockett. 'I thought he'd be taller.' According to Peña's diary, Santa Anna scandalized many Mexican officers by ordering the execution of Crockett and six other prisoners. 'Though tortured before they were killed, these unfortunates died without complaining and without humiliating themselves before their torturers,' he wrote.

Verdict: A bold attempt at a historian's version of the story, but this movie is far too dull to appeal to a wider audience.

The subject of the North Atlantic slave trade and slavery in the United States is still a difficult one for filmmakers to deal with. At the beginning of the film industry, D. W. Griffith's extraordinary and horrific *Birth of a Nation* (1915) romanticized the days of slavery and glorified the Ku Klux Klan. American Civil War drama *Gone with the Wind* (1939) could begin with a misty-eyed recollection about the supposed beauty and elegance of a slaveholding society: 'There was a land of Cavaliers and Cotton Fields called the Old South... Here was the last ever to be seen of Knights and their Ladies Fair, of Master and Slave... Look for it only in books, for it is no more than a dream remembered, a Civilization gone with the wind...'

More recently, filmmakers have tried to portray the horror and obscenity of slave society, with films like *Beloved* (1998) and *Glory* (1989) taking a very different view on the Civil War to *Gone with the Wind*; Steven Spielberg's *Amistad* (1997) showing the middle passage from Africa to the Americas; and Quentin Tarantino's *Django Unchained* (2012) turning slavery into an invigorating Blaxploitation western. But the most effective film on slavery to date is...

1841

Twelve Years a Slave (2013)

Director: Steve McQueen • Entertainment grade: A • History grade: A

In 1841, Solomon Northup – a free black man from New York State – was kidnapped and sold into slavery.

Kidnapping: Solomon Northup (Chiwetel Ejiofor) lives comfortably with a wife, two children, and a decent income from playing the violin. When two men offer him a fortnight's work with a circus in Washington, DC, he agrees. In 1841, the District of Columbia was still a 'slave state' – making the nation's capital dangerous territory for black and mixed-race people. Once there, Northup is drugged. He awakes in chains. The scenes in the film are faithful to Northup's 1853 memoir, also called *12 Years a Slave*. Historians have documented hundreds of kidnapping cases like Northup's, and consider that there must have been more in which such disappearances went unnoticed or were attributed to other causes.

Enslavement: Northup is taken to Louisiana and sold to William Ford (Benedict Cumberbatch). As plantation owners go, Ford is a kindly sort: he delivers sermons and permits his slaves moments of humanity, even giving Northup a violin. But carpenter John Tibeats (Paul Dano) pushes Northup into a fight and then nearly lynches him. Northup is left tied up and dangling from the noose all day, with no slaves daring to rescue him and none of the whites inclined to. In a film filled with unforgettable cinematic moments, this is one of the most striking: it is impossible not to be reminded of the drawn-out agony of a crucifixion. It's also accurate to Northup's book. 'I was growing faint from pain, and thirst, and hunger,' he wrote. Director Steve McQueen's determined appreciation of the sedate, haunted beauty of the landscape, with ghostly cobwebs of Spanish moss trailing over shimmering bayous, throws the evils of violence and slavery into even sharper relief.

People: Northup is passed on to a new owner: the vicious, sadistic Edwin Epps (Michael Fassbender), and his vicious, sadistic wife (Sarah Paulson), the flip side to Scarlett O'Hara. Epps is sexually obsessed with a beautiful slave, Patsey (Lupita Nyong'o). The twisted relationship between this quartet drives much of the rest of the film, helped by terrific performances from all four of them. Few actors can carry so much sadness in their eyes as Chiwetel Ejiofor, and the crucial scenes in which he is powerless to help (and is forced to hurt) Patsey are both accurate to the book and as powerful as cinema gets. There may be an unintentional inaccuracy here, though. In the film, Patsey begs Northup to help her commit suicide by drowning her in the swamp. In the book, as journalist Noah Berlatsky has pointed out, the relevant paragraph is confusingly worded – but it appears Mistress Epps was actually the one who asked Northup to drown Patsey.

Salvation: A Canadian abolitionist turns up at Epps's plantation. He is called Samuel Bass and is played by Brad Pitt, who looks like a cross between a blonde Jesus and a blonde Che Guevara, and acts as if he might be something along those lines, too. At considerable personal risk, he agrees to tell people of Northup's plight and thereby help him escape. A black slave's salvation arriving at the hands of a saintly white man might seem far-fetched, but this – and even much of the dialogue around it – is accurate to Northup's book. Lest anyone imagine Northup's co-writer made it up, historian David Fiske has traced a real man from Ontario who may be the same Samuel Bass.

Verdict: An extraordinarily assured, sensitive, intelligent and beautifully written adaptation of Solomon Northup's story, and one of the most searingly brilliant, painful and truthful historical films you'll ever see.

If you thought the Beethoven movie *Immortal Beloved* was bad, just wait till you see Ken Russell's extraordinary paean to nineteenth-century Hungarian composer Franz Liszt. Liszt became famous across Europe as a pianist and performer. Ken Russell made his movie in the 1970s, a time when everyone was taking a lot of drugs, and cast rock star Roger Daltrey, lead singer of The Who, in the title role.

1847

Lisztomania (1975)

Director: Ken Russell • Entertainment grade: Fail • History grade: Fail

Fame: Franz Liszt (Roger Daltrey) is at a party. 'Liszt, my dear fellow!' says a fellow composer. 'Oh, piss off, Brahms,' Liszt sneers, and adds to his companion Richard Wagner (Paul Nicholas): 'He's a right wanker.' This is the high point of both intellectualism and wit in the film's dialogue. Afterwards, Liszt plays the piano to a throng of screaming teenagers. In the 1840s, long before Elvis, Beatlemania or Justin Bieber, Heinrich Heine coined the term 'Lisztomania' to describe the hysteria of Liszt's fans. Women shrieked, swooned, took cuttings of his hair, collected the dregs from his coffee cups, and even kept the discarded stubs of his cigars between their bosoms.

Romance: In real life, Liszt took up with Princess Carolyne von Sayn-Wittgenstein in 1848. In this film, she is a maniacal dominatrix bat-demon with inverted crosses dangling from her nipples. It's something of a one-sided portrayal. Liszt dons a crinoline and plucks a lyre. Sex-crazed women grab at his skirts. He develops an erection bigger than himself. As his member nears eight feet in length, evil Princess Carolyne prepares a guillotine for it. This isn't an attempt at literal history: possibly Ken Russell misheard someone describing Liszt as Europe's biggest pianist. *Lisztomania* may be the most embarrassing historical film ever made. Wait! It gets worse.

People: Wagner gloats that his music will bring forth 'a man of iron, to forge the shattered fragments of this century into a nation of steel'. He grows fangs, bites Liszt on the neck, sucks his blood, then snogs his daughter Cosima. The real Cosima Liszt left her husband for Wagner, though it didn't happen like this and nobody was a vampire. Liszt and Carolyne try to get married, but the Pope is having none of it. The Pope is a little beardy bloke with a heavy Scouse accent. Good grief. The Pope is played by Ringo Starr. Since he can't marry Carolyne, Liszt takes religious orders. Pope Ringo sends him to exorcise Wagner.

Politics: Wagner – dressed, in a painful literalization of Friedrich Nietzsche's *Thus Spake Zarathustra*, as Superman, complete with red cape – strums an electric guitar and sings about restoring the Teutonic godhead. Like Dr Frankenstein, he has created a monster. The monster is Rick Wakeman (who himself created the monstrous prog-rock soundtrack), done up as Thor. In real life, Nietzsche broke his friendship with Wagner over the religious tone of the composer's opera *Parsifal*. Wagner's revenge was to tell Nietzsche's doctor that the philosopher's headaches were caused by excessive masturbation. A condition one would imagine that the makers of this film understood only too well.

Prejudice: Wagner was a great composer and a nasty piece of work. He was outspokenly anti-semitic, and it is hardly a mitigating factor that many others in the music world at the time (Chopin, for instance) also held these obnoxious views to some degree. Liszt's own feelings about Jewish people, while not so actively hateful, weren't exactly friendly either. Still, *Lisztomania* goes a bit far in blaming Wagner entirely for the existence of Nazism and the rise of Adolf Hitler. He died in 1883, six years before Hitler was born.

War: Wagner is squished beneath his own castle. During his funeral, he rises from his swastika-embossed tomb. In case you haven't yet absorbed Ken Russell's silly point that Wagner is Hitler, Wagner is now actually dressed as Hitler. His electric guitar turns into a machine gun and he rampages around the city, killing Jews. It's played for laughs. I am not making this up. Liszt – who is also now dead – climbs into a heavenly spaceship, flies back to earth and laser-explodes Zombie Vampire Hitler-Wagner. The end. Thank goodness.

The towering American figure of the nineteenth century as far as the film industry has been concerned was Abraham Lincoln, the 16th president of the United States. He is remembered for winning the country's civil war and ending slavery, both in 1865.

The first known Lincoln biopic was made in 1908, under the title *The Reprieve: An Episode in the Life of Abraham Lincoln*. Scores more followed, notably D. W. Griffith's *Abraham Lincoln* (1930); *Young Mr Lincoln* (1935), in which he is played by Henry Fonda; *Abe Lincoln in Illinois* (1940), in which he is played by Raymond Massey. His assassination is the subject of Robert Redford's 2010 film *The Conspirator*. He also appears in *How the West Was Won* (1963), *Bill and Ted's Excellent Adventure* (1989) and *The Lego Movie* (2014).

Last and least, there is *Abraham Lincoln: Vampire Hunter* (2012). You might think a film about Abraham Lincoln secretly hunting vampires wouldn't take itself too seriously. You'd be wrong. Director Timur Bekmambetov is all about moody, Matrix-like visual effects set pieces, with lots of slashing, whirling and choreographed sprays of blood. Writer Seth Grahame-Smith's screenplay, adapted from his own novel, contains only one joke (apart from the title). It's right at the end. Viewers may not make it that far: 105 minutes of dour, plodding vampire slaying feels like four score and seven years.

Instead, historians might recommend this more edifying Lincoln biopic, released the same year:

1865

Lincoln (2012)

Director: Steven Spielberg • Entertainment grade: B+ • History grade: B+

Politics: The film opens towards the end of the civil war, with the slaveholding Confederate South staggering towards defeat. Abraham Lincoln (Daniel Day-Lewis), nearing victory, visits his Union troops. There is little fighting onscreen. Most of the action is talky, and takes place in and around the White House and in the House of Representatives. If you liked *The West Wing*, this may well be up your street: think of *Lincoln* as the prequel. On the other hand, if your tolerance for the intricacies of American legislative procedure is low, this could be a heavy-going two and a half hours.

People: Enter Thaddeus Stevens (Tommy Lee Jones), a Republican radical from Pennsylvania with fire in his belly and all the best lines. He wears a conspicuous wig and a hangdog expression, and if you look up pictures of the real Thaddeus Stevens you will see that both are precisely historically accurate. 'This is the face of someone who has fought long and hard for the good of the people without caring much for any of them,' he growls. 'And I look a lot worse without the wig.' Meanwhile, there's a touch of *The West Wing*'s President Bartlet to Day-Lewis's Lincoln: he hides a searing intellect under all that folksy charm, and even the occasional flash of a human flaw doesn't really undermine his saintliness. Some of the film's best scenes focus on those human flaws, notably in his relationship with his wife, the clever but desperately unhappy Mary Todd Lincoln (Sally Field).

Freedom: Historian Eric Foner has argued that the film exaggerates the importance of the January 1865 debate on the 13th Amendment, and that it gives Lincoln too much personal credit. It comprehensively ignores the roles of black and women activists. Reportedly, Spielberg first conceived the film around Lincoln's friendship with black abolitionist Frederick Douglass, who – very regrettably – isn't in the finished version at all. Furthermore, the 13th Amendment was the result of a 400,000-signature anti-slavery petition organized by the Women's National Loyal League, headed by Susan B. Anthony and Elizabeth Cady Stanton. They aren't in the film either.

Reputations: From a historian's point of view, the transformation in Hollywood's attitude to Thaddeus Stevens over the last century is striking. Back in 1915, he was ridiculed as the villainous race-traitor Austin Stoneman in D. W. Griffith's *Birth of a Nation*. In 2013, he was revered in Spielberg's *Lincoln* as a great liberator and a man far ahead of his time. It is he, even more than the 16th president, who emerges as this film's hero.

In Britain, the most iconic figure of the Victorian age is Queen Victoria herself. Like Abraham Lincoln, she has appeared in a host of serious and unserious movies. She turns up in Jackie

Chan's 2003 martial arts western comedy *Shanghai Knights.* She is romanced by Charles Darwin in 2012 animated caper *The Pirates! In an Adventure with Scientists.* She is played by Peter Sellers in drag in *The Great McGonagall* (1974). One can only imagine her reaction to all of this: 'We are not amused.'

Victoria's life itself has attracted relatively little attention from filmmakers, compared, say, to Elizabeth I. Her marriage to Prince Albert is generally portrayed as straightforwardly happy and comfortable. Not much potential for drama there. After Albert's early death in 1861, Victoria mourned solidly for the next forty years while growing ever more dour and spherical. Perhaps we would now consider her later years to have been characterized by a sort of obsessive depression: they are certainly a challenge to turn into compelling cinema. Rather than taking on her whole life, some filmmakers have focused on a small, romantic slice of it.

1840

The Young Victoria (2009)

Director: Jean-Marc Vallée • Entertainment grade: C+ • History grade: B–

Romance: Speculation is rife about a possible marriage for young Princess Victoria. King Leopold of Belgium is busy grooming his nephew and Victoria's cousin, Prince Albert of Saxe-Coburg Gotha. The film's depiction of this process is notably accurate. As Albert, Rupert Friend captures the real Albert's awkwardness perfectly. He does not capture the tendency to fat that squicked

Victoria out during his first visit to England in 1836. Fortunately, by 1839, Albert had laid off the Lebkuchen and developed a 'fine waist', which the queen admired so much that she married him.

Politics: When her favourite politician, Liberal prime minister Lord Melbourne, loses the election, Victoria is distraught. She refuses to exchange her Liberal-inclined ladies of the bedchamber for Tory-inclined ones who would be favourable to the new PM, Sir Robert Peel. This provokes a major crisis, and results in Peel being unable to form a government. Astonishing as this may seem, it is what happened in 1839. The real Victoria once wrote that she would refuse to be queen of a democracy, and wielded royal influence often.

Dialogue: The thing that lets *The Young Victoria* down is the low opinion it has of its own audience. At one point, Victoria and Albert are shown playing a chess game. There is just enough time to groan at the blatant symbolism before Victoria actually starts to explain it: 'Do you ever feel like a chess piece yourself, in a game played against your will?' Victoria and Albert's predicament was not like chess. They were caught between a variety of predatory interests, including royal factions of England, Belgium and Hanover, as well as Liberals and Tories. It was more like being the two last balls in a game of Hungry Hungry Hippos. Though admittedly showing Victoria and Albert playing Hungry Hungry Hippos might have been something of an anachronism.

Violence: Victoria and Albert are out in their carriage when a young man raises a pistol and shoots at them. Bravely, Albert interposes himself, taking a bullet to save his wife. The would-be assassin, Edward Oxford, is real: he was the first of seven young men who tried to kill the queen at various points in her reign. In real life, he shot two pistols, and missed the royal couple with both. Albert escaped without injury. Conspiracy theories circulated that Oxford had been set up by Victoria's uncle, the King of Hanover. These may or may not have been completely untrue, but the suggestion that Albert got himself shot to save Victoria is definitely completely untrue. It is based not on Victorian history but on 1992's *The Bodyguard*, starring Kevin Costner and Whitney Houston.

Verdict: Historically not at all bad, apart from Prince Albert getting a very different sort of piercing to the one with which his name is associated. And that, by the way, is a myth. Probably.

1865

Mrs Brown (1997)

Director: John Madden • Entertainment grade: B • History grade: B+

Four years after Albert's death, Victoria became attached to her gillie, John Brown.

Taste: John Brown (Billy Connolly) joins Victoria's staff at Osborne House on the Isle of Wight, then moves with her to Balmoral in Scotland. The film invents some *Upstairs, Downstairs* drama, but sticks approximately to the facts. The only conspicuous error is that its Balmoral sets are far too tasteful. Balmoral, like

Osborne, was bought and decorated by Victoria and Albert as a couple, and its interiors were famously hideous. All the wood was painted dark ginger; fake thistles abounded; and anything that stayed still long enough was covered in violently clashing tartans, including curtains, carpets, furniture, linoleum and small children. According to historian Sarah Bradford, the prime minister Lord Rosebery remarked that he 'thought the drawing-room at Osborne was the ugliest room in the world until he saw the drawing-room at Balmoral'.

Protocol: Brown calls Victoria 'woman' rather than 'ma'am', sneaks her drams of whisky, drags her out to ride in freezing temperatures, and takes her to visit her subjects on the estate. She loves all of this. After commissioning memorials to Prince Albert and sulking, the real Queen Victoria's favourite pastime was being grovelled to by thankful peasants. It's also true, as shown in the film, that she refused to relax her rules against smoking in royal palaces, even when begged by her son the Prince of Wales. So strict was Victoria's ban, biographer Lytton Strachey wrote, that 'bishops and ambassadors, invited to Windsor, might be reduced, in the privacy of their bedrooms, to lie full-length upon the floor and smoke up the chimney'.

Republicanism: Victoria's isolation at Balmoral – and her attachment to Brown – fed a wave of republicanism in the nation at large. The film has this right, but Victoria was not the sole cause. Republicanism had its roots in the Chartist movement, and was stoked by the financial crisis of 1866. The naming of the Prince of Wales in a divorce case was also a factor. Still, it's true that Victoria's relationship with Brown was widely disliked and ridiculed. An anonymous 1871 pamphlet (written, it later emerged, by Sir George Trevelyan) was entitled 'What does she do with it?' This was an examination of the Civil List, but the title was meant – and understood – as a double-entendre alluding to what Victoria got up to with Brown.

Romance: The movie is cautious about exactly what Victoria got up to with Brown, showing merely a tender scene of them holding hands on his deathbed. Victorian gossips were less reserved. A European newspaper reported that she secretly married him and had his child (this was in 1869, when she was fifty). The writer Wilfrid Scawen Blunt, who shared a mistress with the Prince of Wales, recorded of Brown's relationship with Victoria that there was 'no doubt of his being allowed every conjugal privilege'. Even Victoria's own daughters began to refer to Brown as 'Mama's lover' – though the Earl of Derby, who recorded this, politely assumed they were joking.

Scandal: Prime Minister Benjamin Disraeli (Antony Sher) decides 'to winkle the old gal out of mourning' and tells the queen to return to public life, basically in order to create some kind of dramatic tension in the movie's final act. In reality, Victoria was never shamed out of her admiration for Brown. After he died, she developed an attachment to another servant – her Hindustani teacher, Abdul Karim. Edward VII destroyed as much as he could find of the evidence of both of these relationships after his mother's death. Victoria insisted on being buried with Brown's photograph, a lock of his hair and his mother's wedding ring – fuelling rumours of a secret marriage. These effects were discreetly hidden by her undertakers with a posy of flowers and some white tissue paper.

Verdict: It's not often that a movie plays down, rather than playing up, a suggestion of historical romance, but Mrs Brown does.

Even if Victoria herself was a bit dull, the Victorian age was anything but. During Victoria's reign, the British Empire formally came into being and stretched its arms to every corner of the world. The idea of a 'Brytish Impire' was first suggested to Elizabeth I by the magician John Dee in 1577. The acquisition of trade rights and (eventually) territory in the east started with merchants and the privately owned East India Company, which was given a charter by Elizabeth in 1600. The Company gradually expanded its influence by trade and conquest until it came to control a vast swathe of Asia. Its rule was ended by the Indian Mutiny, or Indian Rebellion, of 1857. In 1858, the formal British Raj (rule) began, and with it the high period of British imperialism. Victoria was crowned Empress of India in 1876. The empire reached its greatest extent in the 1920s.

British imperialist adventures have always been controversial: they were hotly disputed while they were happening. As the twentieth century went on and the empire dissipated, filmmakers gradually started to find it easier to be critical of imperial life and wars in their movies, too. In recent years, there has been a resurgence of pro-imperial views in history books and historical TV documentaries. This doesn't yet seem to have filtered into feature films, but it will be interesting to see if imperial cheerleading makes it back to our screens in the future. If so, Reel History will be ready to challenge it.

Meanwhile, films produced in former British imperial colonies – notably the former 'jewel in the crown', India – give their own perspective on these troubled histories.

1854

The Charge of the Light Brigade (1968)

Director: Tony Richardson • Entertainment grade: D • History grade: B

The charge of the Light Brigade was led by the 7th Earl of Cardigan on 25 October 1854, during the Crimean War.

Politics: During the Battle of Balaclava, the British Army was commanded by Lord Raglan, and the Light Brigade of cavalry by Lord Cardigan. Ignore the emerging knitwear theme: this was serious stuff. The Crimean War was fought against the Russians by a joint British, French, Ottoman and Sardinian force. This is explained here with animations in the style of *Punch* cartoons by Richard Williams. So the Turkish state (represented, of course, by a turkey in a fez) is molested by a Russian bear, awakening the

British lion. The animations get steadily more surreal, culminating in Queen Victoria slicing up St Basil's Cathedral with a knife and fork and munching its onion domes.

People: The British Army in the Crimea was commanded by Lord Raglan, portrayed here as stiff-upper-lipped by John Gielgud. In real life, his upper lip was stiffer yet. As is correctly shown in the movie, his arm had to be amputated when he was shot in the elbow with a musket ball at Waterloo. While they sawed his arm off – without anaesthetic, of course – Raglan remained stoically silent. The only comment he made was when they chucked his severed limb into a basket. 'Hey, bring my arm back up,' he said. 'There's a ring my wife gave me on the finger.' What a badass.

More people: Supervillain Lord Cardigan (Trevor Howard) loathes simpering Captain Nolan (David Hemmings), calling him 'the Indian'. Though the real Nolan served in the Second Sikh War, it's a far cry to describe him as Indian. He was born in Milan and served in the 10th Hungarian Hussars before joining the British Army. The screenplay has borrowed for him the backstory of Captain John Reynolds, who was indeed part of what was called the 'Indian' faction in the British Army. In the film, Cardigan specifies that only champagne may be drunk at a mess dinner. Nolan orders Moselle wine in a black bottle. Cardigan is so furious he has Nolan arrested. This did actually happen, because Cardigan was that crazy – but with Reynolds in the place of Nolan.

War: The Brits head to the Crimea, an event represented by the animator in alarming fashion. Queen Victoria squats over a map, lifts her crinoline and warships issue forth from… well, one doesn't really want to ask. Soon, the Cossacks are sighted. 'Wussians!' squeals one posh British officer, who like most of his fellows cannot pronounce his Rs. 'Ooh, Wussians!' echoes his friend.

Battle: Nolan delivers a garbled order from Raglan to Cardigan, prompting the disastrous charge itself. The film tries to let him off, half-heartedly shifting the blame for the faulty order on to General Airey. Most historians blame Nolan for messing up the order; it was then misinterpreted by the commander of the Heavy Brigade, Lord Lucan (no, not the disappearing one); and Cardigan carried it out. There is still some dispute over who was responsible for the disastrous charge, but the film is pretty sure it's Cardigan.

Vengeance: Riding out ahead, Nolan is shot at the beginning of the charge. Afterwards, Cardigan is furious again. 'Did you hear the creature?' he barks. 'Shrieking like some tight girl, like a woman fetching off, damn him. Damn all his kind.' General Scarlett replies: 'My lord, you have just ridden over his dead body.' Theatrical though this exchange sounds, it's almost direct quotations from Cardigan's own memory of the conversation.

1857

The Rising: Ballad of Mangal Pandey (2005)

Director: Ketan Mehta • Entertainment grade: A– • History grade: D

Mangal Pandey was a sepoy, an Indian soldier in the army of the East India Company. A few weeks before the famous rebellion of May 1857, also known as the Indian Mutiny, he attempted to start a rebellion of his own. He was hanged, and became a folk hero.

War: The film opens in 1853, when Pandey and his British chum Captain Gordon are fighting the Afghans for some unspecified reason. It's a dramatic scene, but couldn't have happened. The First Anglo-Afghan War finished in 1842, Pandey did not join up until 1849, and his regiment – the 34th Bengal Native Infantry – did not see action in Afghanistan.

Technology: The action moves to Calcutta in 1857, where the Company is determined to introduce its shiny new Enfield rifles. The rifle's cartridges have to have their ends bitten off before they can be used. This turns out to be one of the worst pieces of design in history. They are rumoured to be waterproofed with a mixture of cow and pig fat, making them equally offensive to Hindus, who revere the cow, and Muslims, who are forbidden to eat the pig. These rumours were indeed the spark for the 1857 uprising, though discontent in Pandey's regiment was mostly caused by one British officer's clumsy attempts to convert the sepoys to Christianity.

Economics: The East India Company forces Indian farmers to grow opium, which it smuggles into China. When the Chinese object, the Company sends Indian sepoys to force them to accept the drug trade. 'And they called this the free market,' the voiceover adds bitterly in Hindi, just before Gordon repeats it in English, to make sure that nobody misses it. Unfortunately, the model is accurate. Not exactly Britain's finest hour. But the East India Company was a monopoly, not a free market. Adam Smith, the eighteenth-century father of free market economics, was one of its staunchest critics.

Romance: Pandey falls in love with Heera, a woman forced to work as a prostitute in a whites-only brothel. Legend has it the real Pandey was having an affair with a married woman, whom he had rescued when she tried to commit suicide by throwing herself into the Ganges. That's at least as good a story as the one the film invents.

Military: One of the most pigheaded Brits, Colonel Mitchell, tries to force the sepoys to use the cartridges by aiming cannon at them. Pandey breaks ranks and stands in front of one cannon's mouth. The real Mitchell did order artillery to surround his sepoys at their parade ground, but only after they had looted the arsenal. Pandey could not have been present: Mitchell was in charge of the 19th regiment, not the 34th. And it all happened in the middle of the night, not under the blazing Bengal sun shown in the film. So the personnel, the order of events and the timing are all wrong. Oh well. The costumes are nice.

Violence: The Company brings in the Rangoon Regiment to put down the rising. When the ships arrive, Pandey rushes to the parade ground and opens fire on the Brits himself. In reality, Pandey's premature mutiny was prompted by the arrival of just fifty soldiers from Calcutta, when he was under the influence of opium and bhang. There's no evidence for the film's suggestion that it was difficult to find anyone prepared to hang him afterwards.

Verdict: *The Rising* is a terrific film: powerful, shocking and gorgeous to look at. But this is 1857 the way it should have been, not the way it was.

1879

Zulu (1964)

Director: Cy Endfield • Entertainment grade: B+ • History grade: C+

The Battle of Rorke's Drift on 22–23 January 1879 was part of the Anglo-Zulu War. Fewer than 150 British soldiers, of whom almost a quarter were invalids before the fighting even started, defended a postage-stamp of land against 4,500 Zulu warriors. Though not strategically significant, it is famous for a shock British victory against near-impossible odds.

War: *Zulu* opens with a dramatic tableau of the burning wreckage and strewn British bodies over the battlefield at Isandlwana. It then cuts to a lengthy and interesting, if not entirely pertinent, mass marriage celebration, at the court of the

Zulu king Cetshwayo. This is the only peek into the Zulu side of the story you're going to get, so enjoy the five minutes while it lasts. At Rorke's Drift, a missionary outpost, B Company of the British Army's 24th Regiment of Foot hears that Cetshwayo's Zulus are on the march. In fact, the attack on Rorke's Drift was probably the independent initiative of Cetshwayo's half-brother Dabulamanzi kaMpande, against Cetshwayo's orders. Dabulamanzi commanded the uThulwana regiment, and led the Zulu forces in the attack.

People: Two equally senior officers are present, lieutenants John Chard (Stanley Baker) and Gonville Bromhead (Michael Caine). Chard assumes overall command, having held his commission for three months longer (in real life, three years and three months longer). The real Bromhead wasn't the sharp, steely character shown onscreen. Described by a fellow officer as 'a capital fellow at everything except soldiering', he was reputedly not very bright, and may have been assigned to Rorke's Drift because his partial deafness was thought to limit his ability to command.

Details: Colour Sergeant Frank Bourne is splendidly portrayed by Nigel Green as a bellowing, towering, middle-aged bear of a man, but in reality was a diminutive, skinny twenty-four-year-old, nicknamed 'The Kid'. At least Green has grown some decent Victorian whiskers. There's a disgraceful lack of appropriately fulsome moustaches among the cast: photographs of the real veterans of Rorke's Drift look like candidates for Britain's Best Walrus Impersonator 1879. (Winner: Lieutenant Chard; Mr Congeniality: Lieutenant Bromhead.)

Heroism: Moustaches aside, the veteran who has been most poorly served by *Zulu* is Private Henry Hook (James Booth), shown malingering in the hospital and trying to cadge free booze. The real Private Hook had an exemplary record and was teetotal. The film redeems him when it comes to the fighting: a sudden burst of courage under fire has him shooting and bayoneting Zulus all over the place. While this whole flawed action hero thing works neatly as a cinematic device, it is not in the least bit accurate. Hook's daughter was so offended that she walked out of the film's premiere. Incidentally, Hook's photograph reveals not only that he was another worthy challenger in the walrus contest, but also that he had a distinctive centre parting. This was actually a scar, the legacy of a close encounter with a Zulu assegai, which knocked off his pith helmet when he was defending the hospital. The film leaves this out, and even neglects to make him wear his pith helmet.

Battle: In real life, the last shot was fired around 4 a.m. In the film, there's a showdown at first light, with yet another wave of Zulus turning up. Finally, it all comes down to a sing-off: Zulus versus Welshmen, the latter launching into 'Men of Harlech'. The film's implication that the 24th was a Welsh regiment is two and a half years too early. In 1881, it would move to Wales, but in 1879 it was affiliated to Warwickshire. Most of its men at Rorke's Drift were English and Irish. Correspondingly, its regimental song was not 'Men of Harlech', but 'The Warwickshire Lads'. Great scene, though.

Verdict: The Zulus are a mystery, the Welsh are misplaced, a Victoria Cross recipient is slandered, and no one has enough facial hair. Nonetheless, *Zulu* is a brilliantly made dramatization of Rorke's Drift, and it does a fine job of capturing the spirit for which the battle is remembered.

1885

Khartoum (1966)

Director: Basil Dearden • Entertainment grade: D+ • History grade: C–

Muhammad Ahmad was a Sudanese theocrat and general who in 1881 proclaimed himself Mahdi, a redeemer expected by some Muslims to appear before the Day of Judgement. He conquered large swathes of the Nile Valley and annihilated three Egyptian armies. Gradually, Britain became involved on the Egyptian side. Khartoum covers the section of the war that pitted Muhammad Ahmad against General Charles 'Chinese' Gordon.

Casting: In the 1960s, casting agents must have actually said things like: 'So, we need a Sudanese Nubian… how about Laurence Olivier?' Olivier, in blackface, looks nothing like Muhammad Ahmad. Things don't improve when he speaks. His stab at a Sudanese accent sounds like Sebastian, the singing Caribbean crab from Disney's *The Little Mermaid*, pretending to be a Russian spy. 'Oh, beylovvids!' he says to his beloved followers. 'I am the Mahrhrhdi! The Exxxpected One!' It's particularly unfortunate when the film, inaccurately, has him meet General Gordon (Charlton Heston). Heston plays it straight, leaving Olivier looking even more like he has escaped from a racist panto.

'I'm not a loving man, Muhammad Ahmad, but this land became the only thing that I have ever loved,' Gordon says. 'I am a poor man of the desert, but I am the Mahrhrhdi,' replies Muhammad Ahmad. 'The Exxxxpected One.' Incredibly, this screenplay was nominated for an Oscar.

Imperialism: The middle section of Khartoum gets tangled up in the complicated politics behind British intervention. The story of how Britain stumbled into an imperial adventure in the Sudan is potentially of even greater interest now than it would have been in 1966. The thing it isn't, though, is cinematic. It really does just come down to a lot of men with tufty facial hair sitting around in armchairs and vacillating. To liven things up, the film chucks in a few desert battles, though unfortunately these have been filmed and edited too ineptly to make sense. Meanwhile, a large crowd gathers in London, waving placards and chanting, 'Save Gordon!' This looks suspiciously like a 1960s demonstration, but it is true that public meetings were held in Gordon's support.

Violence: Muhammad Ahmad again summons Gordon to his tent and tries to persuade him to leave: 'You are not my enemy.' 'Oh, but I am!' cries Gordon. 'We are so alike, you and I.' Muhammad Ahmad tires of being patronized, and has a rummage around in some bran tubs. He pulls out the head of *Times* correspondent Frank Power, before presenting Gordon with the hand of his aide, Colonel Stewart. 'Is it not your own ring?' Power and Stewart were murdered by Mahdists, though it was Stewart's head that was sent to Muhammad Ahmad. There was no meeting at which Muhammad Ahmad attempted to intimidate Gordon with lucky dips full of bits of dead people, though he did write him a series of polite letters asking him to leave the Sudan to avoid further bloodshed.

Battle: In a scene inspired by George William Joy's painting *The Last Stand of General Gordon*, the Mahdists storm Khartoum. Gordon steps out to face them calmly. A reverent hush falls, and finally one hurls a single spear through his chest. This is heavily romanticized. The real Gordon came out shooting, but ran out of ammunition on the staircase. The detailed account of one Mahdist suggests he was killed with a gunshot to the chest, not a spear, and that it was a mistake: in the dim light, they mistook him for a Turk. Afterwards, his head is brought on a stick to Muhammad Ahmad, who isn't pleased at all. 'Take it away!' he howls. For a chap with barrels of severed body parts in his tent, this seems uncharacteristically squeamish – but, in real life, Muhammad Ahmad did specifically order that Gordon was not to be killed.

At the beginning of the twentieth century, some of the most famous American outlaws of all history were robbing trains out in the Old West. Their real names were Robert Leroy Parker and Harry Alonzo Longabaugh, but thanks to Hollywood the world knows them as...

1900

Butch Cassidy and the Sundance Kid (1969)

Director: George Roy Hill • Entertainment grade: A– • History grade: B

Crime: The film opens with the admission 'Most of what follows is true.' Butch (Paul Newman) and Sundance (Robert Redford) ride to Hole-in-the-Wall, Wyoming, a pass where outlaws hang out. Their gang is keen to move on to robbing trains, specifically the Union Pacific Flyer. Butch, Sundance and their henchmen stop the train, but meet resistance from a clerk, Woodcock. 'I work for Mr E. H. Harriman of the Union Pacific Railroad, and he entrusted me…' Butch interrupts: 'Will you shut up about that E. H. Harriman stuff and open the door?' Woodcock won't. 'Mr E. H. Harriman himself, of the Union Pacific Railroad, gave me this job, and I got to do my best, don't you see?' 'Your best don't include getting yourself killed,' says Butch, but Woodcock won't budge. The gang blow the door open with dynamite. Woodcock is knocked about a bit, but seems fine. In a film that already upsets viewers who like their westerns gritty and serious, this sounds flagrantly cartoonish – but Charles Woodcock was a real person, and the scene is basically accurate.

More crime: Soon afterwards, Butch and Sundance try another robbery – and, what do you know, it's poor old Woodcock behind the door again. Amazingly, the unfortunate Charles Woodcock really did fall foul of train robberies attributed to Butch Cassidy's Wild Bunch gang twice. For dramatic impact, the film has shifted the circumstances of the first of these incidents – which was the Wilcox train robbery of 2 June 1899, in which a whole railroad car was dynamited apart – to the second incident, which was the Tipton train robbery of 29 August 1900. It is not clear whether Cassidy or Sundance was personally involved in either. Sensitive readers will be relieved to know that, in real life, Woodcock abandoned his capitalist heroics the second time round and just let the robbers in.

Law enforcement: In the middle of the second robbery, a mysterious posse shows up, and begins to chase Butch and Sundance. 'Who are those guys?' they wonder repeatedly. They single out a marshal called Joe Lefors and a Native American tracker called Lord Baltimore. In real life, E. H. Harriman engaged the Pinkerton National Detective Agency to hunt Cassidy's gang. The Pinkertons sent a posse after the outlaws in 1899. The posse did include Lefors, but not Baltimore – he didn't exist. The film's long, inescapable pursuit across the west is fictional. The real Cassidy easily evaded the posse.

Travel: Butch and Sundance take a ship to South America with Sundance's girlfriend Etta Place (Katharine Ross), who, to Butch's irritation, keeps getting in the way of their manly chemistry with each other. They're expecting gold and silver, but arrive in a deserted, dusty, two-llama town. The film skips a respectable sojourn the real trio enjoyed running a ranch in Buenos Aires from 1901, because that would be boring. Soon, armed with some beginners' criminal Spanish lessons courtesy of Place ('Esto es un robo' – this is a robbery), they revert to their old pursuits.

Fate: A few heists later, Butch and Sundance attract the attention of the authorities. The film implies that the Pinkertons tracked them down, which isn't entirely untrue: the agency did continue to receive reports on them. The final shootout in the Bolivian town of San Vicente happened in November 1908, but the fates of Cassidy and Sundance are disputed. Stories of their survival have proved popular over the years, though many historians agree with Cassidy expert Dan Buck, who described one such tale as 'total horse pucky'. The movie's ending is historically unimpeachable.

It's a pity there aren't more movies about nineteenth- and very early twentieth-century Russia. It was an age of extraordinary characters, yet there is, for instance, no great biopic of Tsar Alexander II the Liberator, who freed the serfs and was then assassinated by revolutionaries. He appears in a couple of minor European films and adaptations of Jules Verne's novel *Michael Strogoff*, but that's it. Of course, during the twentieth century American filmmakers often found it hard to sell Russian subjects to audiences fired up with Cold War fury; and Soviet filmmakers didn't generally pitch movies about how wonderful the tsars were.

The period also produced some of the greatest literature in history – Gogol, Turgenev, Dostoevsky, Chekhov... and perhaps the biggest name of them all, Lev Tolstoy.

1910

The Last Station (2009)

Director: Michael Hoffman • Entertainment grade: C • History grade: B+

Count Lev Nikolayevich 'Leo' Tolstoy, author of *War and Peace* and *Anna Karenina*, is considered to be one of the greatest writers of all time. He had a long, tempestuous marriage to Sofya Andreyevna Tolstaya.

Locations: The film begins in 1910 at Yasnaya Polyana, the estate where Leo Tolstoy (Christopher Plummer, with excellent lookalike beard) wrote his great works. The real Yasnaya Polyana is now immaculately preserved as a museum. *The Last Station* was filmed at the Schloss Stülpe in Brandenburg, Germany, a comparable (though perhaps even grander) house. Alongside his writing, Tolstoy was a moral philosopher, advocating vegetarianism, celibacy and non-violence.

Celibacy: Earnest young disciple Valentin Fyodorovich Bulgakov (James McAvoy) is appointed by sinister Tolstoyan purist Vladimir Grigorievich Chertkov (Paul Giamatti) to act as Tolstoy's secretary. He is shown into Tolstoy's study, and embraced by the great man. 'Sit down!' bellows Tolstoy. 'I was born on that sofa!' Bulgakov is a bit freaked out, but historically this is accurate: the sofa on which Tolstoy was born stayed in his study at Yasnaya Polyana, and indeed is still there (though the house was occupied by invading German forces during World War II and there is now a hole in it, made by a Nazi soldier's bayonet).

Tolstoy admits to being a poor Tolstoyan himself, struggling especially with his own belief in celibacy. He kept trying to give up sex throughout his life, yet sired thirteen children with his wife (plus, according to him, at least one with someone else). Bulgakov's own struggle with celibacy in the film – swiftly lost after the introduction of a hearty wood-chopping lass called Masha (Kerry Condon) – is fictional, as is Masha herself.

Conflict: Chertkov asks Bulgakov to spy on Tolstoy's wife, Sofya (Helen Mirren): 'She's very, very dangerous.' For many years, Sofya Tolstaya's historical reputation was that of a selfish harridan who got in the way of her husband's greatness. Recent scholarship has rebalanced this image, noting that Chertkov himself was responsible for spreading many of the nastiest stories about her. This film is strongly influenced by the more recent view, depicting Chertkov as a villain and Sofya as a passionate, neurotic figure, driven to despair. 'I'll throw myself under a train, like Anna Karenina!' Sofya yells at Tolstoy. 'You don't need a husband, you need a Greek chorus!' he yells back. It's soap-operatic dialogue, but a historically justifiable take on their relationship. *The Last Station* goes soft on Tolstoy himself, rendering him an amiable patriarch gliding benignly above most of the conflict. In his 1889 novella *The Kreutzer Sonata*, the main character fights his 'swinish' sexual desires and ends up murdering his wife. Many readers at the time saw the book as a violent fantasy attack on Sofya.

Breakups: Sofya's rage grows: she smashes crockery, entangles herself furiously in a curtain, and at one point shoots several bullets into a picture of Chertkov (in real life, she did let off a gun – though reportedly it was a child's toy, shooting only caps). Mirren and Plummer – both sublime actors – do their best with the histrionic screenplay. But even they can't redeem a make-up bedroom scene in which Mirren is obliged to say, with a nearly straight face, 'I'm still your little chicken, and you're still my big cock.' Then poor Plummer must snuggle up to her, making chicken noises. Clucking hell.

Death: With his marriage in full meltdown, the 82-year-old Tolstoy leaves Yasnaya Polyana in the middle of the night on 28 October 1910. He travels as far as Astapovo, but is then too ill to continue. The film's depiction of Tolstoy's last days, spent in the station-master's house surrounded by the world's press and his massively dysfunctional family, is more or less accurate. It is also accurate about Sofya's experience. According to Bulgakov's memoirs, on hearing that he had walked out on her, she tried to drown herself in the pond: 'I had seen Sofya Andreyevna's body lying face-up and open-mouthed in the water, her arms spread helplessly as she sank,' he wrote. He, along with a footman and Sofya's daughter Alexandra (Anne-Marie Duff), pulled her out. The film is also right that Tolstoy's children and Chertkov would not let Sofya see her husband until he was unconscious – though it cannot resist adding a slight hint of a reconciliation.

Verdict: Handsome but hammy, *The Last Station* gets nowhere near Tolstoy's emotional profundity – but its historical research is commendable.

Many filmmakers have attempted to tackle the sinking of the 'unsinkable' *Titanic* in 1912. In fact, the first movie on the subject was released just 29 days after the thing itself sank: a one-reel short called *Saved from the Titanic*, starring the 22-year-old actress Dorothy Gibson. Gibson herself had been saved from the *Titanic*: she and her mother both escaped on Lifeboat No. 7. She appeared in the film wearing the same clothes she had been wearing on the ship, but the experience was apparently not easy for her. She was reported to have suffered a nervous breakdown after reliving her trauma in the film and never made another.

A Night to Remember (1958) is probably still the best-regarded film about the sinking by *Titanic* enthusiasts. *Raise the Titanic* (1980) is a Cold War adventure movie in which Jason Robards and Alec Guinness must find the sunken ship and retrieve a MacGuffin. (Alfred Hitchcock popularized the term 'MacGuffin': it is a plot device, commonly an object, that the protagonist of a film must pursue to push the plot forward. It does not matter what the MacGuffin is. The point is that the protagonist must want it, and the villain must want to stop him or her getting it.)

Raise the Titanic (1980) was a box-office disaster, making only around a quarter of its production value back. As its producer Lew Grade famously remarked afterwards, 'It would have been cheaper to lower the Atlantic.' By contrast, another movie about the *Titanic* became (in its time) the highest-grossing film in history – the first to bring in over $1 billion. It won eleven Oscars.

1912

Titanic (1997)

Director: James Cameron • Entertainment grade: B+ • History grade: B–

One April night in 1912, the biggest, newest and most famous passenger ship in the world collided with an iceberg. In less time than it takes to watch James Cameron's film, RMS *Titanic* provided one of history's clearest examples of pride coming before a fall.

Details: Costumes and sets have been meticulously researched, and some shots were filmed on the real wreck. Admittedly, if you look at the IMDb's goofs page, you will find pedants complaining about the colour of the wicker furniture, and some inaccurately positioned door handles. If you're the sort of person whose day is ruined when you spot that 'The button on the left side of Jack's borrowed jacket is a "Kingsdrew" button, first made in 1922', it's never too late to seek professional help. If you're not, the ship is entirely convincing.

Characters: Several of the film's characters are based on real people, though the leads, Jack (Leonardo DiCaprio) and Rose (Kate Winslet), are fictional. Rose is realistic enough: a well-bred but destitute young lady, about to be married off to a suave cad with cash pouring out of his trousers. Jack is less believable as a Wisconsin urchin who has somehow ended up as a jobbing fine artist ('Monet!' he gasps, waving his hands at Rose's art collection. 'Look at his use of colour here! Isn't he great?').

Romance: Jack tells Rose he trained by sketching women in the brothels of Paris. Amazingly, she accepts this excuse for being in the brothels of Paris, and even proceeds to have sex with him on the cargo deck. Luckily for her, the first antibiotic treatment for syphilis was marketed in 1910. Perhaps Jack was inspired by the painting hanging in Rose's cabin: Picasso's *Les Demoiselles d'Avignon*, a portrait of five prostitutes. (For anyone upset by anachronistic jacket buttons: that painting was definitely not on the *Titanic*. It can still be seen in New York.)

Society: Credibility is stretched even further by the depiction of life in first class as boring and miserable, while the happy proletarians down in third are having a knees-up. In reality, throughout most of history, it has been much nicer being rich than being poor. Moreover, *Titanic*'s operator White Star segregated single male and female passengers in most third-class areas, limiting the scope for heterosexual onboard jollies.

Controversy: The film shows third-class passengers being locked in their quarters to facilitate the escape of the aristos up top. There is some debate over whether or not this really happened. But the survival rates of passengers by class are striking: while over 60 per cent of first and 40 per cent of second got off the ship, only 25 per cent of third did.

6

Oh, What Lovely Wars

The First World War (1914–18) was a conflict unlike any seen before in history. So many nations, so much new military technology, so many dead: afterwards, the world map substantially redrawn, and a series of economic, social, political, cultural and military reverberations set off that would define the twentieth century.

There are far too many fascinating World War I films to list here. A few recommendations: *The Four Horsemen of the Apocalypse* (1921), the enthralling smash hit silent movie that launched Rudolph Valentino's superstar career, and which reveals an equivocal and complicated attitude to wartime heroism in the wake of the war itself; *All Quiet on the Western Front* (1930), an American adaptation of a German novel about trench warfare, and G. W. Pabst's similar German film *Vier von der Infanterie* (1930) – literally *Four of the Infantry* but known in English as *Westfront 1918*; and *Shoulder Arms* (1918), a Charlie

Chaplin comedy about fighting in France, which captures the military humour of the time.

Here are another two of the best films about the soldiers' experiences:

1915

Gallipoli (1981)

Director: Peter Weir • Entertainment grade: A– • History grade: A–

Gallipoli was a campaign of World War I, a joint offensive by Allied forces intended to capture Constantinople and secure a sea route to Russia. It was also the first major engagement for Anzac, the Australian and New Zealand Army Corps. Gallipoli incurred one of the highest death tolls of the war while failing to achieve its objective.

Joining up: The film opens in rural Western Australia in 1915, where a group of farmhands are reading news reports from Gallipoli. 'The Turkish defences included wire entanglements on land and sea, and deep pits with spiked bottoms,' reads one. 'Bastards!' exclaims another. 'That's it,' says a third. 'I'm gonna join up.' Who knew a spiked bottom could be so persuasive? The film's fictional hero, Archie, befriends fellow sportsman Frank, and the two of them hike across the desert to join the 10th Light Horse Regiment in Perth. Such persistence may seem unlikely, but there are plenty of true stories to match it. One real recruit rode 300 miles on horseback out of the Kimberley, and then hopped on a boat to Fremantle, over 2,000 miles away, to sign up for the 10th Light Horse.

Training: The boys are shipped off to Egypt for training. This appears to involve playing rugby on the Giza Plateau, in between the pyramids and the Sphinx. Mena Camp, where the Australians trained, was indeed around ten miles outside the centre of Cairo, near the pyramids. The depiction of training camp life is pretty accurate, down to the sexually transmitted disease prevention lectures and laboured practical jokes. On the other hand, the 'antique' figurines that the lads get sold in the bazaar look suspiciously like the gold sarcophagus of Tutankhamun, discovered by Howard Carter in 1922.

Military: Finally, the regiment makes its way to Turkey. The troops are forced to land on Anzac Beach in the middle of the night under heavy fire. In real life, that day's fighting alone saw 682 Australians killed or injured. The rest of the film is played out against an unceasing soundtrack of explosions and gunfire, just like real life in the trenches. It is true, as shown, that there were corpses lying around all over the place. If anything, the film doesn't go far enough. Men digging new trenches would regularly uncover the decomposing bodies of their fallen comrades. Unsurprisingly, Anzac troops stationed in the trenches started coming down with an unpleasant infection, involving vomiting and septic sores.

Battle: The moving climax depicts the Battle of the Nek, a doomed push against the Turkish trenches by the 8th and 10th

Light Horse. Much criticism has been made of Peter Weir for casting the fictional commanding officer, Robinson, as a Brit. In fact, Robinson is speaking with a posh Australian accent – and wearing an Australian uniform. He is clearly not supposed to be a Brit. The film even refrains from criticizing the two Britons most commonly held responsible for the disaster of Gallipoli, namely Winston Churchill and Lord Kitchener. Meanwhile, what really happened at the Nek was similar to the story shown, only with different characters: an appalling case of miscommunication and misjudgement by colonels Jack Antill and F. G. Hughes. Lt Col Noel Brazier was the real officer who went back and forth between the two, trying to persuade them to stop sending troops over the top. The signal for a final row of 150 men to put themselves straight into the line of Turkish fire was indeed given while the commanding officers were dithering about their decision.

1916

Paths of Glory (1957)

Director: Stanley Kubrick • Entertainment grade: A– • History grade: C

Strategy: The film begins on the French front in 1916. General Broulard (Adolphe Menjou) tells General Mireau (George Macready) that he must take a German position known as the Anthill. His reward will be a new star. 'I'm responsible for the lives of 8,000 men,' Mireau says. 'What is my ambition against that?' He is tempted, though. After some presumably self-justifying thought, he heads for the trenches to tell Colonel Dax (Kirk Douglas) to take the Anthill.

Class: Mireau's stroll around the trenches is a splendidly dark snapshot of the class differences between officers and men in World War I. 'Ready to kill more Germans?' he asks the soldiers, all chipper as if he's proposing a Sunday afternoon game of bridge.

War: When Dax and his men advance into No Man's Land, the Germans are already shooting and shelling. Witnessing the slaughter that follows, French reinforcements refuse to leave their trenches. Enraged, Mireau orders his artillery to fire on his own trenches to force the men in them to go over the top. Mireau and Dax are fictional characters, but this story (adapted from Humphrey Cobb's novel) is based on real events. On 7 March 1915, French general Géraud Réveilhac ordered his artillery to fire on his own soldiers when they refused to advance at Souain in the Champagne region. As in the film, the artillerymen refused to fire on their own comrades.

Justice: Dax calls off the assault. Mireau isn't at all happy with his soldiers. 'They've skimmed milk in their veins instead of blood!' he bellows. He wants to shoot a hundred of them, but Broulard talks him down to three. In real life, thirty men stood trial, though only four were convicted. They were Théophile Maupas, Louis Lefoulon, Louis Girard and Lucien Lechat. Maupas, who had an exemplary record as a soldier, corresponds vaguely to the character of Pierre Arnaud (Joseph Turkel) in the film. The trial is a sham. The men are sentenced to be shot by firing squad.

Glamour: Meanwhile, there's a party in the general's palace, complete with fine food, fine wine and pretty ladies in satin dresses. Away from the dancing, Dax protests to Broulard about the firing squad. 'There are few things more fundamentally encouraging and stimulating than seeing someone else die,' Broulard replies cheerfully. (He is echoing the famous quote from Voltaire's *Candide* about Britain's Admiral John Byng, executed 1757: 'il est bon de tuer de temps en temps un amiral pour encourager les autres.') Finally, Dax spills the beans about Mireau trying to fire on his own men.

Reputations: In the film, Broulard is shocked by Mireau's action, and justice comes quickly. In real life, things weren't so neat. After the four men were executed, Réveilhac remained in his post until he was given three months' leave in February 1916 (because, according to a senior officer, he seemed to have 'reached the limit of his physical and mental abilities'). He was later made a Grand Officer of the Legion d'honneur. The French authorities repeatedly refused to investigate the case. Eventually, thanks to the efforts of Maupas's widow Blanche and Lechat's sister Eulalie, a court cleared the men in 1934. General Réveilhac died peacefully at the age of 86 in 1937.

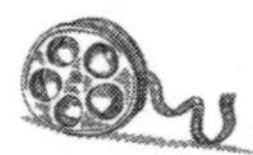

While the war raged on in Europe, other conflicts mushroomed. In Ireland, the fight for home rule led by Michael Collins continued. Collins led the negotiations that established the Irish Free State.

1916

Michael Collins (1996)

Director: Neil Jordan • Entertainment grade: B • History grade: D

Casting: The film begins with the Easter Rising of 1916, after which Collins (Liam Neeson) and his compatriots surrender to the British. Neeson carries off Collins's intense, earthy charisma. There's just one problem: when Neeson made this, he was forty-four. In 1916, Collins was twenty-five. He was assassinated at the age of thirty-one. Accurately, Collins is shown asking young men to kill for the Irish Republican cause – but the fact that Neeson is visibly twice their age changes the tone, making him look more like a behind-the-scenes manipulator than a fellow fighter.

Imperialism: After the Easter Rising, the film depicts the cold-blooded firing squad executions of its leaders by the British authorities. In real life, that event pushed many Irish (and quite a few British) people into sympathy with the Republican cause. In the film, it is brilliantly and unflinchingly handled. It's more of a challenge to maintain sympathy for the Republicans when they, too, start killing people, but most of the time director Neil Jordan does an impressive job of balancing the humanity of the individuals concerned with an accurate picture of the fierceness of the fight.

Violence: At Croke Park football ground, a crowd is watching a match. British armoured vehicles roll into the ground, and, without warning, open fire on players and spectators. There was a horrific massacre at Croke Park by the Auxiliaries and the Black and Tans in 1920, known as Bloody Sunday (not to be confused with the 1972 Bloody Sunday). If you've watched this scene, you'll be surprised that only fourteen civilians died: the British are shown firing into dense crowds with the machine guns mounted on their armoured vehicles. In real life, though, the armoured vehicles stopped outside Croke Park. The shooting was done by hand. The reality of Bloody Sunday is terrible – yet apparently not terrible enough for this movie, which exaggerates it. 'The reason I did it really is because I wanted the scene to last thirty seconds,' Neil Jordan said. That thirty seconds costs this movie a lot of credibility. British imperial history is chock-full of massacres, genocides, unjust wars, famines and so on. With so many real atrocities to choose from, you don't need to make things up.

Murder: The movie shows political leader Éamon de Valera (Alan Rickman) setting Collins up to lead negotiations in London, knowing it will be impossible to secure full republican status or a united Ireland. Secretly, he hopes that Collins will take the fall for those concessions. That is a historically justifiable view. What is not so justifiable is that the film goes on to imply strongly that de Valera was behind Collins's assassination. A fictional teenage boy (played by a young Jonathan Rhys Meyers) is shown acting as de Valera's loyal spy and messenger, and afterwards shooting Collins in an ambush. In real life, though they fought each other in the civil war, de Valera wanted to negotiate with Collins. He was not involved in the ambush: actually, he tried to stop it. 'I don't mean to imply that de Valera had anything to do with the assassination,' said Jordan. Really? Then why identify de Valera's boy as the assassin, and why end the movie on a quote from the real de Valera which is made to sound bitter and possibly guilty: 'History will record the greatness of Michael Collins, and it will be at my expense'?

One of the most famous and most mysterious men of the First World War was T. E. Lawrence. He was a British officer who campaigned with Arab regulars, and he was immortalized in one of the finest biopics in film history:

1916

Lawrence of Arabia (1962)

Director: David Lean • Entertainment grade: A • History grade: C–

Landscapes: In 1916, Lawrence (Peter O'Toole) is sent from Cairo into the Arabian desert to find Prince Faisal of Mecca. It's essential to watch this film on the biggest screen you can find, at the highest resolution possible. Director David Lean filmed it on sumptuous 70 mm stock instead of the usual 35 mm, which allowed for incredible sharpness. The desert shots are mindblowing: glimmering mirages, whirling clouds of sand, teeny weeny people and camels inching their way across massive, spectacular landscapes (notably Wadi Rum in Jordan, where Lawrence and Faisal based themselves for a while in real life). Really not one to see on your smartphone.

Bromance: Crossing the desert, Lawrence meets Sherif Ali of the Harith. Despite several attempts to cast white actors in this role, including Alain Delon and Horst Buchholz, and the leftfield suggestion of casting Bollywood legend Dilip Kumar, the filmmakers were eventually obliged to settle on a genuine Arab: Egyptian superstar Omar Sharif. The result is one of the hottest screen couples in history, with the crackling jealous and macho tension between the impossibly handsome O'Toole and the equally impossibly handsome Sharif hovering on the brink of the sexual. This may not be entirely historically accurate, but it has some grounding. The real Lawrence wrote admiringly of what he called 'man-on-man loves', and biographers usually conclude that he must have been at least a bit gay. His autobiography, *The Seven Pillars of Wisdom*, opens with a love poem, 'To S. A.' This was not Sherif Ali – he didn't really exist. Omar Sharif's character in the film is a fictionalized composite of several Arab leaders. 'S. A.' is sometimes thought to be Selim Ahmed, Lawrence's assistant and rumoured lover.

People: The other Arab leaders in the film, Prince Faisal and Auda abu Tayi, are played by Alec Guinness and Anthony Quinn respectively. The screenplay underplays their roles so as to big up Lawrence's – though the real Lawrence had already bigged himself up a lot. Faisal's lines are smartly written and dryly delivered, which at least allows him wit and dignity, though he gets none of his real-life action. Auda is more of a problem. His character is portrayed as an unreformed savage who cares only for violence, treasure and his own pompous self-image. In fact, he was a serious and intelligent leader, who deserved more credit for the crucial taking of Aqaba than Lawrence. Auda's family were deeply offended by the film, and reportedly spent years trying unsuccessfully to sue the producers.

Character: Several incidents in Lawrence's life are represented with major dramatic licence – including the fate of Gasim (I. S. Johar), who Lawrence first rescues from the desert and afterwards is forced to execute. The first of these things happened; the second sort of did, though Lawrence did not have to shoot the same man he rescued. In real life, he shot one called Hamed, in a separate and earlier dispute between Syrians and Moroccans. What the film does, though, is use these incidents to build an idiosyncratic but insightful picture of Lawrence, played indelibly by Peter O'Toole: a complicated, egomaniacal and physically masochistic man, at once godlike and all too flawed, with a tenuous grip both on reality and on sanity. It's so well done that a historian might even forgive stuff like the filmmakers getting the date of the United States joining World War I wrong. (In real life that happened before, not after, the capture of Aqaba.)

Violence: The movie depicts an incident that has long bothered Lawrence biographers: what happened, or didn't, at Deraa. Lawrence wrote in *The Seven Pillars*, and in two private letters, that he was imprisoned there by district governor Hajim Bey (José Ferrer) and tortured, sexually assaulted and perhaps (his descriptions are vague) raped. The film hints at this, but could not show much. Some historians consider the whole Deraa incident a fantasy, partly because Lawrence described it sensually ('a delicious warmth, probably sexual, was swelling through me' he wrote of being flogged, then kicked in the ribs), and partly because he was seen by witnesses looking unhurt afterwards. In 1924, Lawrence wrote to George Bernard Shaw's wife Charlotte confessing that 'to earn five minutes' respite from a pain which drove me mad, I gave away… my bodily integrity'. Historian Scott Anderson suggested sympathetically that Lawrence may have submitted to the rape to avoid further torture, and afterwards embroidered his tale with 'the kind of violence that offers an absolution of guilt by making all questions of will or resistance moot'. Whatever happened, the film is right that Lawrence became even more withdrawn and peculiar after Deraa.

Imperialism: *Lawrence of Arabia* takes a critical view of British imperialism in the Middle East – showing it as cold, calculating and widely resented by the locals. The sharpest lines are given to Sherif Ali, memorably when Lawrence (who has adopted Arab dress) returns to the British headquarters. 'In Cairo, you will put off these funny clothes,' he says bitterly. 'You will wear trousers and tell stories about quaintness and barbarity.' Lawrence is furious: 'You are an ignorant man,' he snaps back. Later, he is seen in Cairo, self-consciously wearing a pair of trousers. It's accurate: after the war, Lawrence tried to escape his 'of Arabia' identity, going so far as to change his name twice.

Russia was a major player in World War I and was at the same time riven by its own internal troubles. There had been a revolution against Tsarist rule in 1905, but the reforms thereafter were not enough. During the war, discontent grew within the army. It also grew on the streets. In 1917, there was a series of revolutions. The tsar was forced to abdicate.

Western filmmakers have been fascinated by the fall of the tsar and the horrible fate of his family ever since. The first film about those events was *The Fall of the Romanoffs* (1917), made in the United States before the Romanovs themselves had even been executed. Like many films about the Romanovs, it included the mystic monk Grigori Yefimovich Rasputin: a figure largely blamed in popular culture, though not so strongly by historians, for hastening the demise of the tsars. Rasputin's closeness to the Tsarina Alexandra did cause upset in real life – but the tsarina believed that he had the power to help her haemophiliac son and heir to the throne of all the Russias, the tsarevich Alexei. Hammer Studios cast Christopher Lee in *Rasputin, The Mad Monk* (1966); he is great fun, but the film around him is not.

Soviet director Elem Klimov made a film about Rasputin called *Agoniya* (1973–75), known in English as *Agony*. It displeased the authorities and was not shown in the Soviet Union until 1981. Meanwhile, there have been several movies about the supposed fate of Anastasia, the tsar's youngest daughter, who was rumoured to have escaped the firing squad and fled to Europe. As a sidelight on the revolution, it's well worth seeing *Reds* (1981), directed by and starring Warren Beatty. It's an impressively balanced and immaculately researched biopic of John Reed, an American journalist who witnessed the October Revolution, and a terrific movie to boot.

Also noteworthy is the 1932 film *Rasputin and the Empress*, featuring all three siblings of the famous Barrymore acting family: Lionel as Rasputin, his sister Ethel as Rasputin's rumoured lover Tsarina Alexandra, and their brother John as Prince Chegodieff, a fictionalized version of one of Rasputin's killers, Prince Felix Yusupov. The real Princess Irina Yusupov, Felix's wife and Tsar Nicholas II's niece, sued MGM for the inaccurate representation of her in this movie. Even though her name had been changed in the film to Princess Natasha, she won the suit in an English court and received a settlement reportedly of $250,000 from MGM in the United States. As a result of this lawsuit, films made thereafter have almost always included a disclaimer along the lines of 'All characters appearing in this motion picture are fictitious. Any resemblance to actual persons, living or dead, is purely coincidental.'

Reel History, of course, knows better than to trust that.

1917

Nicholas & Alexandra (1971)

Director: Franklin J. Schaffner • Entertainment grade: C+ • History grade: B+

People: In 1904, Tsarina Alexandra (Janet Suzman) finally gives birth to an heir, Alexei. 'I thought we'd go on having girls forever,' she admits to the tsar (Michael Jayston, a dead ringer for the real thing). They have already produced four little grand duchesses. Meanwhile, at a political meeting, stony-faced Lenin (Michael Bryant) and exasperated Trotsky (Brian Cox) meet a bubbly young

Borat lookalike calling himself Stalin (James Hazeldine). The film has elided a couple of events here: the Bolshevik–Menshevik split of 1903, in Belgium, and the All-Russian Bolshevik Conference of 1905, in Finland, at which Lenin first met Stalin. London folklore holds that Lenin and Stalin actually first met when they had a pint together before that conference at the Crown Tavern on Clerkenwell Green, but the evidence for this isn't exactly solid.

Religion: Nicholas and Alexandra arrive at a party full of guffawing aristocrats, all of whom are ignoring the oppressed proletariat and practically guzzling Fabergé eggs. One guest stands out: boggly-eyed political liability Grigory Rasputin (played splendidly by a pre-*Doctor Who* Tom Baker). He tells racy stories. Grimacing, Nicholas slopes off to find the vodka – but Alexandra is enraptured. When her infant son is diagnosed with haemophilia, she turns to Rasputin and the power of prayer. Or the power of whatever it is he does. This stokes the brewing revolution. The film stages a brilliant recreation of the horrific massacre of Bloody Sunday.

Violence: The Russian people get their parliament, and Pyotr Stolypin (Eric Porter) as prime minister. It's now 1913, the tercentenary of the Romanov dynasty, so the tsar appears before his subjects. 'God help me, but I do love it when they stand and wave,' he murmurs. Afterwards, Stolypin is shot at the opera by a revolutionary while the tsar and his terrified daughters watch from the royal box. This remarkable scene is accurate – though, since Stolypin was assassinated in 1911, two years before the tercentenary, it's in the wrong place.

War: When the First World War comes along, Nicholas is convinced that the Kaiser, whom he calls 'Cousin Willi', will help Russia. 'With due respect to your cousin,' growls his adviser Sergei Witte (Laurence Olivier), 'the Kaiser is a deceitful megalomaniac. If he is offering to help, then it is time to pray.' Witte is right. The war is a complete disaster.

Politics: The film focuses accurately on Nicholas and Alexandra's pigheadedness in the face of change. It could have gone further. 'Be firm,' she wrote to him in real life, '"Russia loves to feel the whip" – it's their nature – tender love and then the iron hand to punish and guide. How I wish I could pour my will into your veins.' He replied: 'Tender thanks for the severe written scolding,' and signed himself 'Your poor little weak-willed hubby.' The film's big challenge is to make these dreadful people into sympathetic characters.

Abdication: The tsar abdicates (and, in the film's most powerful scene, must tell his wife that he has done so). He and his family are moved to Tobolsk, and thence to Ekaterinburg. Hard though it is to care much for the ex-tsar and tsarina, both of whom have been running at full tilt towards their fate, you might expect to feel a twinge of pity for their children. Curiously, though, and on scant historical evidence, the film portrays the thirteen-year-old tsarevich as the image of his unspeakable mother. He gives precocious, entitled speeches, injures himself for attention, berates his father for losing the crown, and says of his guards, 'I'd like to kill them all.' Bad luck, kiddo. That's not the way this goes.

The interwar years saw flappers, a great depression and the rise of dictators. An interesting sidelight on the politics of those years is the intriguing film *Lion of the Desert*, featuring Rod Steiger as Benito Mussolini. Steiger was reprising the role of the Italian dictator from the 1975 Italian movie *Mussolini: Ultimo Atto*, known in English as *Last Days of Mussolini*, which also features Franco Nero and Henry Fonda.

1929

Lion of the Desert (1981)

Director: Moustapha Akkad • Entertainment grade: B • History grade: B–

Sidi Omar al-Mukhtar led guerrilla resistance to Italian rule in the province of Cyrenaica in eastern Libya until he was captured and hanged in 1931.

Casting: Omar Mukhtar is honoured in Libya as an Arab hero who offered staunch resistance to imperialism. This biopic casts in almost every Libyan-speaking role an American or European actor – notably, John Gielgud as Sharif al-Ghariyani, and Anthony Quinn as Omar Mukhtar himself. If you're thinking 'typical Hollywood', think again. Far from being a Hollywood movie, *Lion of the Desert* was funded by Libyan dictator Muammar Gaddafi. Perhaps Gaddafi thought western audiences would take his film more seriously if he cast A-list British and American actors. They didn't. *Lion of the Desert* failed to roar at the box office, taking by some reports about $1.5 million against Gaddafi's $35 million investment. Which is a pity, because – if you can get past the Gaddafi association – it's actually a pretty good movie.

War: In 1929, Benito Mussolini (Rod Steiger, who contrives to be even camper and shoutier than the real Duce) decides to crush the Libyan rebellion. He sends Rodolfo Graziani (Oliver Reed) to take over the governorship. In reality, Graziani wasn't appointed until 1930, and then only as vice-governor. In the movie, Graziani's tenure has been conflated with that of his predecessor, Domenico Siciliani. Graziani took over a disastrous military campaign that had been going since 1923. Against Italian tanks and aeroplanes, Omar Mukhtar's total active fighters numbered between 1,000 and 3,000, on horseback and for the most part lightly armed. Nevertheless, these Arab guerrillas trounced Mussolini's armed forces almost on a daily basis, fighting over 250 skirmishes and engagements even in a slow year.

Genocide: Graziani realizes that he cannot defeat Omar Mukhtar with conventional methods. 'I propose to concentrate the Bedouin,' he says. 'Put them behind wire in camps and keep them there until we find it prudent or safe to release them.' This is true. Though the Italian administration had mooted setting up concentration camps before Graziani's arrival in Libya, it is fair to say that Graziani was the man most responsible for putting this into practice. The film's depiction of the policy itself is accurate. In 1930, up to 100,000 Bedouin men, women and children – about half the entire tribal population of Cyrenaica at the time

– were herded into desert camps. The official Italian statistics are unreliable. Even so, it is plain that by 1933 only between one-third and half of the people in the camps had survived.

People: Gaddafi's money certainly bought the filmmakers some impressive battle scenes – filmed, of course, in real Libyan locations. Omar Mukhtar is brought down when his horse is shot. Reportedly, he was pinned under it, though the film has him thrown aside. Omar Mukhtar is captured and taken to Benghazi where, in the movie's best scene, Graziani interviews him. Quinn conveys Omar Mukhtar's steadfastness and dignity. Reed somehow captures the tone of the real Graziani's 1932 memoir *Cirenaica Pacificata*, which reveals that the Italian commander was almost jealous of his Arab foe's strategic brilliance, his moral purity, and even his martyrdom. *Lion of the Desert* nearly makes Graziani too sympathetic. He is shown graciously returning Omar Mukhtar's spectacles, which were stolen in a previous battle. In fact, transcripts of the secret proceedings around Omar Mukhtar's show trial at Benghazi reveal that the guerrilla leader had to ask for them back – a request his interrogators considered outrageous.

Execution: Twenty thousand concentration camp inmates and Cyrenaican notables were forced to watch Omar Mukhtar's death. The film attempts to provoke an emotional response by focusing on a small boy in the crowd, implying that he is the next generation of Libyan rebel. Unfortunately, the result is schmaltzy. The scene did not require further adornment: the hanging of an unbowed, elderly guerrilla (Omar Mukhtar estimated his age as seventy-three; some historians claim sixty-nine) would have been more than affecting enough.

The biggest scandal of the interwar years was the abdication of King Edward VIII after only a few months on the throne. Edward – who was known as David by his family – wanted to marry his American lover, Wallis Simpson. But Mrs Simpson had already been divorced twice. The king was (and is) Defender of the Faith, the head of the Church of England. Until 1981, the Church would not marry people who had been divorced. The king could not have married in his own church or reasonably maintained his position at its head if he so publicly broke with its teachings.

Because he insisted on marrying Mrs Simpson, the king was obliged to abdicate his throne. Edward VIII became the Duke of Windsor, and his younger brother Albert (known as Bertie), Duke of York, became King George VI – very reluctantly, for he was a deeply private man afflicted with a stammer, and had no desire for such a public life. Bertie's elder daughter Elizabeth became heiress presumptive to the British throne, and would later rule as Queen Elizabeth II.

It was one of the great stories of the twentieth century, but the abdication hasn't featured in many movies – though there have been dozens of TV dramas about it. In 2012, Madonna directed *W.E.*, a frothy movie about a modern American woman obsessed with Wallis and Edward. It attempted to dismiss the well-evidenced allegations that the Duke and Duchess of Windsor, as they became, were all too interested in Adolf Hitler and Nazism. Critics and filmmakers roundly dismissed it back.

Far more successful was this tale of David's successor – his brother Bertie, known to the world as King George VI:

1936

The King's Speech (2011)

Director: Tom Hooper • Entertainment grade: A– • History grade: B+

People: Bertie (Colin Firth) was from boyhood affected by a stammer, which made his public life exceptionally difficult. The film is right in suggesting that he endured various therapies to address it, though this historian could find no reference to support the scene in which he is made to fill his mouth with marbles, like Eliza Doolittle. Perhaps the filmmakers were thinking of Charles I, another stammering king: he tried to correct his speech by filling his mouth with pebbles and talking to himself. The film has Bertie going to therapist Lionel Logue (Geoffrey Rush) in the late 1930s, a decade after the two really began working together. The importance of their relationship as depicted in the film is something of an overstatement.

Family: George V (Michael Gambon), the martinet father of David and Bertie, is shuffling off his mortal coil. Guy Pearce perfectly captures David's self-pitying brattishness, and his coldness towards his family: when the real David was informed of his father's imminent death, he refused to return from a safari holiday in Africa and instead spent that evening seducing the wife of the local commissioner. Pearce does not perfectly capture David's accent. Owing to a childhood spent almost entirely with nannies, the Prince of Wales spoke in private with a Cockney inflection – and later, in exile, developed an American twang.

Royalty: It's difficult to play Winston Churchill without slipping into caricature. Timothy Spall can't manage it, pouting, scowling and waddling around like The Penguin. Just as bad is the film's implication that Churchill counselled Bertie to take over during the abdication crisis. In fact, Churchill was one of David's fiercest supporters, advising him: 'Retire to Windsor Castle! Summon the Beefeaters! Raise the drawbridge! Close the gates! And dare Baldwin to drag you out!' Churchill also rewrote David's abdication speech, splendidly delivered by Pearce in the movie. Before Churchill got his hands on it, David allegedly wanted to open with: 'I now wish to tell you how I was jockeyed off the throne.' Churchill replaced this with the more dignified: 'At long last I am able to say a few words of my own.'

Family: The film takes it upon itself to impart dignity to Bertie when David abdicates. Instead of the sombre scene in the movie, with both brothers calmly signing the abdication, Bertie spent an hour sobbing on the shoulder of his mother, Queen Mary. 'I feel,' he declared, 'like the proverbial sheep being led to the slaughter, which is not a comfortable feeling.' He never got used to it: 'How

I hate being a king!' he once said. 'Sometimes at ceremonies I want to stand up and scream and scream and scream.'

Politics: *The King's Speech* was criticized by several reviewers for glossing over Bertie's support for Neville Chamberlain's policy of appeasement towards Adolf Hitler. True, the film could have made more of George VI's support for Chamberlain – and, indeed, of his personal preference for Lord Halifax to take over as prime minister rather than Churchill on Chamberlain's resignation. But shoehorning a whole load of heavy stuff about the Royal Family's many political imperfections into *The King's Speech* wouldn't have advanced the film's theme of Bertie's private struggle with his public role. Considering that all Bertie really did wrong was to support Chamberlain (a mainstream opinion at the time) and that he wasn't the sharpest tool in the box anyway (he came 68th out of 68 in his final examinations at naval college), to pillory him onscreen might have seemed vindictive. Portraying Bertie as an appeaser also wouldn't have helped audiences like him – but the truth is sometimes inconvenient like that.

Queen Victoria had been the first British Empress of India. Bertie, who was her great-grandson, would be the last emperor. The reason for that had much less to do with Mohandas Karamchand Gandhi than film audiences may have been led to think, but it is undeniable that Gandhi – known as the 'Mahatma', or 'Great Soul' – became a globally recognizable figurehead for the cause of Indian independence in the 1930s.

Gandhi has appeared as a character in plenty of Indian movies, including *Gandhi, My Father* (2007), in which he is played by Darshan Jariwala. His son Harilal – with whom he had a very difficult relationship – is played by Akshaye Khanna. In slapstick comedy *Lage Raho Munna Bhai* (2006), gangster Munna Bhai (Sanjay Dutt) masquerades as a professor of history, and when he gens up on Gandhi's work he begins to see his spirit (played by Dilip Prabhavalkar). He uses Gandhian ideas to help ordinary people solve their problems. There is also the downright bizarre *Gandhi to Hitler*, also known as *Dear Friend Hitler* (2011). The film features Raghuvir Yadav as Hitler, Neha Dhupia as Eva Braun and Nalin Singh as Josef Goebbels. Gandhi (Avijit Dutt) is shown trying to persuade the Führer to embrace non-violence.

More seriously, there's the big one: Richard Attenborough's epic *Gandhi*, made with the posthumous blessing of Gandhi's friend and India's first prime minister, Jawaharlal Nehru (who died twenty-two years before the film eventually made it to the screen). Nehru had originally wanted Alec Guinness to play Gandhi, and said the man himself would have been amused to be played by a Briton. Later, when Richard Attenborough was nominated as director, the guardians of Gandhi's legacy thought that no one was good enough to play the Mahatma. So saintly was he that he should not be represented onscreen at all, except perhaps by a ball of glowing light. According to legend, Attenborough replied: 'I'm not making a movie about fucking Tinkerbell.'

In the end, he cast Ben Kingsley – whose performance is sublime, nuanced and impeccably accurate, even down to the determined walk. Viewers sometimes assume this is yet another example of a white actor being cast in the historical role of a person who was not. In fact, Ben Kingsley is of Gujarati heritage, like Gandhi. He changed his birth name of Krishna Bhanji to Ben Kingsley because his real name was limiting his choice of roles in British and American productions.

1900–48

Gandhi (1982)

Director: Richard Attenborough • Entertainment grade: B • History grade: C+

Politics: The first half of the film follows Gandhi's career from his political awakening in South Africa through to the Amritsar Massacre. On 13 April 1919, British Brigadier-General Reginald Dyer cornered several thousand men, women and children in a walled garden in Amritsar, where they were listening peacefully to political speeches. Without warning, he opened fire. Even the low official figures admitted at least 379 were killed, 1,200 injured. Richard Attenborough's recreation of this event is gut-wrenchingly horrible and precisely accurate. As the film correctly implies, Amritsar immediately radicalized Jawaharlal Nehru, among others. It does not acknowledge that the effect on Gandhi was slower. His first reaction was to criticize the victims for having 'taken to their heels' rather than face death with composure. It was over a year later when he finally handed back his British Empire medal and declared himself in favour of independence.

People: The film's most glaring bias is its depiction of Mohammad Ali Jinnah, leader of the Muslim League and ultimately founder of Pakistan. It shows Jinnah sitting around with Congress leadership in Gandhi's ashram after the 1931 Round Table Conference, being mean to the Mahatma: 'After all your travels, after all your efforts, they sent you back empty-handed.' Jinnah attended the Round Table Conference, from which everyone came away empty-handed, including him – so this would have been an odd thing to say. It's even odder to picture Jinnah casually hanging out with Congress leadership in the 1930s: he had left the party in 1920, deploring Gandhi's 'pseudo-religious approach to politics'. The film writes him off as a motiveless baddie, seemingly making a career out of hanging around looking sinister while wearing natty suits and smoking cigarettes. (The suits and cigarettes are accurate. The *New York Times* called Jinnah 'one of the best dressed men in the British Empire', and he got through fifty Craven A cigarettes every day.)

War: During World War II, Gandhi is shown saying sadly that 'Jinnah has cooperated with the British.' He did, but let's not forget that – whatever their crimes as imperialists – the British were on the right side in World War II. At the time, Jinnah's cooperation was viewed by many as more morally defensible than Gandhi's non-cooperation. The film steers well clear of exploring Gandhi's thoughts on Axis powers, some of which might have made a western audience choke on its popcorn. For instance, his suggestion that Jews should sacrifice themselves to Hitler to demonstrate their moral superiority: 'I can conceive the necessity of the immolation of hundreds, if not thousands, to appease the hunger of dictators,' he wrote in 1939, adding in 1946 that 'the Jews should have offered themselves to the butcher's knife. They should have thrown themselves into the sea from cliffs.'

Power: After Partition, Calcutta was ripped apart by Hindu-Muslim violence. Gandhi announced he would fast until it stopped. It did, in little more than a day. Surprisingly, the film downplays this, showing Gandhi weakened and struggling in Calcutta. In real life, this fast was one of the most stunning demonstrations of the moral power for which he was justly famous. As Lord Mountbatten, then Governor-General of India, wrote to him: 'In the Punjab we have 55,000 soldiers and large scale rioting on our hands. In Bengal our forces consist of one man, and there is no rioting.' That, surely, is a great soul in action.

Verdict: *Gandhi* is beautifully filmed and moving, but its uncomplicated Mahatma is less interesting than the real thing.

Just as for World War I, historians are spoiled for choice with movies about World War II. There are heart-stopping recreations of wartime experiences, such as *Saving Private Ryan* (1998), *Schindler's List* (1993), *The Bridge on the River Kwai* (1957) or *Das Boot* (1981). There are action movies, such as *The Great Escape* (1963). There are witty yet moving reflections on love and war like *Casablanca* (1942) or *A Matter of Life and Death* (1946). There are profoundly haunting takes on the human toll, like *Grave of the Fireflies* (1998). There are brilliant comedies, like *The Great Dictator* (1940), *To Be or Not to Be* (1942) and *The Producers* (1967).

There are also heaps of films on World War II that are over-sentimentalized, silly, slapdash or just plain wrong. Among those is...

1941

Pearl Harbor (2001)

Director: Michael Bay • Entertainment grade: D • History grade: C

On 7 December 1941, the Japanese navy devastated the American Pacific fleet in a surprise attack on Pearl Harbor, Hawaii. The raid killed 2,403 people, and dragged the United States into World War II.

Politics: Ben Affleck stars as the fictional Rafe McCawley, a plucky USAF pilot who sees action in all three of the film's battles. That's impossible, for a start: the Eagle Squadrons in the Battle of Britain only accepted civilian Americans. Cue some scenes in Britain, a cold place full of beer, stately homes and obsequious officers who spend all their time telling Americans how wonderful they are at fighting wars. Is this supposed to be making some sort of point?

Dialogue: Rafe is having some injections in his bottom, courtesy of pretty nurse Evelyn (Kate Beckinsale). For some reason he decides this would be an ideal moment to ask her out. He tries to tell her that he likes her, but it comes out as 'Miss, I really, really lick you.' Ha ha! A Freudian slip! Evelyn giggles as if it's sexy. In the 1940s, though, to 'lick' someone meant to beat them up.

Romance: Undeterred, Rafe turns up to meet Evelyn later. 'I got some genuine French champagne,' he boasts. 'From France.' This scene is set in December 1940. We can only hope Rafe bought the bottle at least seven months earlier, because northern France has been completely occupied by the Germans since June. Offering to punch a lady and then plying her with Nazi booze: if this character were really in the 1940s, he would need to work on his seduction technique.

People: Cuba Gooding Jr appears for a cameo as Doris Miller, one of the real heroes of Pearl Harbor. Miller, a ship's cook, carried sailors to safety during the attack, then grabbed an anti-aircraft gun and took on the Japanese planes. In the film, he only interacts with the main characters in one scene, when Evelyn tends to his injuries. (She does this without a chaperone, even though she is white and he is African-American. Bearing in mind that the armed forces were actually increasing segregation in their hospitals at the time, this is hard to believe.) The real Miller was a stand-out figure at Pearl Harbor. It's a shame the film relegates him to a token role.

Warfare: There are too many faults in the detail of warfare here to list, but military history enthusiasts will find plenty to get their regimental knee-breeches in a twist about. If you notice things like wrong-model Warhawks, prepare for three hours of teeth-grinding rage. The Doolittle Raid opens another can of mistake worms, not least the implication that the Americans bombed Tokyo to resolve a love triangle between Rafe, Evelyn and Rafe's best buddy. But by this point you might be too busy laughing at Alec Baldwin shouting 'Max power!' to care.

Details: In the 1940s, everyone smoked relentlessly. The 2001 film has a strict no smoking onscreen policy. Apparently, this is because smoking is bad for you. Which is true, but then again the movie shows people playing games of chicken in planes over populated areas, driving across open fields through machine gun fire in cars fully tanked up with petrol, and launching a full-scale military attack on America. All of which are even more bad for you than smoking. Ask your doctor.

One of the events of history most appallingly bowdlerized by cinema must surely be the story of Enigma, the German cipher machine. Breaking the Enigma code was crucial to Allied intelligence and to victory. In real life, it was first cracked by the Polish Cipher Bureau in the 1930s – but they decoded a code generated by a specific cipher setting on the machine. At that stage the cipher settings on the machine were changed only once every few months, so this was useful. But the total number of possible settings on the machine was almost 159 quintillion (i.e. 159 million million million). During World War II, they changed every day, which meant a more efficient method of cracking the code had to be found.

From 1940, codebreakers at Bletchley Park in England – including Dilly Knox, John Jeffreys, Peter Twinn and Alan Turing – devised ways of automatically decoding Enigma keys. In 1941, the British ship HMS *Bulldog* captured a complete Enigma machine along with codebooks from the German submarine U-110. From the summer of 1941, British intelligence could decipher any Enigma-coded message.

This story has been mashed into a pulp by the film industry in a trilogy of travesty. In *Enigma* (2001), the Poles are edited out along with all the real British cryptanalysts. The famously gay Alan Turing is replaced by a straight character called Tom Jericho (Dougray Scott), who romances Hester Wallace (Kate Winslet). Then there are the following two films, both of which are standout examples of the worst excesses of historical filmmaking:

1941

The Imitation Game (2014)

Director: Morten Tyldum • Entertainment grade: C+ • History grade: Fail

Childhood: *The Imitation Game* jumps around three time periods – Turing's schooldays in 1928, his cryptographic work at

Bletchley Park from 1939–45, and his arrest for gross indecency in Manchester in 1952. It isn't accurate about any of them, but the least wrong bits are the 1928 ones. Young Turing (played well by Alex Lawther) is a lonely, awkward boy, whose only friend is a kid called Christopher Morcom. Turing nurtures a youthful passion for Morcom, and is about to declare his love when Morcom mysteriously fails to return after a vacation. Turing is summoned into the headmaster's office, and is told coldly that the object of his affection has died of bovine tuberculosis. The film is right that this awful event had a formative impact on Turing's life. In reality, though, Turing had been warned before his friend died that he should prepare for the worst. The housemaster's speech (to all the boys, not just him) announcing Morcom's death was kind and comforting.

Romance: In the 1939–45 strand of the story, Turing has grown up physically – though not, the film implies, emotionally. He is played by Benedict Cumberbatch, who is always good and puts in a strong performance despite the clunkiness of the screenplay. The film gives him a quasi-romantic foil in cryptanalyst Joan Clarke (Keira Knightley), dubiously fictionalized as the key emotional figure of Turing's adult life. The real Turing was engaged to her for a while, but he told her upfront that he had homosexual tendencies. According to him, she was 'unfazed' by this.

Technology: Obsessively, Turing builds an Enigma-code-cracking machine, which he calls Christopher. It's understandable that films about complicated science usually simplify the facts.

This one has sentimentalized them, too: fusing *A Beautiful Mind* with *Frankenstein* to portray Turing as the ultimate misunderstood boffin, and the Christopher machine as his beloved creation. In real life, the machine that cracked Enigma was called the Bombe, and the first operating version of it was named Victory. The digital computer Turing invented was known as the Universal Turing Machine. Colossus, the first programmable digital electronic computer, was built at Bletchley Park by engineer Tommy Flowers, incorporating Turing's ideas.

Espionage: *The Imitation Game* puts John Cairncross, a Soviet spy and possible 'Fifth Man' of the Cambridge spy ring, on Turing's cryptography team. Cairncross was at Bletchley Park, but he was in a different unit from Turing. As Turing's biographer Andrew Hodges, on whose book this film is based, has said, it is 'ludicrous' to imagine that two people working separately at Bletchley would even have met. Security was far too tight to allow it. In his own autobiography, Cairncross wrote: 'The rigid separation of the different units made contact with other staff members almost impossible, so I never got to know anyone apart from my direct operational colleagues.' In the film, Turing works out that Cairncross is a spy; but Cairncross threatens to expose his sexuality. 'If you tell him my secret, I'll tell him yours,' he says.

The blackmail works. Turing covers up for the spy, for a while at least. This is wholly imaginary and deeply offensive – for concealing a spy would have been an extremely serious matter. Were the makers of *The Imitation Game* intending to accuse Alan Turing, one of Britain's greatest war heroes, of cowardice and treason? Creative licence is one thing, but slandering a great man's reputation – while buying into the nasty 1950s prejudice that gay men automatically constituted a security risk – is quite another.

Sexuality: The final section of the film, set in 1951, may be the silliest, and not only because the film might have bothered to check that Turing's arrest actually happened in 1952. Nor only because a key plot point rests on the fictional Detective Nock (Rory Kinnear) using Tipp-Ex, which didn't exist until 1959 (similar products were marketed from 1956, but that's still not early enough for anyone to be using it in the film). Nock pursues Turing because he suspects him of being another Soviet spy, and accidentally uncovers his homosexuality in the process. This is not how it happened, and the whole film should really get over its irrelevant obsession with Soviet spies. In real life, Turing himself reported a petty theft to the police – but changed details of his story to cover up the relationship he was having with the possible culprit, Arnold Murray. The police did not suspect him of espionage. They pursued him with regard to the homophobic law of gross indecency. He submitted a five-page statement admitting to his affair with Murray – evidence that helped convict him.

Justice: The film is right that the 'chemical castration' Turing underwent after his conviction was unjust and disgusting. Turing was pardoned in 2013, but the pardon was controversial. Many campaigners believe, as Turing himself did, that consensual sex between men should never have constituted an offence at all. Tens of thousands of less famous men were similarly prosecuted between 1885 and 1967, and their convictions stand.

1942

U-571 (2000)

Director: Jonathan Mostow • Entertainment grade: C– • History grade: Fail

War: It's spring 1942, and an American submarine is making its way through the Atlantic. The target: a stricken German U-boat. Posing as a German supply crew, the American sailors plan to board the U-571 and steal its Enigma. Just a few problems here. First, the real submarine U-571 was never captured, though it was sunk by an Australian plane off Ireland in 1944. Second, by 1942, Allied intelligence already had several Enigma machines. The first capture took place in February 1940, when the U-33 was taken by HMS *Gleaner* off the coast of Scotland. Three Enigma rotors were found, according to some sources, in a German sailor's trousers. Third, as eagle-eyed readers may already have noticed, the Enigma had actually been deciphered for almost a year before this film is set – and months before the US entered World War II.

Inspiration: The film seems to be based on the real story of Operation Primrose. On 8 May 1941, German submarine U-110 attacked an Allied convoy that included the British ship HMS *Bulldog*. Damaged by depth charges, U-110 surfaced and was boarded by the *Bulldog*'s crew, who collected all the papers they could find (no one spoke German, so they couldn't be selective), and an Enigma machine. Bletchley Park already had several Enigmas at this point. *Bulldog*'s triumph was recovering the codebooks.

Casting: A generally B-list and exclusively American cast is headed up by Matthew McConaughey, Bill Paxton and Harvey Keitel, with the tokenish addition of T. C. Carson as an African-American cook. After the German crew is taken prisoner, Carson jeers at them: 'It's your first time looking at a black man, ain't it? Get used to it!' It's absolutely true that Nazi Germany persecuted black people. Whereas the United States in 1942 was a model of racial equality, and… oh. Never mind. Obviously, at some point during pre-production, someone asked the question: 'But how can we make this film even more ridiculous?' Fortunately, the answer was readily to hand: cast nineties poodle rocker Jon Bon Jovi as the chief engineer.

Missions: The men successfully swipe the Enigma machine, but soon find themselves pursued by a very angry German destroyer. Quickly, they realize they must get the Enigma machine to Britain, or die in the attempt. If they are captured by the Nazis, they will be tortured, and Allied cryptography may be revealed. Or, as Lieutenant Bon Jovi might put it, we've got to hold on to what we've got. It doesn't make a difference if we make it or not. Whoa, oh, living on a prayer.

Mortality: Amid any number of explosions and deaths, the original scene in which Lieutenant Bon Jovi was decapitated by a bit of flying debris was cut. Instead, he is shot through the heart, and you're to blame. Baby, you give love a bad name. Sorry, that's not true. Actually, he falls over the side. But he does go out in a blaze of glory.

Details: The director actually has the audacity to end on a title card dedicating his film to the memory of the real sailors who captured Enigma machines. Yes, that same memory he has just desecrated. This is exactly the most tasteless gesture the filmmakers could have made.

Verdict: The only honest thing about *U-571* is its tagline: 'Nine men are about to change history.'

There are many films about the experience of soldiers during the war. Here are three of the most interesting, from a historical point of view:

1944

A Bridge Too Far (1977)

Director: Richard Attenborough • Entertainment grade: D • History grade: A–

Operation Market Garden was a daring attempt to force forward into northern Germany by Allied forces in 1944. Led by Field Marshal Bernard Montgomery, it planned to drop paratroopers in the German-occupied Netherlands, seize bridges behind enemy lines, and make way for a full invasion. In the event, the Germans managed to delay the Allied advance by blowing up one bridge at Son, and defending another at Arnhem during a prolonged battle. The operation failed.

People: Most of the film's characters are either real people or closely based on real people, and – in a refreshing change from the weirdness of watching Nazis speak colloquial English in more recent films like *Valkyrie* (2008) – Germans speak German, Dutch speak Dutch, and Brits say things like 'I'm awfully sorry, but I'm afraid we're going to have to occupy your house.' It's even possible to overlook Sean Connery talking like Sean Connery, seeing as his character, Maj-Gen Roy Urquhart, was a Scotsman; albeit a Scotsman who had attended St Paul's School and Sandhurst. The chief linguistic offender is Gene Hackman, who plays Polish general Stanislaw Sosabowski with an accent floundering somewhere between vampire and pirate. Meanwhile, Ryan O'Neal distinguishes himself from the refined performances given by the rest of the A-list ensemble by delivering every one of Brig-Gen James Gavin's lines as if he were reading it from an idiot board to an audience sitting on the other side of a canyon.

War: Committed Second World War buffs may spot microscopic inaccuracies, such as a few anti-tank guns being painted the wrong colour, but overall the recreation of the battles was acclaimed by real veterans. The action scenes are a triumph, visceral and memorable: swarms of planes, massive explosions, hundreds of paratroopers floating through the sky like jellyfish through the sea. If you never tire of watching things blow up while big old bits of machinery rumble around, you're going to be happy as Larry. (Larry – in the form of Laurence Olivier – turns up, too, playing a fictional Dutch doctor.) But the cast, while impressive, is so large that few characters manage more than a cameo appearance.

The fighting scenes, while impressive, drag on so long the mind wanders. The attention to every aspect of the operation, while impressive, hampers narrative pace and direction. By the beginning of the third hour, it seems Attenborough is trying to make his audience feel like they, too, have trudged for days through muddy Dutch fields without food or sleep. Which is an achievement of sorts.

Blame: Conspicuous by his absence from the film is 'Monty' Montgomery himself. As a result, there's a sense that responsibility for the operation's failure rests mostly with Lt Gen 'Boy' Browning (Dirk Bogarde). In the closing scenes of the film, Browning is permitted a subtle dig at the still-unseen Monty ('He thinks the operation was 90 per cent successful') and says that he always felt the Allies 'tried to go a bridge too far'. In reality, Browning made that comment directly to Monty before the operation began.

Trivia: The production had several veterans of Market Garden on hand, including John Addison, composer of the splendid score, who served with XXX Corps. Dirk Bogarde was there for real, too, though his memoirs imply that he spent most of September 1944 'liberating' champagne from local wine-cellars and avoiding the advances of an amorous, eccentric major-general known as 'Uncle'. According to Bogarde, Uncle was 'gobbling up half the Highland Infantry' and thought wearing helmets into battle was 'common' and 'not the behaviour of a gentleman'. In this light, William Goldman's tally-ho-old-boy screenplay begins to sound quite convincing.

Verdict: It's a fantastic historical and cinematic achievement but, if you're not a war obsessive, watching all 176 minutes of this may actually be a bridge too far.

1943

Cross of Iron (1977)

Director: Sam Peckinpah • Entertainment grade: C+ • History grade: B+

The German invasion of the Soviet Union during World War II began in 1941. By 1943, troops were in retreat, and the tide of the war had begun to turn against Adolf Hitler.

People: Troops of the Wehrmacht 17th Army have retreated across the Taman Peninsula to the Kuban bridgehead. Indestructible platoon leader Sergeant Steiner (James Coburn) is stuck serving under Captain Stransky (Maximilian Schell), an oily Prussian aristocrat who has transferred to the Eastern Front with the explicit intention of winning the distinction of the Iron Cross. Steiner couldn't give a hoot for Iron Crosses, and he actively dislikes oily Prussian aristocrats. These characters are fictional, though some sources suggest Steiner may have been inspired by real-life Sergeant (Feldwebel) Johann Schwerdfeger. Willi Heinrich, author of the novel on which this film was based, served on the Eastern Front in the 101st Jäger Division – as did Schwerdfeger.

Politics: *Cross of Iron* is unusual among World War II movies in that the Germans are the heroes, though it carefully distances its protagonists from actual Nazism. The ordinary soldiers show no interest in politics at all, aside from resentment of their officers. The officers can see that Hitler's disastrous military strategy is losing the war, and are already trying to work out how to play things when it is over. Stransky comes close to master-race theory when he claims that he has 'ethical and intellectual superiority' in his blood – but also states firmly that he has never been a Nazi. Instead, he's a Prussian aristocratic supremacist, who disdains the low-born Hitler as readily as he would disdain anyone else who didn't have several pages and a fancy engraving in the *Almanach de Gotha*. The film's most obvious Nazi is SS recruit Private Zoll (Arthur Brauss), and it's probably not a coincidence that the screenplay reserves for him the stickiest of all its endings.

War: When the Soviets attack, it is Steiner, not Stransky, who earns the Iron Cross. This, and Steiner's refusal to tell a lie so that Stransky can have one too, cements the loathing between the two men. There follows another mighty battle. Director Sam Peckinpah shot the war footage in what was then Yugoslavia, where he had been promised real Soviet tanks. There weren't many knocking around by 1976, though, and Richard Attenborough had snaffled most of them for his Netherlands-based production of *A Bridge Too Far*. *Cross of Iron* had to stage some of its major shots with just two.

Women: On their way to rejoin their army, Steiner's platoon captures a farmhouse which is occupied by a detachment of hot female Soviet soldiers. Hundreds of thousands of Soviet women did serve on the front line, and doubtless some of them were hot, so to an extent this is realistic. Some critics have considered *Cross of Iron*'s depiction of the Soviet women to be misogynist, though, reducing them to hopeless, uncommitted fighters and sexual predators. In fact, Soviet women were allowed a more active role in combat than the women of any other nation during World War II, and took it up with gusto. Many were highly decorated as soldiers, pilots and snipers.

1944

Objective, Burma! (1945)

Director: Raoul Walsh • Entertainment grade: B+ • History grade: D–

Allied forces began their campaign to retake Burma from Japanese forces in 1944.

People: American general Joseph Stilwell is planning the invasion of Burma. 'Here's where we start paying back the Japs,' he growls, chewing on a cigarette in a dainty holder. General Stilwell did indeed smoke a cigarette in a holder, though you wouldn't have dared take the mickey out of it. He had one of the sharpest tongues in the army, earning him the nickname 'Vinegar Joe', and didn't soften it for anyone – not even his good lady wife. 'We have had a hard scrap in this bitched-up jungle,' reads one typical billet-doux he sent her from Burma in March 1944.

Casting: The American soldiers at the Burmese front are passing time playing baseball and giving each other manicures. Really. The fictional Captain Nelson (Errol Flynn) calls them to the briefing shack and tells them it's time to put down their cuticle cream and get on with the war. Casting Flynn as a war hero was controversial. He was born in Australia, and took American citizenship in 1942 – but did not join the military. Unbeknown to the public, he had applied repeatedly. He was rejected on account of his health record, which included recurring malaria and tuberculosis, a heart attack, and an exotic array of venereal diseases. Warner Bros didn't want to tell his fans that their action superstar couldn't join the forces because he was a physical wreck, so Flynn just had to brazen out the jibing that he was a coward.

Military: Nelson and his men are to be dropped behind enemy lines to take out a radar station. Their unit is based on the 5307th Composite Unit (Provisional), whose operation in North Burma in 1944 was known as Galahad, and who were nicknamed 'Merrill's Marauders' by the press after their commander, Frank Merrill. The raid shown in the film is fictional, though it does fit with the unit's mission: known in the military, which is never shy of a double-entendre, as long-range jungle penetration. Aimed, in this instance, at a place called Jambu Bum. Stop giggling at the back.

Details: *Objective, Burma!* was made immediately after the events it depicts and before the end of World War II. It's a piece of almost instant history – and, as such, the technical and cultural details of military life are spot on. The filmmakers had access to real planes, uniforms and equipment. Captain Nelson cheers up his cold, hungry and terrified men with a regular dose of amphetamines. 'All right, boys, here's the pill that kills the chill,' he says breezily. There was no point toning this stuff down, for the film was made with an audience of real soldiers in mind – and they would have spotted inaccuracies faster than any historian.

International relations: It's not a surprise that *Objective, Burma!* doesn't give equal weight to the Japanese point of view. More problematic at the time of its release was the fact that it implied Burma was liberated entirely by Americans. In real life, the majority of Allied forces in Burma were British, South African, Indian or Chinese. Notoriously, the British 14th army in Burma were known as the 'Forgotten Army'. It wasn't especially dignified of Hollywood to have forgotten American allies quite so quickly.

Controversy: Merrill's Marauders were inspired by Orde Wingate's Chindits, special forces who were mostly British, Indian, Gurkha, Chinese and Burmese. *Objective, Burma!* isn't as bad as *U-571* in terms of misattributing wartime achievements to Americans: at least the Marauders did actually exist, and played a part. Still, it's easy to see why the film caused massive offence in Britain and among troops of many nationalities in the China-Burma-India theatre when it was released in 1945. Warner Bros withdrew it from British cinemas after a week, and only re-released it in 1952, with extra documentary footage that included a fleeting hat-tip to Major-General Wingate.

'The History of the world is but the Biography of great men,' wrote Thomas Carlyle in 1840, establishing what is known as the Great Man theory of history – the idea that events are shaped by extraordinary individuals. The Great Man theory was trounced by everyone from Lev Tolstoy to Karl Marx, but Hollywood still loves it. The biopic has always been one of its favourite ways of telling historical stories.

World War II biopics include *Valkyrie* (2008), with a miscast Tom Cruise playing would-be Hitler assassin Claus von Stauffenberg; *MacArthur* (1977), with an anaemic Gregory Peck failing to capture the real General MacArthur's coruscating personality and wit; *To Hell and Back* (1955), which features real veteran Audie Murphy, one of the most decorated American soldiers of World War II, playing himself; and *Sophie Scholl – Die Letzten Tage* (2005), in English *Sophie Scholl: The Final Days*, a German film about an iconic figure in the German resistance to the Nazis.

Three of the best are *Patton* (1970), with George C. Scott giving one of the greatest historical performances of all time as the American general; *Desert Fox* (1951), with James Mason as the controversial German field marshal Erwin Rommel, considered by many to be a military genius and opponent of Hitler; and of course this:

1945

Downfall (2004)

Director: Oliver Hirschbiegel • Entertainment grade: A– • History grade: A–

As World War II drew to its conclusion, Soviet forces began to shell the centre of Berlin on 20 April 1945.

People: The film is bookended by documentary footage of the splendidly named Traudl Humps, Hitler's private secretary from 1942–45. In 1947, she wrote a memoir. It was published in 2002 under her less thrilling married name, Traudl Junge. The film draws extensively on it, especially for the relationship between Adolf Hitler (Bruno Ganz, in the performance of a lifetime) and his girlfriend, Eva Braun (Juliane Köhler). Junge paints Eva as a needy, delusional figure – dancing around her old living room 'in a desperate frenzy, like a woman who has already felt the faint breath of death'. Another eyewitness, Gerhardt Boldt, said she was 'rather affected and theatrical'. This is the Eva who makes it to the screen, and she's a historically credible one.

Characterization: The film's most famous scene is no less brilliant for the fact that it is often comically resubtitled on YouTube. When Hitler's generals tell him he can't mobilize troops that don't exist, he flies into a fury: 'What I should have done is liquidate all the high-ranking officers, as Stalin did!' Historian Giles MacDonogh, who took some issue with the film for its gentle treatment of SS Brigadeführer Wilhelm Mohnke and heroic characterization of concentration camp medical researcher Ernst-Günther Schenck, approved of its portrayal of Hitler: 'What I really liked about the film was the suggestion that Hitler was acting. He was a remarkably good actor. He bit carpets to frighten people, and it worked.' (Reportedly, Hitler writhed on the floor biting at the carpet during his famous tantrums, earning himself the nickname *Teppichfresser* – rug muncher.) 'Eva Braun says he is acting in the film, and that the real "Adolf" was different. I don't think we will begin to understand Hitler until we wipe away the portrait imposed on him by wartime propaganda.' The Hitler of *Downfall* is horribly realistic. 'Hitler was, after all, a human being,' noted historian Sir Ian Kershaw in a glowing review of the film, 'even if an especially obnoxious, detestable specimen.'

Isolation: As the Soviets close in, many of Hitler's people either desert him or commit suicide. Of his close political associates, almost no one remains but Joseph Goebbels. Actor Ulrich Matthes, playing Goebbels, has black hair swept smoothly back, a beaky nose and eyes so dark they seem not to have whites at all. He looks quite a lot like Goebbels, but even more like Feathers McGraw, the evil penguin from *The Wrong Trousers*. No wonder Hitler finally realizes that all is lost.

Death: The film's Traudl (Alexandra Maria Lara) is in the bunker kitchen, entertaining the six children of Joseph and Magda Goebbels, when their 'Auntie Eva and Uncle Hitler' go into their private quarters for the final time. A shot rings out. 'Bullseye!' shouts nine-year-old Helmut Goebbels, thinking it is an explosion outside. Later, after the bodies have been carried away, Traudl goes into Hitler's room and sees the Führer's blood on the upholstery. According to Traudl Junge's memoir, this is all precisely as it happened. In real life, she also remembered being sickened by the 'heavy smell of bitter almonds' – the scent of Eva Braun's used cyanide capsule.

More death: The film shows a resolute Magda Goebbels (Corinna Harfouch) writing to her son from a previous marriage: 'The world that will come after the Führer and National Socialism is not worth living in, and for that reason I have brought the children here as well.' Then, she feeds a sleeping draught to her other six children. When they're asleep, she crushes cyanide in each of their mouths. This awful scene is accurate, according to telephonist Rochus Misch, who was in the bunker at the time. Traudl Junge and others suggest that the children were injected with morphine, rather than drinking a sleeping draught. The outcome was the same, and the quote from Magda Goebbels' letter in the film is correct.

Verdict: *Downfall* is an intelligent, thoroughly researched recreation of Hitler's last days, and a terrific movie.

7

Modern Times

The World War II alliance of the United States and the Soviet Union proved to be shortlived. By the end of the 1940s, the Cold War had set in: an enduring and eventually nuclear-enhanced state of permanent discomfort between the capitalist west and the communist east. Films about the Cold War in the United States include Clint Eastwood's floundering biopic *J. Edgar* (2012), in which Leonardo DiCaprio struggles under layers of older-person make-up to play FBI director J. Edgar Hoover; and the much sharper and more stylish *Good Night, And Good Luck* (2005), in which George Clooney directs himself, David Strathairn, Robert Downey Jr and Patricia Clarkson as broadcasters standing up to Red Scare figurehead Senator Joseph McCarthy.

The Cold War coincided with the decline of the remaining European empires, notably the British and French. One of the most controversial and brilliant historical films about decolonization is Gillo Pontecorvo's *The Battle of Algiers* (1966), which uses real and fictionalized characters to tell the story of the Front de

Libération Nationale (FLN)'s insurgency against French colonial rule in Algeria in the 1950s. So accurate is *The Battle of Algiers* that it has been shown within terrorist groups and military and police agencies as part of training exercises. It was screened at the Pentagon by the Directorate for Special Operations and Low-Intensity Conflict in 2004, apparently to inform strategy in Iraq.

What was then called the Third World has provided the setting for some of the most interesting Cold War movies. Raoul Peck's *Lumumba* (2000) stars the French actor Eriq Ebouaney as Congolese independence leader Patrice Lumumba, targeted for assassination by the CIA (though he was eventually killed by the Belgians in conjunction with his domestic enemies). *The Comedians* (1967), scripted by Graham Greene from his own novel, is a brilliant story of life inside the surreal nightmare of François 'Papa Doc' Duvalier's Haiti, starring Richard Burton and Elizabeth Taylor. Duvalier was the inspiration for Dr Kananga, the drug lord Caribbean dictator in Ian Fleming's James Bond novel *Live and Let Die*. He was played by Yaphet Kotto in the 1973 movie, which stars Roger Moore as Bond. The Vodouist villain in Disney's animated feature *The Princess and the Frog* was originally to be named Dr Duvalier; in the final version he is known, less controversially, as Dr Facilier.

Cinema's search for Cold War figureheads has led it repeatedly to focus on the most glamorous of all revolutionaries: Argentine doctor Ernesto Guevara de la Serna, better known as Che Guevara. Che's worldwide fame came from a single photograph snapped in 1960 by photographer Alberto Korda for the Cuban newspaper *Revolución*. Che had appeared only briefly by the side of a podium during a four-hour public speech by Fidel Castro. Korda made a single print of the picture, and called it Heroic Guerrilla. It hung in his studio and was not seen in public until it was picked up by an Italian publisher and turned into a poster in 1967.

Che's whereabouts were, at the time, unknown. It later emerged that he had been attempting to foment revolution in Bolivia, where he was murdered by Bolivian special forces backed by the CIA. His image quickly became a global icon, and is estimated by the Victoria & Albert Museum to have been the most reproduced photograph in history.

The first Che feature film was *Che!* (1969), starring Omar Sharif as Che Guevara and Jack Palance as Fidel Castro. His story has also been told over two historically accurate but bloated and tedious biopics, *Che Part One: The Argentine* and *Che Part Two: The Guerrilla*, directed by Steven Soderbergh and starring Benicio del Toro. He appears in Alan Parker's film version of the musical *Evita* (1996), played by Antonio Banderas, opposite Madonna as the Argentine first lady Eva Perón. In real life, the two never met, though the young Guevara did once write Evita a letter asking her to buy him a jeep. It was a joke. Probably you had to be there.

1952

The Motorcycle Diaries (2004)

Director: Walter Salles • Entertainment grade: B • History grade: A–

Casting: Medical student Ernesto Guevara and his biochemist friend Alberto Granado set out on their motorcycle from Buenos

Aires, heading by a roundabout route for North America. According to press reports, Rodrigo de la Serna, playing Alberto, is a second cousin to the real Che Guevara. DNA isn't everything, though: the unrelated Mexican actor Gael Garcia Bernal, playing Ernesto, much more closely resembles Guevara in 1952. Indeed, when the real Ernesto was well groomed, it was often said that he looked like a movie star. But that didn't happen too often, for he had a lifelong aversion to grooming. He once wore a pair of underpants for two months, and then gleefully won a bet that they would stand up by themselves. Thankfully, that isn't in the film.

Romance: The first stop on the men's trip is Miramar, south of Buenos Aires, where they visit Ernesto's girlfriend Chichina. He gives her a puppy, named (in English) Come-back, to indicate that he intends to, well, come back. In the film, she gives him $15 to buy her a bathing suit when he reaches the United States. In real life, according to one of Che's biographers, the money was for a scarf. Other than that, this is accurate.

Media: The motorcycle breaks down near a small Chilean town. Alberto and Ernesto are broke – but they have an idea. They give an interview to the town paper, claiming to be touring leprosy experts, and then use the piece to impress the locals into giving them free stuff. This is also true. The mechanic who subsequently fixes their bike invites them to a dance. By now, Chichina has dumped Ernesto, and he is nursing a broken heart. He is nursing it by trying to cop off with the mechanic's wife.

Scandal: The film subtly cleans Ernesto's conduct up in comparison to his own description of the evening. It depicts the mechanic's wife, as the real Guevara wrote, acting 'pretty randy', but glosses over the fact that Ernesto too was 'full of Chilean wine'. When she refused him, 'I was in no state to listen to reason and we had a bit of a barney in the middle of the dance floor,' he admitted. Like in the movie, Ernesto and Alberto were chased out of the dance hall by a mob of angry Chileans. But the film uses dramatic licence when it has them bust out their bike from the mechanic's garage and speed off in the nick of time. In reality, they stayed another night, had lunch with a family next door to the garage, and left without incident in the afternoon.

Politics: In the mining settlement near Chuquicamata, Alberto and Ernesto meet an impoverished couple who fear persecution on the grounds that they are communists – which, at the time, Ernesto was not. From 1948 until 1958, the Chilean Communist Party was banned and its adherents prosecuted under the Law for the Defence of Democracy. The poet Pablo Neruda was among those who fled the country. The scene in the movie sticks closely to Guevara's account. There's one striking difference. In the film, we are later told that Ernesto gave Chichina's $15 to the couple. In real life, both Ernesto and the $15 eventually made it to Miami – and, though Ernesto never saw Chichina again, he did apparently send her that scarf.

Che Guevara played a key role in forming and nurturing the Soviet-Cuban relationship, which led to the Cuban Missile Crisis. That crisis has inspired a couple of films of its own. It forms the central plot in mutant superhero movie *X-Men: First Class* (2011), which is really quite enjoyable, though not even slightly historically accurate. Much closer to the truth – or, at least, to Robert F. Kennedy's account of what happened – is *Thirteen Days* (2000), based on his book of the crisis and starring Kevin Costner as John F. Kennedy's appointments secretary, Kenny O'Donnell. The film doesn't have a Soviet or Cuban perspective, and is lavishly pro-Kennedy – but it's a reasonably faithful recreation of events in Washington DC.

John F. Kennedy's murder on 22 November 1963 was experienced as a tremendous shock around the world. The Warren Commission, charged with investigating the assassination, concluded that he was murdered by Lee Harvey Oswald, acting alone. Some found this verdict hard to accept, and the case has spawned dozens of conspiracy theories, blaming JFK's murder on everyone from the Soviets to the Mafia to anti-Castro Cubans to pro-Castro Cubans to the CIA to the FBI to Kennedy's vice-president and successor, Lyndon B. Johnson. The conspiracy theories have been dramatized as *Executive Action* (1973), starring Burt Lancaster; *Flashpoint* (1984), with Kris Kristofferson; *Ruby* (1992), with Danny Aiello as Lee Harvey Oswald's assassin Jack Ruby; and pseudo-documentary *Interview With the Assassin* (2002).

As far as serious historians are concerned, none of these is even slightly accurate. Even if you believe any of the conspiracy theories – and it is a question of belief, for there is no solid proof for any of them – they can't all be true. But in the absence of a smoking gun for whichever theory you favour, you could always just make a whole load of evidence up so that it sounds more convincing. That's what Oliver Stone did when he made the granddaddy of JFK conspiracy movies...

1963

JFK (1991)

Director: Oliver Stone • Entertainment grade: B • History grade: Fail

Truth: *JFK* opens with a documentary montage, presenting Kennedy (very questionably) as a radical progressive who upset the establishment and therefore found himself on the road to assassination. This is mixed in with recreated fictional footage, and segues into the movie itself without distinction – making a discreet but definite claim for documentary-level accuracy. Our hero is New Orleans district attorney Jim Garrison – who, in another subtle bid for trustworthiness, is played by 1991's biggest mainstream Hollywood star, Kevin Costner. There's no doubt about it: Oliver Stone wants you to believe this is the truth. Many do. Between two-thirds and three-quarters of Americans believe there was a conspiracy behind John F. Kennedy's murder – a belief that, pollsters Gallup noted, was sustained by this movie.

The film's case: Nagged by fears that shady characters in his own district might have been involved in the president's assassination,

Garrison puts together a case. He has three key witnesses. David Ferrie (Joe Pesci) is a mercenary working with anti-Castro Cuban exiles. He breaks down and confesses the entire plot to Garrison, complete with CIA and Cuban exile involvement. Immediately afterwards, he is murdered by his co-conspirators. Willie O'Keefe (Kevin Bacon) is a gay prostitute involved with the conspirators. He too confesses the whole plot to Garrison, exactly in line with Ferrie. Finally, Garrison goes to Washington to meet an unnamed government insider, 'X', played with unabashed brilliance by Donald Sutherland. In a coruscating monologue, 'X' explains the full breadth and depth of the conspiracy, bringing in the entire military-industrial complex behind the American government.

The real case: On the strength of this evidence, the case for a conspiracy would appear overwhelming. There's just one problem: it's all wrong. David Ferrie was a real person, but always maintained his innocence. His big plot confession scene is a figment of the filmmakers' imaginations. Were he alive, it would constitute a massive libel. Ferrie died of natural causes – a coroner's verdict that the real Garrison, as district attorney, would have been ideally placed to challenge, had he seen any suggestion of foul play. He did not challenge it. The movie's 'X' is fictional, based loosely on air force colonel L. Fletcher Prouty, who was not part of Garrison's investigation but did serve as a technical adviser on this movie. Prouty's credibility was demolished in a critique of *JFK* by investigative journalist Edward Jay Epstein. The mega-conspiracy to which 'X' alludes is drawn from a famous spoof, *The Report From Iron Mountain*, published in 1967 and revealed in 1972 by its author to have been a hoax.

That leaves the case hinging on Willie O'Keefe – another fictional character. In reality, Garrison's equivalent key witness was Perry Russo, a heterosexual insurance salesman. Russo's testimony was not particularly lively until Garrison administered a dubious 'truth serum' of sodium pentothal – known to make people suggestible – and subjected him to questioning under hypnosis. At that point, Russo 'remembered' all sorts of wacky things. In the movie, Garrison is conspicuously not shown jacking his witness up on barbiturates or hypnotizing him. Because that would make his case look like a shoddy pile of incoherent fantasies wrung out of vulnerable people by suspect means.

Ballistics: The film's stirring finale is a splendidly enacted courtroom scene, during which Garrison pulls apart the case for a lone gunman on grounds of what he calls the 'magic bullet theory' – demonstrating that the bullet that the Warren Commission claims killed Kennedy and injured Texas governor John Connally performed all sorts of unlikely twists, turns and pauses in midair. Again, the evidence in the film seems overwhelming. Again, that's because it's just not true. Garrison's onscreen case is based on a partial selection of flawed reconstructions. One example is the film's allegation that this bullet changed direction to move upwards as it passed through Kennedy's neck. This comes from an analysis of the bullet hole in the back of his jacket. In fact, a photograph taken three seconds before the assassination shows Kennedy's jacket rucked up above his shoulders. Once you take that into account, it looks like the bullet's trajectory continued normally downwards and was consistent with a shot from the book depository. The only thing dodging around like a magic bullet here is the movie itself, veering erratically between misconceptions and outright lies in a determined effort to avoid the facts.

Verdict: *JFK* is a cleverly constructed, tightly written and sometimes breathtakingly well-acted movie – and one of the most appalling travesties of history you're ever likely to see.

For anyone interested in the real story of the Kennedy assassination, the 2013 film *Parkland*, starring Paul Giamatti and Zac Efron, is an enthralling and exceptionally historically accurate feature film about 22 November 1963. It is based on Vincent Bugliosi's 1,600-page tome *Reclaiming History: The Assassination of President John F. Kennedy*, also released in a more manageable 700-page version as *Four Days in November*. Bugliosi agrees with the verdict of the Warren Commission. Much of his longer volume is devoted to ripping apart various conspiracy theories. For many historians, *Parkland*'s consistent focus on the known, supportable facts will be a huge relief. Viewers who aren't familiar with the case may find *JFK* a more compelling watch, but *Parkland* gets pretty much everything as close to right as we can currently know.

The Sixties were an age of political assassinations: Lumumba, Che Guevara, JFK and RFK (the latter depicted in Emilio Estevez's star-studded but rather plodding 2006 movie *Bobby*), Ngo Dinh Diem, the leaders of South Africa, Togo, Nigeria, the Dominican Republic, Burundi, Somalia, Syria, Iran,

Jordan, and allegedly United Nations Secretary-General Dag Hammarskjöld. There were also the two most iconic African-American civil rights activists of the 1960s: Malcolm X and Martin Luther King. Spike Lee's *Malcolm X* (1992), starring Denzel Washington, is a brilliant and powerful account of the former's life, though it cuts a few historical corners. On Martin Luther King, there is this:

1965

Selma (2014)

Director: Ava DuVernay • Entertainment grade: B+ • History grade: A

In 1965, Dr Martin Luther King Jr led a campaign in Selma, Alabama, to secure voting rights for black citizens.

Controversy: In December 1964, Martin Luther King (David Oyelowo, perfect) meets President Lyndon B. Johnson (Tom Wilkinson) to discuss the issue of black people being denied their legal right to vote. Johnson wants King to wait. 'Let's not start another battle when we haven't even won the first,' he says, referring to the Civil Rights Act of 1964, which he signed into law with King standing right behind him. 'And you know what the next battle should be? The elimination of poverty. I'm calling it the War on Poverty… This voting thing is going to have to wait.' *Selma* has run into controversy over its portrayal of Johnson. Critics have seized on a comment by one of King's aides, Andrew Young, who has said that the real meeting was not confrontational.

However, the scene in the film is very close to the account in *The Autobiography of Martin Luther King*, a volume of King's own writings collected by Clayborne Carson in 1998. King remembered that he had told Johnson that the voting rights issue was serious and immediate. 'Martin, you're right about that. I'm going to do it eventually, but I can't get a voting rights bill through this session of Congress,' Johnson replied. 'Now, there's some other bills that I have here that I want to get through in my Great Society program, and I think in the long run they'll help Negroes more, as much as a voting rights bill.' King pushed him, and Johnson continued: 'I can't get it through, because I need the votes of a Southern bloc to get these other things through… it's just not the wise and the politically expedient thing to do.' These words may have been said confrontationally or calmly, but they're a lot like what Johnson says in the movie. King's account makes it clear that he was not satisfied by Johnson's response and that he started the Selma campaign despite Johnson's cold feet. The film portrays this accurately.

More controversy: Former Johnson assistant Joseph A. Califano has alleged that Johnson and King 'were partners in this effort. Johnson was enthusiastic about voting rights and the president urged King to find a place like Selma and lead a major demonstration.' Califano's memory of these events is at odds with much of the historical record, including other first-hand accounts. Eric F. Goldman, special consultant to Johnson and to his White House office, wrote in his 1969 book *The Tragedy of Lyndon Johnson*: 'He [Johnson] was no great admirer of Martin Luther King, among other reasons because he questioned how well his judgment would hold up over the long pull. LBJ was also no enthusiast of mass demonstrations. To a man of his turn of mind, the Negroes would do themselves more good by using their energies and their resources working on their politicians to get beneficial legislation.'

Even more controversy: It is true, as some critics have pointed out, that Johnson had asked his acting attorney general to work on black voting rights in mid-1964. As Goldman noted, though: 'The assignment was long-range and was to be kept out of the press. Lyndon Johnson had no intention of handing Barry Goldwater more Southern votes in the election of 1964.' By 4 February 1965, after King and others had been arrested, Johnson was still dodging press questions on whether he intended to use troops to protect demonstrators in Selma, arguing that anyone concerned with voting rights should use the courts to enforce the Civil Rights Act. 'Because Johnson evaded the issue, King now publicly declared his intention to press for a voting rights law,' wrote one of Johnson's biographers, Robert Dallek. The film does not, as Califano alleges, suggest that Johnson was 'only reluctantly behind the Voting Rights Act of 1965'. It suggests that he attempted to delay putting legislation before Congress for political reasons and that he tried to avert a public showdown between King and the governor of Alabama, George Wallace (Tim Roth). This is accurate.

Impact: *Selma* does a magnificent job of recreating important historical scenes, such as the events of 7 March 1965 – known as Bloody Sunday – in which Alabama state troops and local police attacked peaceful marchers. 'The whole nation was sickened by the pictures of that wild mêlée,' wrote King's widow Coretta Scott King. 'Tear gas, clubs, horsemen slashing with bullwhips like the Russian Czar's infamous Cossacks, and deputies, using electric cattle prods, chasing fleeing men, women, and children all the way back to Brown's Chapel.'

Dialogue: In the screenplay, all of King's fabulously distinctive phrases had to be unpicked and convincingly respun. His speeches remain under copyright, and his famously litigious estate has licensed the film rights exclusively to Dreamworks and Warner Bros for a biopic of King being developed by Steven Spielberg – so director Ava DuVernay could not use any of King's own words.

Balance: *Selma* is ultimately balanced on Johnson, letting him have his moment of glory with the best speech of his presidency, 'We shall overcome'. It is also balanced on King, revealing his flaws as well as his strengths. In one of its best scenes, his wife Coretta (Carmen Ejogo) confronts him about his frequent extramarital affairs. He emerges from the film as a hero – but not a saint.

Verdict: A well-researched, accomplished and fair-minded historical biopic, set around a sensationally good lead performance. Don't believe the hype.

The United States' military involvement in Vietnam and Cambodia – part of its Cold War struggle against communism – was one of the most controversial wars of the twentieth century. There are plenty of fine American films about the war: *The Deer Hunter* (1978), *Coming Home* (1978), *Apocalypse Now* (1979), *Good Morning Vietnam* (1987), *Full Metal Jacket* (1987), *Casualties of War* (1989) and so on. Here is one of the worst – John Wayne's *The Green Berets*, which is such a travesty of history that it fired up real Vietnam veteran Oliver Stone to make his ferociously anti-war film *Platoon* (1986) in response – followed by one of the best:

1964

The Green Berets (1968)

Director: John Wayne & Ray Kellogg • Entertainment grade: E+ • History grade: Fail

Production: During the early 1960s, criticisms began to grow of US involvement in Vietnam – to the consternation of big-screen cowboy and deep-dyed patriot John Wayne. Wayne believed in the righteousness of the American cause, and wanted to make a film about it. His source material (largely discarded for the final screenplay) was a gung-ho novel by Robin Moore, *The Green Berets*, based on Moore's experiences with Special Forces in Vietnam in 1963. Wayne wrote to President Lyndon B. Johnson to secure government approval. 'If he made the picture he would be saying the things we want said,' presidential adviser Jack Valenti assured

Johnson. The Pentagon allowed Wayne lavish use of props and military bases for filming; it also retained script approval, and insisted on extensive and detailed changes to plot and dialogue.

Politics: The film begins with a lengthy prologue showing what good ol' boys the Special Forces are. But there is a liberal journalist – those guys are the *worst* – called George Beckworth (David Janssen). He has gotten the silly idea in his commie-loving head that this war might be a bit nasty. Fortunately, Special Forces set him right at the press conference. 'What's going on here is communist domination of the world!' claims Master Sergeant Muldoon (Aldo Ray). John Wayne, playing the fictional Colonel Mike Kirby, looks on approvingly.

International relations: Off they all go to Vietnam, with Beckworth in tow. 'This trip is going to make LSD feel like aspirin,' one of the soldiers tells him, making an unsubtle presumption about the recreational habits of pinko liberal hippie types. The army base at Fort Benning, Georgia, stood in for Da Nang in the film, not entirely convincingly. They meet local South Vietnamese Captain Nim (George Takei). 'My home is Hanoi,' says Nim. 'I go home too some day. You see. First kill all stinking Cong. Then go home.' All the Vietnamese characters in the film talk like this. 'This'd be a great country if it weren't for the war,' says Kirby with a sigh, inadvertently hitting on a truth.

Freedom and democracy: The Americans spend all their time in Vietnam doing nice things, like offering medical assistance to needy peasants and hugging adorable children. Meanwhile, the Viet Cong are a massive, faceless force of evil, murdering children and raping women. Beckworth suddenly realizes that America is totally in the right. Take that, liberals! In fact, a year after this film was released, a *New Yorker* investigation by Daniel Lang would reveal that such atrocities as this film attributes to the North Vietnamese were being committed by American troops. His report formed the basis for Brian De Palma's considerably more accurate film *Casualties of War.*

Friendship: No suggestion of that sort of thing here, of course. Instead, *The Green Berets* sets up a supposed-to-be-charming relationship between goofy Sergeant Petersen (Jim Hutton) and an orphaned Vietnamese boy called Hamchuck (Craig Jue). Viewed in the twenty-first century, this doesn't so much warm the heart as disquiet the stomach. Maybe the scene in which Petersen invites the pre-teen boy to share his bed looked cute in 1968. These days, you'd call the police.

War: The film's big war set piece is inspired by the Battle of Nam Dong in 1964, in which Viet Cong fighters took on US Special Forces. It makes no particular gesture towards the reality of this incident. The sequence is long and tedious, and there's another forty minutes of the film to go after it: the run-time of this beastly thing is almost two and a half hours, though it feels much longer. The last act spins off into a wacky subplot about the American kidnap of a Viet Cong general. Special Forces put him in an orange jumpsuit and whisk him away to an off-the-grid detention facility. Like so many bits of this film, it may leave modern audiences with an unpleasant sense of déjà-vu.

Verdict: On *The Green Berets*' release in 1968, the *New York Times* said it was 'unspeakable... stupid... rotten... false in every detail... It is vile and insane. On top of that, it is dull.' At least the Soviets made good propaganda movies.

1973

The Killing Fields (1984)

Director: Roland Joffé • Entertainment grade: A– • History grade: A–

Richard Nixon ordered an incursion into Cambodia in 1970 as a corollary to the war in Vietnam. With the country under an American-installed government, the Khmer Rouge gained widespread support. After American withdrawal in 1975, it instituted a regime that made George Orwell's *1984* seem like a feelgood tale of heartwarming friendship between a man, his brother and their pet rat. Between 1975 and 1979, the Khmer Rouge coerced most of Cambodia's people into forced labour, and murdered something in the region of 1.5–2 million – around 20–30 per cent of the entire population.

Violence: *The Killing Fields* follows the story of Dith Pran, a Cambodian fixer, and his patron, *New York Times* journalist Sydney Schanberg. The first few scenes show the two of them travelling to the town of Neak Luong, which the Americans accidentally bombed, in 1973. Putrid water fills enormous craters where homes used to be. Refugees stagger around the makeshift field hospital, begging Schanberg to take their photographs and show the world the truth of what is happening. Immediately, it's clear that this film is not going to patronize its audience by gift-wrapping the story.

Casting: In an inspired piece of casting, Dith is played by Haing S. Ngor, a doctor and real-life veteran of the Khmer Rouge's labour camps. This was Ngor's first performance, and it deservedly won him an Oscar. Sam Waterston is well cast as Schanberg, and John Malkovich gives a memorable performance as photographer Al Rockoff. On the other hand, the real Rockoff has always insisted that Schanberg was a lying coward, and that both Malkovich's performance, and many of the details in the scenes that take place inside the French Embassy in Phnom Penh, are inaccurate.

Slavery: When the journalists are forced to leave, Dith is left to the mercy of the new regime. He passes himself off as a taxi driver, pretending not to speak English or French. The languages would immediately give him away as being middle class and having worked with foreigners, either of which would have earned him a summary execution. The two and a half years Dith spent in Dam Dek, a village-cum-slave camp near Siem Reap, are unavoidably compressed, but the film does an excellent job of recreating the sense of living in constant fear and confusion. Characters speak in Khmer, without subtitles – leaving the mostly non-Khmer-speaking audience, like the prisoners in the camp, reliant on instinct to work out what's going on.

Escape: Some of the facts of Dith's escape have been switched around, but the significant historical details are all present and correct: the Vietnamese invasion, Dith's flight over the border to Thailand, and the shocking recreation of the killing fields themselves. These vast dumping grounds, where the Khmer Rouge left the bodies of their victims, were described by the real Dith as being pitted with water wells full of corpses, 'like soup bones in broth'. In reality, Dith stayed around for longer under the Vietnamese occupation than the film allows, even becoming mayor of Siem Reap. However, the closing scenes, shot in a real Cambodian refugee camp in Khao-i-Dang, Thailand, provide plenty of authenticity. They also include the film's one artistic misstep: ending on the fatuous strains of John Lennon's *Imagine*.

The 1950s to the 1980s saw the dawn of the space age. Driven partly by scientific curiosity, partly by Cold War military strategy and partly by schoolboy (or occasionally schoolgirl) fantasy, governments poured money into the exploration of the galaxy. In 1976, a Soviet film called *Tak Nachinalas Legenda* (*Thus Began the Legend*) told the story of the first man in space, Yuri Gagarin. A Russian biopic titled *Gagarin: Pervyy v Kosmose* (*First in Space*) was released in 2013; it was praised by Russian space experts, but some critics and viewers felt it made Gagarin into too simplistic a hero.

Ron Howard's brilliant *Apollo 13* (1995) stars Tom Hanks as astronaut Jim Lovell, fighting to get a lunar mission craft safely home after an explosion onboard. But the best American film about the space race is:

1959

The Right Stuff (1983)

Director: Philip Kaufman • Entertainment grade: A– • History grade: A

People: Philip Kaufman's epic yet gripping film begins with test pilot Chuck Yeager (Sam Shepard) going for a drink in a local bar, and casually signing up to break the sound barrier. 'If you ask me, I think the damn thing doesn't exist,' he says gruffly. Then he falls off his horse while riding it around the desert in a daring competition with his firecracker wife Glennis (Barbara Hershey). He breaks two ribs, but pretends to be fine so they won't take him off the mission – and then successfully pilots the Bell X-1, becoming the first man to go faster than the speed of sound. Yeager appears to have sprung straight from the Big Book of American Heroes – strong jaw, cowboy hat, horse sense, stoic manner – but he really was like this, and doubtless still is. He last broke the sound barrier in 2012, aged 89, in an F-15. Total badass.

Technology: Meanwhile, President Dwight D. Eisenhower (Robert Beer) and Senator Lyndon B. Johnson (Donald Moffat) are upset that the Soviets have gone and launched Sputnik-1 into the outer space that is rightfully America's before they got their act together. 'How the hell did they ever get ahead of us?' Johnson bellows. The answer is swiftly and amusingly illustrated when his aides cannot find the plug socket to get the meeting-room projector working. The chief scientist is unflustered. 'Our Germans are better than their Germans,' he says, alluding to the fact that both the Soviet and US rocket and space programmes after the war owed a great deal to former Nazi scientists.

Recruitment: The Americans plan to retaliate with the first manned space flight, though some think they should use an animal rather than a person. 'The first American in space is not going to be a chimpanzee,' growls Eisenhower. Possible candidates for astronauts included surfers, acrobats and rally drivers ('They already have their own helmets,' says a scientific adviser, chirpily. 'I don't know if that's a factor.'). The film is right that it was Eisenhower who insisted that astronauts be drawn from a field of test pilots – even though they would have little role in actually piloting the craft.

Achievement: The star of the Mercury Seven – the first astronaut group – is John Glenn (Ed Harris), for he is both handsome and incredibly good at spouting wholesome patriotic platitudes in front of newsmen. 'I just thank God I live in a country where the best and the finest in a man can be brought out,' he says. Then Soviet cosmonaut Yuri Gagarin becomes the first man in space, beating the Americans again. Alan Shepard (Scott Glenn) has to settle for being the second, and has to deal with desperately needing a wee before takeoff and having to go in his own spacesuit. This is accurate.

Controversy: Tom Wolfe's book *The Right Stuff*, a flashily written oral history of the space programme, which served as the basis for this film, has been controversial for its portrayal of astronaut Virgil 'Gus' Grissom (Fred Ward). Grissom's Liberty

Bell 7 craft sank in the sea after the hatch opened too quickly on landing. Some blamed Grissom for panicking and opening the hatch himself. Grissom blamed it on a technical error. The film treads a safe line, avoiding showing the critical moment and thus leaving the question of what happened open. In fact, Grissom may well not have been at fault – and the film is kinder to him than the book. Whatever the truth, the incident lets the film show accurately the pressure that was on these men. 'I wanted to eat in the White House!' his wife bawls afterwards. 'I wanted to talk to Jackie [Kennedy] about… things!' Grissom was killed a few years later in the Apollo 1 fire of 1967.

The biggest scandal of the 1970s was Watergate, which brought down the 37th president of the United States, Richard M. Nixon. There have been several good films about this story, including Ron Howard's eminently watchable if factually patchy *Frost/Nixon* (2008). Nixon also appears, less seriously, in *Forrest Gump* (1994), alternative history comedy *Dick* (1999), and the sequel to Cuban Missile Crisis movie *X-Men: First Class*, the immensely enjoyable and completely fictional *X-Men Days of Future Past* (2014), in which he gets excited about secret weapons programmes to fight mutant superheroes.

Oliver Stone's *Nixon* (1995), a sweeping biopic starring Anthony Hopkins as the president, is highly strung and historically dodgy. The best film on Nixon remains one in which he does not actually appear:

1974

All the President's Men (1976)

Director: Alan J. Pakula • Entertainment grade: B+ • History grade: B+

People: The film begins, as did the Watergate affair, with five men breaking into the headquarters of the Democratic National Committee (DNC) on 1 June 1972. The DNC was based in the Watergate office, hotel and residential complex in the Foggy Bottom neighbourhood of Washington DC. The late Frank Wills, the real-life security guard who discovered the break-in, played himself in this movie. The story is first taken up by junior journalist Bob Woodward (Robert Redford) as a minor incident. Soon, though, it begins to bloat out in all directions. Ben Bradlee (Jason Robards), the executive editor of the *Washington Post*, brings the more experienced Carl Bernstein (Dustin Hoffman) on board to work with him.

Investigation: Woodward and Bernstein begin to dig – and here students of the history of journalism may marvel at how much more difficult all this investigative work was in the days before mobile phones and the internet, especially when at one point they have to go through all the hard-copy borrowing records at the Library of Congress by hand. The film shows correctly that their most mysterious source was known as Deep Throat, a high government official turned whistleblower, nicknamed after a notorious pornographic film of the time. The film never reveals who Deep Throat was, but that's fair enough: his identity was not publicly confirmed for almost thirty years after it was made. In

2005, former FBI associate director Mark Felt finally admitted it had been him.

People: Thanks to Deep Throat and other sources, Woodward and Bernstein are soon led to the appropriately acronymed Committee to Re-Elect the President (CRP, pronounced CREEP) and some remarkable characters – including E. Howard Hunt, a disillusioned former CIA officer, and FBI agent G. Gordon Liddy. Deep Throat is particularly memorable on Liddy. 'I was at a party once, and Liddy put his hand over a candle, and he kept it there,' Deep Throat says. 'He kept it right in the flame until his flesh was burned. Somebody said, "What's the trick?" And Liddy said, "The trick is not minding."' Great as this story is, any historical film buff will instantly spot that it has been borrowed from one of the opening scenes of *Lawrence of Arabia*.

Consequences: As Woodward and Bernstein continue to dig, they uncover extensive evidence of dirty tricks, which the tricksters call 'ratfucking': stuffing ballot boxes, planting spies in the opposition and running up fake campaign literature. The conspiracy seems to suck in nearly everyone in Washington. In real life, sixty-nine people were indicted as a result of the Watergate investigations, and forty-eight pled or were found guilty. Plus, of course, President Nixon resigned on 9 August 1974 – still a unique event in American history.

Dialogue: In an iconic scene, Deep Throat tells Woodward and Bernstein to 'Follow the money'. So catchy and apt has this phrase proved that it is now often attributed to Felt, even though he never said it. It does not appear in the *Washington Post* coverage of the affair, nor in Woodward and Bernstein's book, also called *All the President's Men*. In fact, screenwriter William Goldman – who also wrote *Butch Cassidy and the Sundance Kid*, *The Princess Bride* and *Marathon Man* – invented the line for the movie.

The final film in this section forms part of the build-up to one of the biggest stories of the 1980s and 1990s: the end of apartheid in South Africa. For viewers interested in a very different aspect of African politics of the 1970s, it's worth looking up *The Last King of Scotland* (2006). The film is a fictionalized take on the history of Uganda in that period, but features an unforgettable and rightly Oscar-winning performance from Forest Whitaker as the dictator Idi Amin. He charms, he swaggers, he rages and he terrifies, all so powerfully that, when a clip of documentary footage comes up at the end, the real Amin himself looks like Whitaker's stunt double.

Gandhi director Richard Attenborough turned his attention to South Africa for *Cry Freedom*, a film released while the struggle against apartheid raged on. On the same period and subject, but focusing on a fictional story, is MGM picture *A Dry White Season* (1989), starring Marlon Brando and Donald Sutherland. It was directed by Euzhan Palcy, who thereby became the first black woman director to be produced by a major Hollywood studio.

1976

Cry Freedom (1987)

Director: Richard Attenborough • Entertainment grade: C+ • History grade: C

Along with Nelson Mandela and Robert Sobukwe, Steve Biko was one of the most important anti-apartheid leaders in mid-twentieth-century South Africa.

Politics: Liberal newspaper editor Donald Woods (Kevin Kline) has convinced himself that Steve Biko (Denzel Washington) is an anti-white racist. Biko has been 'banned' by the regime – meaning that he cannot associate with more than one person outside his immediate family at any one time, nor travel outside a specific area. Woods goes to meet him. In the film, Woods politely objects to Biko's message, and Biko responds with a gentle sermon on the plight of black South Africans. It's considerably toned down from the authentic version recounted in Woods's memoir, in which Woods lost his temper, shouting: 'I don't have to bloody well apologize for being born white!' Biko's real-life response was good-natured, but more powerful and confrontational than the one in the film. He explained that he tried to discourage hatred of any sort, but his priority was to liberate black people, not to worry about the hurt feelings of white liberals. Director Richard Attenborough, much lauded for the *Gandhi* he created, projects an almost identical personality on to this icon. But if there was a Gandhian in South Africa it was Mandela, not Biko – and neither man espoused non-violence.

Race: 'We don't want to be forced into your society,' says Biko. 'I'm going to be me as I am, and you can beat me or jail me or even kill me, but I'm not going to be what you want me to be.' But while the film lets Biko say that, it strives to present him as it wants him to be – humble, chaste, non-violent – not who he was. The real Biko spoke fierily, wittily and colloquially, peppering his speech with 'hey, man'. The film Biko talks like a slightly dull vicar from Suffolk. The real Biko's simultaneous long-term relationships with a wife and a lover, not to mention dalliances with many other women, are all but airbrushed out. 'One cannot give a full account of the personality of Steve without mentioning his powerful sexuality', the real Woods wrote. The film tries, and is the poorer for it. So this movie, honouring a black hero who staked his identity on refusing to conform to white liberal expectations, redesigns him… to conform to white liberal expectations.

Law: Woods goes to the country garden estate of police minister Jimmy Kruger (John Thaw, who is superb). Woods asks Kruger to lay off persecuting Biko. Kruger plays nice at the time, but later secretly turns on Woods – sending the police after him instead. Meanwhile, Biko is arrested. He sustains a suspicious head injury, and dies in custody. Shamelessly, the authorities claim he did it himself, with a hunger strike. 'Biko's death leaves me cold,' Kruger snarls at a press conference. This line, unpleasantly enough, is accurate. The pronunciation is not. Almost everyone in the cast (except Washington) mispronounces the name Biko. The man himself said it bee-core, to rhyme with 'seesaw' – not bee-koh, to rhyme with 'neato'.

Violence: Woods, too, is banned by the regime. He eventually flees the country. At the very end of the film, he has a flashback to the Soweto uprising. On 16 June 1976, police opened fire on protesting school students. Recreated here, the scenes of the massacre are devastating. They are also jarring – because they're so much more dramatic than the last hour of the film, which has focused on how Woods slipped past his ban and got out of South Africa. Certainly, Woods's experience was remarkable. But when the viewer is suddenly presented with hundreds of children being shot in the streets, you've got to wonder if 'white guy escapes' is the story most in need of telling here.

Verdict: A well-meaning film about the white liberal experience in South Africa – but, if you want to know about Steve Biko, look elsewhere.

8

Living in the Now

As the 1980s began, the Cold War still had a hold across the globe. The state of mutual antagonism between the United States and the USSR was now heavily backed by nuclear weapons and space technology. To handle this massive responsibility, the American people elected their first Hollywood president: former movie star Ronald Reagan. Reagan, who had appeared in notable movies like *Dark Victory* (1939) as well as less lauded productions like chimp comedy *Bedtime for Bonzo* (1951), never entirely stopped acting. Threatening to veto tax increases, he quoted Clint Eastwood from one of the Dirty Harry movies: 'Go ahead… make my day.'

Reagan was a big fan of Sylvester Stallone's *Rambo* films, which he quoted with regard to policy, and of George Lucas's sci-fi movie *Star Wars* (1977). From the latter, he appropriated the term 'evil empire' to describe the Soviet Union, and the subtitle 'a new hope' to describe his own policies. When his government set up the Strategic Defense Initiative, a massive ground- and space-based programme designed to protect the United States from nuclear attack, the media christened it Star Wars. As Reagan's biographer Michael Rogin points out, it may have had more to do with *Murder in the Air* (1940), in which Reagan himself played Secret Service man Brass Bancroft. It is Bancroft's job to protect a new defensive weapon designed to destroy any attacking missile – just like the SDI.

Star Wars writer-director George Lucas loathed the use of his title to describe SDI. In fact, according to Lucasfilm's official history of *Star Wars*, 'in portraying the ascent of Senator Palpatine, who becomes the evil Sith Emperor, Darth Sidious, Lucas says he had Richard Nixon in mind' – like Reagan, a Republican president. Lucas sued two pro-SDI advocacy groups in 1985 in an attempt to prevent them using the term Star Wars to describe it, but lost.

It was characteristic of the Cold War that the main United States–Soviet Union conflict found its expression in dozens of proxy wars and smaller conflicts. There are a clutch of films about the Cold War in the 1980s, but much of the archive material from that era remains closed – so filmmakers are still not working with the full picture. A lot of films about this era are distinctly unsatisfying. Either they let the United States off the hook too easily in the hope of not offending a wide audience – like *Charlie Wilson's War* (2007), in which Tom Hanks plays a Texas congressman getting chummy with the mujahideen in the 1980s – or they fictionalize so heavily as to lose credibility, like Oliver Stone's *Salvador* (1986).

Ben Affleck's *Argo*, which won Best Picture at the 2013 Oscars, offended historians, Britons, New Zealanders, Canadians and Iranians with its version of events. The real operation was a joint

US-Canadian project: the Canadians are written out of the film until a hastily added postscript appears just before the credits. The Brits and New Zealanders who helped are written out too, except that it is alleged in the film that British diplomats turned desperate American refugees away from their embassy (which is not true: in real life, the British welcomed the Americans in before they were passed over to the Canadians). But *Argo* does at least improve on *Charlie Wilson's War* and *Salvador* by turning a remarkable Cold War story into a genuinely enjoyable movie.

1979

Argo (2012)

Director: Ben Affleck • Entertainment grade: A– • History grade: C

On 4 November 1979, Iranian revolutionaries occupied the American Embassy in Tehran and took more than fifty Americans hostage. Six diplomats escaped. Canadian officials and the CIA launched a secret joint operation to get them out.

Politics: In 1953, the CIA and MI6 engineered a coup to overthrow Mohammad Mosaddegh, the democratic president of Iran, and replace him with a military-backed absolute monarchy. By 1979, democratic opposition to the shah hardened into revolutionary fervour and found itself, fatefully, on the same side as Islamic fundamentalism. *Argo* presents this context imaginatively, though fleetingly and perhaps too vaguely. The sequence in which revolutionaries storm the US Embassy is brilliantly realized, though. If you wait for the end credits, a series of real photos are shown alongside the movie's recreations so you may admire its accurate visual recreations.

Operation: The six escaped Americans are taken in by Canadian ambassador Ken Taylor (Victor Garber). If you're thinking they'd be awfully conspicuous in a big group like that, you'd be right. In real life, they were split into two groups of three, one staying with Taylor and one with immigration officer John Sheardown. Back in Virginia, CIA agent Tony Mendez (Ben Affleck) comes up with a way to get them out. With the help of his friend John Chambers (John Goodman) – a makeup artist who won an honorary Oscar in 1969 for his work on *Planet of the Apes* – he sets up a film company. The plan is to set up a fake production, arrange a location recce in Iran, and pass the six diplomats off as Canadian filmmakers. Afterwards, they will simply walk out through Mehrabad Airport. Madcap as this sounds, it's true.

Plot: 'We decided we needed a script with "sci-fi", Middle Eastern, and mythological elements,' Mendez wrote in his account of the real operation. 'Something about the glory of Islam would be nice, too.' They secure the rights to one called *Argo*. In real life, *Argo* was based on the novel *Lord of Light*, a dystopian orientalist space epic by Roger Zelazny. Director Ben Affleck couldn't use any elements of *Lord of Light* in his *Argo*, because in real life he didn't have the rights. So the *Argo* in *Argo* is a fake version of a fake movie. The real fake *Argo*, as it were, was based on Hindu-Buddhist mythology – not quite Middle Eastern or a glorification of Islam, but the CIA seemed to think it was close enough. The fake fake *Argo* in this movie is a *Star Wars* rip-off. They've got a big blue Wookiee and everything.

Action: Mendez persuades the six to play along, but the exfiltration is a nail-biter. First, Iranian officials show them round a bazaar, where they must convincingly play their roles and are exposed to spying eyes. Then, at the airport, they have to pass off their dodgy paperwork and negotiate their way round the revolutionary guards. Will they get out before the spying eyes from the bazaar match up with other intelligence to identify them? It is terrifically exciting. It is also almost entirely fictional. Not least because the idea that regime officials were moments away from capturing the six at the airport credits Iranian bureaucracy with lightning efficiency.

More action: The real operation went 'as smooth as silk', according to Mendez, aside from a brief holdup over a mechanical problem with the plane. The choppy version in *Argo* certainly makes for a much more exciting film. For a historian, though, the last third of the run-time feels almost like the end of *Adaptation*, when the high-velocity, high-concept style of the movie within the movie seems to take over the movie you're watching, and the barriers between fact and fiction and fantasy break down, and you might just need to sit down with a nice cup of tea until reality stops spinning.

Verdict: A smart, gripping and witty historical action thriller – though there are so many interwoven layers of reality and fiction here that it wouldn't be surprising if the blue Wookiee whipped off his furry head to reveal he was really the Ayatollah.

Contemporary with Ronald Reagan's presidency in the United States, Margaret Thatcher was prime minister of the United Kingdom. As a right-wing radical and reformer she was an intensely divisive figure. She has now had several television biopics and this movie, released a few months before she died in 2013 – plus Janet Brown plays her flirting with a parrot she thinks is James Bond at the very end of *For Your Eyes Only* (1981).

1984

The Iron Lady (2012)

Director: Phyllida Lloyd • Entertainment grade: C+ • History grade: C

Structure: *The Iron Lady* tells its story as a series of flashbacks experienced by the ageing Thatcher (Meryl Streep), suffering from dementia and haunted by the imagined ghost of her husband Denis (Jim Broadbent). Streep is terrific, carrying off Thatcher in her prime and Thatcher in her dotage with equal aplomb. Regrettably, so much of the film's screentime has been devoted to the dotage – and so many of the flashbacks are, unlike Thatcher herself, preoccupied with her role as a wife and mother – that little time is left for the interesting stuff. A few of those who are relegated to blink-and-you'll-miss-'em status, or don't appear at all: Cecil Parkinson, Nigel Lawson, Norman Tebbit, Willie

Whitelaw, Keith Joseph, Charles Powell, Bernard Ingham, Neil Kinnock, Arthur Scargill and Ronald Reagan.

Class: Back to 1950, when young Margaret (née Roberts) is being interviewed as a prospective Conservative candidate for Dartford. In the film, this takes place at an intimidating formal dinner. One of the guests is businessman Denis Thatcher. Grocer's daughter Margaret is daunted by the cutlery. Denis whispers: 'Start on the outside and work your way in.' This did not happen to Margaret Roberts. Instead, it has been lifted from the 1990 film *Pretty Woman*, starring Julia Roberts (no relation) as a Los Angeles prostitute. During the real Dartford selection meeting, Margaret Roberts sat on a podium next to her father and discussed the welfare state. Instead of attacking it, she claimed some credit for the Conservatives for setting up the Beveridge Commission – the inquiry that led to its foundation. It is true, though, that Denis was in the audience.

Parliament: In 1970, Thatcher becomes education secretary. She irritates the prime minister, Edward Heath, in cabinet meetings by expressing views that go beyond her remit. This is true, though in real life her lines were sharper than in this movie. For instance, when appointing a new chairman of the BBC, Heath dismissed one candidate: 'He's got much too high an opinion of himself.' The real Thatcher interrupted from the end of the table: 'Well, most men do, Prime Minister.' Soon, Thatcher is elected leader of the Conservative Party. The film suggests she did this by getting a fabulous blow-dry. Good grief.

War: Thatcher is elected prime minister and soon makes herself unpopular, both within her own party and in the country at large. Fortunately for her political career, Argentina invades the Falklands. The film attempts to explain the sinking of the *Belgrano*, showing that Thatcher knew the Argentine cruiser was sailing away from the exclusion zone when she gave the order to sink it. Everything happens in a situation room, complete with beepy radar screens, people running around looking important, and a table covered in model ships. According to Rear-Admiral J. F. Woodward, commander of the Falklands task force, there was no such fuss when he sent a colleague to secure Thatcher's agreement to the sinking. 'This was achieved in remarkably short order,' he remembered, 'reputedly in the entrance hall at Chequers.' The film skips the government's cover-up. Famously, a year later, Thatcher was still denying that the *Belgrano* was sailing away from the task force when it was attacked.

Ousting: By the end of the 1980s, Thatcher's economic miracle crumbles into recession. There are riots over the poll tax. Her attitude to Europe isolates her from her own party. The film gives a tantalizing but all too brief glimpse of the political drama that brought her down: the turning of her close ally, Sir Geoffrey Howe (Anthony Head), the ambition of Michael Heseltine (Richard E. Grant). It almost tries to excuse Thatcher's legendary rudeness to Howe by implying she was beginning to lose it at the time. In fact, being tough and inflexible was always her style. Even back in the 1970s, close ally Airey Neave walked out of a meeting with her, claiming he had never been spoken to so rudely in his life. This movie would be more satisfying for Thatcher's admirers and critics alike if they had cut the fluff and let the Iron Lady be what she was: hard as nails.

Verdict: Meryl Streep's knockout performance lifts *The Iron Lady* out of complete mediocrity, but the film around her is wishy-washy and unfocused. Whether you love or loathe Margaret Thatcher, those are not things you can say about her.

One of the most iconic leaders of the late twentieth century, and one of those with the most films made about them, was South Africa's Nelson Mandela. Imprisoned by the apartheid regime for twenty-seven years, he went on to lead his country to freedom and reconciliation. Mandela has been played in TV movies by Danny Glover in *Mandela* (1987) and by Sidney Poitier in *Mandela and de Klerk* (1997), opposite Michael Caine as F. W. de Klerk. In cinematic releases, he has also been played by Clarke Peters in *Endgame* (2009), with Chiwetel Ejiofor as Thabo Mbeki; and by Terrence Howard in *Winnie Mandela* (2011), with Jennifer Hudson as his wife Winnie.

The extremely dubious *Goodbye Bafana* (2007) stars Dennis Haysbert as Mandela in an adaptation of the widely discredited memoir of Mandela's prison guard James Gregory (Joseph Fiennes). Mandela was reportedly urged to sue the real Gregory for misrepresentation, though he decided not to when the South African prisons department distanced itself from the book. Much better, though not a masterpiece, is *Invictus* (2009), starring Morgan Freeman as Mandela and Matt

Damon as South African rugby captain François Pienaar. It's a well-acted and mostly well-made film about post-apartheid reconciliation, marred only by its inability to make the game of rugby seem exciting. The crucial match is just random shots of players crashing heavily about, disconnected from any sense of what is actually going on in the game, and – disastrously – filmed in slow-motion with solemn music. 'So what does this mean?' a helpful audience-proxy character asks at one point. A viewer might conclude that director Clint Eastwood has only a vague familiarity with the sport he is trying to depict, and even less enthusiasm for it.

The best performance as Mandela so far – which outshines the film around it – is:

1990

Mandela: Long Walk to Freedom (2013)

Director: Justin Chadwick • Entertainment grade: B • History grade: B+

Casting: This biopic, based on the late Mandela's own autobiography, turned out to be so aptly timed as to verge on the spooky: the subject's death was announced during its London premiere. It stars British actor Idris Elba who, it must be admitted, looks nothing like Nelson Mandela. Nonetheless, he is a terrific actor, and blessed with an appropriately powerful physical presence. The young Mandela cut an imposing figure: over six feet tall, a boxer, a hotshot lawyer and leader of a violent armed struggle. He was a tougher guy than the TV characters Elba is famous for playing, Stringer Bell and John Luther, and – to judge by many stories – very nearly as appealing to the ladies. Elba has this down.

Violence: Since the real Mandela's death, some of his supporters have criticized the right wing in the west for calling him and the African National Congress 'terrorists', while others have claimed his 'terrorism' as a vital part of his struggle. The word 'terrorism' is problematically emotive for historians. There isn't much difference between a 'freedom fighter' and a 'terrorist', except that we think the former is justified in blowing stuff up and the latter isn't, and that's the sort of subjective judgement historians aren't supposed to make. Mandela himself made no secret of the fact he co-founded and led Umkhonto we Sizwe, a paramilitary organization aligned with the African National Congress and the South African Communist Party. It blew quite a lot of stuff up, as this film clearly shows.

More violence: William Nicholson's screenplay presents anti-apartheid violence in context of the constant brutal violence the white supremacist regime was meting out to black South Africans. 'For fifty years we have been talking peace and nonviolence,' says Mandela in the film, explaining his move to arms. 'As violence in this country was inevitable, it would be unrealistic and wrong for African leaders to continue preaching peace and nonviolence at a time when the government met our peaceful demands with force,' said the real Mandela in his speech at the Rivonia Trial. Thankfully, the film does not sentimentalize Mandela as the world's cuddly old grandfather. At the same time, it shows you why he felt pushed to radicalism by the appalling regime he was up against. High historical marks for achieving this balance.

Romance: Mandela's passionate, troubled relationship with his second wife, Winnie Madikizela-Mandela (Naomie Harris), is at the heart of the story. Winnie's enthusiasm for violence even in the internecine struggle between anti-apartheid activists is not glossed over, and nor is her apparent enthusiasm for 'necklacing' – a sadistic method of execution in which the victim is bound with a rubber tyre, doused with petrol and burned to death. 'I am terribly brutalized inside,' the real Winnie admitted to the BBC in 1986. 'I know my soul is scarred. But what has happened is that hasn't brutalized me to an extent of being consumed in hate.' The film could be accused of simplifying this complicated woman, but it's already two and a half hours long and it isn't really about her.

Humour: While the political and historical efforts of this film are impressive, it does underplay one crucial element of Mandela's personality: his wit. A classic example came in 1997, when journalists asked him how he felt on meeting the Spice Girls. 'I don't want to be emotional,' deadpanned the man who had endured twenty-seven years of imprisonment, ended apartheid, won South Africa's first real democratic election and ultimately become the most revered statesman on earth, 'but this is one of the greatest moments of my life.'

Since 1991, Somalia has been in a state of ongoing civil war. The Battle of Mogadishu, fought in its capital during October 1993, was at the time the biggest US military firefight since the Vietnam War. An attempt by American Special Forces to kidnap two chief aides of Somali warlord Mohammed Farah Aidid went disastrously wrong, triggering an all-out battle. Under the UN banner, American, Pakistani and Malaysian forces fought Aidid's militia.

1993

Black Hawk Down (2001)

Director: Ridley Scott • Entertainment grade: C • History grade: C

Exposition: 'This isn't Iraq, you know,' says one officer. 'Much more complicated than that.' Maybe in 2001, when *Black Hawk Down* was released, you could just about get away with that line. In any case, the conflict in Somalia is indeed complicated. The film opens with a slew of explanatory title cards, revealing it expects its viewers to be a fairly dense bunch. One reads 'Somalia, East Africa.' As opposed to Somalia, Massachusetts?

Violence: Since *M*A*S*H**, American military bases have tended to be portrayed on film as wild and sleazy places. Not so in *Black Hawk Down*, where the men use their downtime to play chess, illustrate children's books and debate the rules of Scrabble. One soldier's entire characterization is that he insists on making proper cafetière coffee. Meanwhile, Staff Sergeant

Eversmann (Josh Hartnett) holds forth about how profoundly he respects the Somali people. So does everyone else, apparently, and the troops' nickname for the locals – 'skinnies' – is merely a sign of affection, rather than a tasteless slur in a country where 300,000 people have just died of starvation. 'Bakara Market is the Wild West,' announces one Ranger. 'But be careful what you shoot at because people do live there. Hooah!' In the subsequent fighting, soldiers are shown carefully avoiding shooting at any women or children (two groups inevitably lumped together as helpless victims by the movie, which avoids dealing with Somalia's notoriously large number of child soldiers, and only once shows a woman with a gun). The audience can only conclude that, in real life, the several thousand civilian casualties must all have been hit by bullets ricocheting off genuine, kite-marked warlords.

War: *Black Hawk Down* doesn't hide the fact that the battle was the result of a perennial US military blindspot: underestimating the efficacy of guerrilla warfare. The run-time is almost entirely taken up by visceral battle sequences, in which high-tech American equipment proves to be little use against determined street fighters. If there's a director who can make a massacre look picturesque, it's Ridley Scott. Showers of sparks glow amid the ruins; market stalls are elegantly swagged with bandoliers; curls of smoke rise from spent bullet casings as they hit the ground; blood spurts forth in graceful fountains. American soldiers die in slow-motion, accompanied by mournful string or piano music. Somalis just fly into the air, explode and disappear.

Politics: The film was much criticized for pitting noble, civilizing white heroes against faceless, savage black villains. It's true that Special Forces are less racially diverse than the US military overall, but it is still a bit conspicuous that *Black Hawk Down* chooses an entirely white cast of main characters from among them. It's also a bit conspicuous that the very few Somali-speaking characters (mostly played by Brits of West African and Caribbean descent) don't do anything except scheme, gloat, menace and be untrustworthy. Meanwhile, the Pakistani and Malaysian soldiers who fought in the battle have been written out altogether. When American troops return to a Pakistani base after the operation, they are greeted by the film's only visible Asians: three beturbaned waiters, meekly offering glasses of water and fluffy white towels. So irritated was former Pakistan president Pervez Musharraf at this slight that he denounced the movie in his autobiography – though, as things turned out, Hollywood was the least of his problems.

On 6 April 1994, a plane carrying the Rwandan president Juvenal Habyarimana was shot down over the airport at Kigali. This triggered massive civil unrest between the majority Hutu and minority Tutsi people. It is usually estimated that more than 800,000 Rwandans, mostly Tutsis, were murdered in the following three months – a number almost equivalent to the entire British and colonial military death toll for the whole of World War I.

The Rwandan genocide has inspired several feature films, including *Shooting Dogs* (2005), known in the United States as *Beyond the Gates*, featuring John Hurt and Hugh Dancy; *Shake Hands with the Devil* (2007), telling the story of General Roméo Dallaire as adapted from his own autobiography; and the powerful American-Rwandan film *Munyurangabo* (2007), which is also the first feature film ever made in the Kinyarwanda language. The TV movie *Sometimes in April* (2005), directed by Raoul Peck and starring Idris Elba, touches on events at the Hotel des Mille Collines, as does...

1994

Hotel Rwanda (2004)

Director: Terry George • Entertainment grade: B+ • History grade: C+

People: Paul Rusesabagina (played brilliantly by Don Cheadle, who earned an Oscar nomination for Best Actor but lost out to Jamie Foxx as Ray Charles in *Ray*) is the kind of hotel manager who knows how to keep all the local generals sweet with Cohiba cigars and Glenmorangie whisky. Gradually, tension builds outside the Hotel des Mille Collines' smoothly whitewashed walls – until the president's plane is shot down, and the whole country seems to go off like a bomb.

International relations: Paul gets his family and friends into the hotel by bribing a local general. The United Nations, represented by the fictional Colonel Oliver (Nick Nolte, over-acting), are about as much use as the proverbial chocolate teapot. 'We're here as peacekeepers, not as peacemakers,' burbles Oliver, as children are hacked to death with machetes all around him. Somewhat unfairly, Oliver is based on real-life Canadian UN General Roméo Dallaire. The UN has been criticized for its failure to respond effectively to the genocide in Rwanda, but Dallaire was not to blame – in fact, most reports indicate he did everything he could.

Intervention: Western journalists aren't much better than western soldiers, in *Hotel Rwanda*'s view. 'We're not leaving the hotel grounds unless we have an armoured car,' the chief reporter tells cameraman Jack (Joaquin Phoenix). 'That's the ground rules.' Disgusted, Jack replies: 'The ground rules? Where do you think we are, fucking Wimbledon?' The film is sharply critical of the international community for failing to take action. 'How can they not intervene?' Paul asks Jack. 'I think if people see this footage, they'll say "oh my goodness, that's horrible",' says Jack, 'and then go on eating their dinners.' Historically speaking, though it may make some people uncomfortable, *Hotel Rwanda*'s critical view is supportable. The UN itself accepted that it had failed in Rwanda back in 1999, five years after the genocide, and repeated its admission for the twentieth anniversary.

Controversy: *Hotel Rwanda* runs into greater controversy as its depiction of Rusesabagina approaches the saintly. It suggests Rusesabagina provided the hotel's services on a charitable basis and only issued bills to keep up the pretence of being a legitimate business rather than a refuge – but some survivors have alleged that he extorted money from them, or that he refused to let some people in who did not have means, or that he forced them to vacate their rooms if they couldn't pay. *Hotel Rwanda*'s director, Terry George, responded angrily to these allegations, accusing Rusesabagina's critics of running a 'smear campaign'. Making measured judgements on traumatic and highly politicized events like those of the Rwandan genocide is the most difficult part of any historian's job. There are always wildly different opinions and enormous contradictions in the evidence. It's hard for any outsider to know what really went on in the Hotel des Mille Collines, but historically minded viewers would do well to remember that the film's version of the story is only one version – and it is disputed.

Happy endings: At the end of the film, Paul and his wife Tatiana (Sophie Okonedo) are evacuated by the UN to a well-organized refugee camp at Kabuga. Here the film diverges from Rusesabagina's own version of the story as told in his memoir, *An Ordinary Man*. The real Rusesabaginas were transported by the Rwandan Patriotic Front, not by the UN. Kabuga, he wrote, 'was no camp in the conventional sense. It was a looting zone… I, too, was among those who had to forage for food.' It is true, as the film shows, that the Rusesabaginas were reunited with their two infant nieces in Kabuga, but they were not so well looked after as they appear to be in the film. 'Both of the children were covered in dirt and appeared to be starving and barely alive,' Rusesabagina wrote. 'They had been living for months on ground-up chicken feed.' Kabuga was run like a prison, he wrote: 'Weeping filled the air.' It's easy to see why the film has altered the truth – the sense of security and order returning allows it to create a happy ending. In real life, unfortunately, happy endings are harder to come by.

The death of Diana, Princess of Wales in August 1997 provoked international mourning and a flurry of conspiracy theories. Here are two historical films about that story: one terrible, one terrific.

1997

Diana (2013)

Director: Oliver Hirschbiegel • Entertainment grade: Fail • History grade: C

Portents: The film begins on the night of 31 August 1997 in Paris. Pausing in a corridor, the Princess of Wales (Naomi Watts) turns as she hears a mysterious, baleful noise. It's not obvious what this harbinger of doom is supposed to be. Perhaps it's the collected groans and howls of the poor souls who sat through earlier screenings. Anyway, it sets the tone for the movie: delusional, banal and often ridiculous.

Misery: The story flashes back to 1995. Lonely Di hangs out in Kensington Palace, boiling baked beans for one, playing the *Moonlight Sonata*, and hurling the remote control at the television when Prince Charles is on. Her life is boring and depressing, a feeling the filmmakers recreate with maximum accuracy for the audience. Her private secretary tells her she must attend a ceremony to launch a nuclear submarine. 'A nuclear submarine?' she whines plaintively. 'I want to help people.'

Romance: The husband of Diana's acupuncturist is in hospital. Visiting him, Diana encounters dishy heart surgeon Hasnat Khan (Naveen Andrews). This is indeed how the two met, though they cannot be held responsible for the film's agonizing imagined dialogue. 'Hospitals fascinate me,' deadpans Diana. 'When I visit hospitals, I get excited.' Not wanting to be outdone on sinister platitudes, Hasnat says: 'You don't perform the operation. The operation performs you.' If only they'd given this script to David Lynch and played it as a surreal, dystopian horror movie. Or just stuck it in the shredder.

People: Despite the film's apparent conviction that it is telling one of history's great love stories, its narrative is basically that two people who haven't the slightest flicker of chemistry between them commit high treason in soft focus, then spend most of the film tortuously breaking up. Though the peddlers of memoirs and mid-market newspapers have scavenged every last tidbit from this affair, sensible historians admit knowing little about it. Diana never went on the record and nor, in any great detail, has the real Dr Khan – though he confirmed the existence of a relationship to police during the investigation into Diana's death.

More romance: It has evidently suited some of those close to the late princess to claim that Hasnat was her 'true love' while his successor, Dodi Fayed, was a flash in the pan. Maybe this is true or partially true, or maybe it's just what they want to believe. The movie swallows it whole, in the process reducing its principals to flimsy cutouts who wouldn't make the grade in a Mills & Boon novel. Director Oliver Hirschbiegel, whose brilliant *Downfall* deserved its great acclaim, may go down in cinema history as the man who made Adolf Hitler come across as a more three-dimensional character onscreen than Princess Diana.

Politics: The real Diana's support for the campaign to ban landmines was genuinely pioneering and admirable. Here, her 1997 trip to mine-strewn Angola is just a white saviour fantasy, performed mainly to impress Hasnat. You haven't seen a beautiful blonde royal use dark-skinned people as mute, grateful props quite so shamelessly since Season 3 of *Game of Thrones*. She calls Hasnat back in London. 'Did they print the pictures of all the kids with their arms and legs blown off?' she asks. 'No,' he tells her. 'Bastards!' she cries.

Relationships: Diana lets herself into Hasnat's flat. It's a mess. She makes the questionable decision to tidy it up. Reports have suggested this really happened. Had the filmmakers possessed a modicum of wit, though, they'd have marshalled some adorable woodland creatures to help her scrub the plates with their fluffy bottoms. Alas, they have not. 'Yes, I've been a mad bitch,' she confesses. 'Yes, I've been a stalker.' Hasnat punishes her by sending her to Pakistan to deal with his fearsome mother – who, displaying a tenuous grasp of history, blames Diana for the partition of India. The princess consoles herself by going to Italy to cure a blind man's sight. Or something. Everyone knows how it's going to end, of course – but let's hope that whatever form all these relationships took in real life, they were a lot more rewarding than this movie.

1997

The Queen (2006)

Director: Stephen Frears • Entertainment grade: B– • History grade: A–

Casting: Tony Blair has just won a landslide election victory, and goes to the palace to irritate the Queen with his disregard for protocol until she testily asks him to form a government. Michael Sheen's impression of Blair (seen also in *The Deal* and *The Special Relationship*) is eerily accurate. Playing the Queen, Helen Mirren makes a reference to her first prime minister, Winston Churchill. 'He sat in your chair in a frock coat and hat,' she tells Blair, archly. 'He was kind enough to give a shy young girl like me *quite* an education.' 'I can imagine,' Blair replies, with a nervous giggle. The audience might also permit itself a nervous giggle at this point: is Mirren going to sex up the Queen? How are we to remove from our minds the image of the aging postwar Churchill trying it on with Her Maj after a few sherries? Mercifully, from this point on, Mirren's performance and the film around it pursue a more reserved and more convincing characterization.

People: The Queen and Prince Philip are woken up with news of the accident. The film shows the two of them sharing a bed (not to mention, in a later scene, him cheerfully leaping into it with the words 'Move over, cabbage!'). When Michael Fagan broke into the Queen's bedroom at Buckingham Palace in 1982, it was acknowledged publicly that the royal couple does not share a bedroom.

Family: There's a great scene in a Land Rover, where Prince Charles, talking to the Queen about her subjects, asks, 'Why do they hate us so much?' and she replies, 'Not *us*, dear.' Beyond that, the film can't seem to decide whether Charles is a grieving husband in touch with the public mood, or a snivelling opportunist terrified of the people's wrath. Meanwhile, Alex Jennings, playing him, looks so much like Edward VIII that viewers may have to remind themselves they aren't watching a movie about a different twentieth-century British royal crisis. Thanks to the archive footage, several other characters, including Diana herself and her brother Earl Spencer, effectively play themselves. During Spencer's famous speech at Diana's funeral, Mirren really shows why she deserved her Oscar, giving him a perfect imitation of the royal stink-eye.

Politics: The contrast between cloistered, timeless royal life at Balmoral and the *West Wing*-like hustle of the Blairite administration in London is historically credible, and beautifully observed. Sometimes, it's almost too realistic, like when Blair meets his advisers wearing a Newcastle football shirt emblazoned with his own name and the number 10. Crivens. He shocks the Queen by telling her that one in four people want to abolish the monarchy. After her public capitulation to their demands, though, he says this has 'all gone away'. Polls can be found to confirm that 25 per cent anti-royal statistic, though it might strike you as being actually quite low. But the way the film presents it is misleading. The level of support for republicanism in Britain has remained remarkably consistent at around 15–20 per cent for decades, including before and after Diana's death.

Verdict: A commendable piece of historical filmmaking, quiet and dignified in exactly the way that the Queen herself, according to this film at least, wanted to be.

On 11 September 2001, four American domestic flights were hijacked. One plane was flown into each of the two towers of the World Trade Center in New York, one was flown into the Pentagon, and one – United Airlines flight 93 – crashed in a field in Pennsylvania. The shocking television pictures of the events in New York made such a powerful impression that it was inevitable movies would follow. Oliver Stone's *World Trade Center* (2006) starred Nicolas Cage as Port Authority police officer John McLoughlin, one of the heroes of the day; Mira Nair's *The Reluctant Fundamentalist* (2012), based on Mohsin Hamid's novel, took a fictionalized look at the context for the attacks.

Bollywood films about 9/11 have often focused on the experience of being wrongly identified as a terrorist, such as *My Name is Khan* (2010) and *New York* (2009). Life imitated art imitating life for Shah Rukh Khan, the megastar lead of *My Name is Khan*. He was detained by immigration authorities on entry into the United States in 2009 and 2012. On the first occasion, the Indian Embassy in the United States intervened to have him released; on the second, officials from Yale University vouched for him. Khan said that he believed he was detained on account of his Muslim name.

2001

United 93 (2006)

Director: Paul Greengrass • Entertainment grade: C • History grade: C

Involvement: All characters in the film are based on real people, and several (notably aviation authority operations manager Ben Sliney) play themselves. Historically, having people play themselves may be a step too far. It is surely impossible for anyone who was actually involved to be impartial about the story or their role in it, especially with a subject as emotive as 9/11. Nonetheless, the restrained early scenes are a convincing reminder of the disbelief and confusion that day.

Evidence: It's only when the film gets into what happened on the flight that it begins to stray into dubious territory. Every eyewitness died, and piecing together what can be remembered from thirty-seven mostly brief and unrecorded voice calls made from the plane does not provide a clear or necessarily reliable picture. The film was finished before a transcript of the cockpit voice recording was released. Therefore, these scenes can only be a work of imagination, and indeed they were largely improvised by the cast. What makes it unnerving is that they are presented as an accurate recreation, unfolding more or less in real time, complete with documentary-style camerawork and title cards. It's the very realism that's suspect here, for there are no grounds for claiming that the scenes on the plane are anything other than fiction.

People: Subtly, *United 93* introduces a nationalistic, pro-War on Terror tone – notably in its treatment of German passenger Christian Adams, the one non-American hostage. In the film, Adams is the only person shown suggesting cooperation with the hijackers: 'I think we shouldn't provoke them. Just do what they want.' Adams's wife, it was reported, had declined to contribute to the film's production. The actor who played Adams claimed that he was a thoughtful man who 'never made any rash decisions'. It's a big jump to go from that to depicting him as an appeaser. In reality, no one knows who led or participated in the storming of the cockpit, though one man, Todd Beamer, was overheard by a telephone operator saying, 'Let's roll!' The film makes him something like an action hero. Maybe he was, but then again maybe Christian Adams was, too.

Violence: Pushing their way to the cockpit, hostages corner and seemingly beat to death two of the hijackers. This is pure fantasy. Presumably, watching blood spurt from kicked terrorists is intended to satisfy the audience that Team America got payback. Apparently, it's not enough to appreciate the real heroism in the story: the hostages' brave actions helped bring the plane down in a field, potentially saving hundreds of lives it might have ended had it hit its target.

Propaganda: The pre-release cut of this film had a final title card that read 'America's war on terror had begun.' It hadn't. George W. Bush first used the phrase 'war on terror' five days later. American and British military operations in Afghanistan began on 7 October 2001. This final card was seen by some reviewers as making *United 93* a propaganda movie. Bearing in mind that it would have followed the speculative scene in which ordinary Americans ignore the spineless Euro-wimp and go all out to kick terrorist ass, it's hard not to agree. The filmmakers thought the better of it. In the released version, the final card reads 'Dedicated to the memory of all of those who lost their lives on September 11th 2001.' Less controversial, though it's curious they didn't find a way of phrasing that laudable sentiment that excluded the hijackers.

Verdict: *United 93* is superbly made and authentic in feel, but the choices it makes about what happened on the plane – and who gets to be a hero – are open to serious question.

The wars in Afghanistan and Iraq that followed the 9/11 attacks are still almost in the realm of current events. Veteran left-wing filmmaker Oliver Stone's George W. Bush biopic *W.* (2008) stars Josh Brolin in a fine performance as the dopey president. Perhaps surprisingly, Stone goes easy on Bush, blaming many of his failings on Donald Rumsfeld, Dick Cheney and an ice-cold father. As Bush himself said: 'I'll be long gone before some smart person ever figures out what happened inside this Oval Office.'

Doug Liman's *Fair Game* (2010) and Paul Greengrass's *Green Zone* (2010) are highly accomplished films and impressively researched, as far as the history can yet be researched with so many of the documents still classified. They take a critical slant on the American case for war and its prosecution respectively, which will sit well with some viewers and badly with others. Kathryn Bigelow's rather more ambivalent *Zero Dark Thirty* (2012), about the raid to kill Osama bin Laden, ran into controversy over the question of whether it endorsed torture, or wrongly depicted torture as essential to the hunt for bin Laden.

With events still so fresh and raw, any film made about the 'war on terror' is likely to upset somebody. This one certainly did:

2002

American Sniper (2014)

Director: Clint Eastwood • Entertainment grade: D+ • History grade: D–

Chris Kyle, known to his contemporaries as 'Legend', was a US Navy SEAL who served in Iraq in the early 2000s. He is considered the deadliest sniper in American history, with a recorded 160 confirmed kills out of 255 probable kills. He later served as a bodyguard for Sarah Palin.

Bad guys: Director Clint Eastwood – last seen at the Republican National Convention in 2012, telling an empty chair off for invading Afghanistan – reduces everything in the film to primary colours and simple shapes. Chris Kyle (Bradley Cooper) joins the SEALs after he sees the 1998 US Embassy bombings on TV (these had nothing to do with his decision in real life). When he gets to the front line, all Iraqis resisting the American occupation are unquestionably identified as AQI (Al Qaeda in Iraq), making them legitimate targets. They're also referred to in the script as 'savages', entirely unironically, as they are throughout the real Kyle's memoir (also called *American Sniper*).

In case you don't believe they're savages, the main Iraqi characters – who remain almost entirely unspeaking – are clearly very bad guys. There's a mostly fictional sniper called Mustafa (Sammy Sheik), a former Olympic marksman, who is mentioned in one paragraph of Kyle's book but in the film becomes his sharp-shooting, marine-murdering nemesis. In real life, Kyle wrote of Mustafa, 'I never saw him, but other snipers later killed an Iraqi sniper we think was him.' In the film, of course, Kyle and Mustafa battle to the death.

Then there's a fictional terrorist called The Butcher (Mido Hamada), who wears a long black coat and attacks small children with electric drills. The Butcher may be vaguely based on Ismail Hafidh al-Lami, known as Abu Deraa, blamed for thousands of deaths in the mid-2000s. But the main point is that he's horrible. Everyone Kyle kills is horrible. The war is a lot easier to support when no Americans ever make any mistakes and everyone who opposes them is really obviously horrible. You're either with us or against us. Freedom and democracy are advanced by guns and drones. God bless America.

Good guys: Every kill Kyle makes, even on split-second decisions, is 100 per cent righteous and saves American lives. The skull logo of Marvel Comics' murderous vigilante The Punisher is on his vest and his armoured vehicle, yet nobody asks whether that sort of symbolism is going to help win Iraqi hearts and minds. He is a true patriotic American with a whacking great tattoo of a crusader cross on his arm. That bit is true: 'I had it put in in red, for blood', he wrote. 'I hated the damn savages I'd been fighting. I always will. They've taken so much from me.'

He suffers after his tours of duty – but only, he says, because he wanted to kill more bad guys to save more marines. He develops a thousand-yard stare and attacks his own dog at a barbecue. *American Sniper*'s message is that Kyle is the real victim of the war. Not any of those Iraqis he shot. They deserved it, because – as it has established to its own satisfaction – they were savages. As for non-savage Iraqis who may have reasonable grounds to complain about what happened to their country following the invasion, they must all be in some other movie.

Sources: This film alters Kyle's book significantly, but the reliability of his account may also be open to question. In 2014, former wrestler turned politician Jesse Ventura won over $1.8m in damages from Kyle's estate after a jury decided he had been defamed. Kyle claimed he had punched Ventura in a bar after Ventura said Navy SEALs 'deserved to lose some' for their actions in Iraq. Ventura said he had never even met Kyle. In a separate case, Kyle told a writer that he had shot and killed two armed men who attempted to carjack him in Dallas. Reporters were unable to confirm this with county sheriffs and medical examiners, all of whom insisted no such incident had ever taken place. Kyle further claimed that he and another sniper had sat on top of the New Orleans Superdome during the aftermath of Hurricane Katrina, and killed thirty armed civilians he thought were making trouble. Again, this story could not be confirmed by any of the relevant authorities.

One investigating journalist wrote that these tales 'portray Kyle as if he really were the Punisher, dispensing justice by his own rules. It was possible to see these stories as evidence of vainglory; it was also possible to see them as attempts by a struggling man to maintain an invincible persona.' Maybe some of these brags were true, and maybe they weren't. A lot of this film certainly isn't – and all the complicated questions it leaves out would have made a much more interesting film than the Bush-era propaganda it shovels in.

If the industrial revolution defined the late eighteenth and early nineteenth centuries, the technological revolution defined the late twentieth and early twenty-first. Home computers became common in the 1980s; the internet boomed in the 1990s and 2000s; smartphones proliferated in the 2010s.

It is not at all easy to make historical movies about technology or business. The action tends to be static: it's hard to make great drama out of people sitting down and talking into phones or tapping data into computers. The options for sex, violence, chases and explosions are limited; complex exposition doesn't make a great substitute. The characters are all too often nerdy.

Nonetheless, there have been historical movies about the internet age. David Fincher's *The Social Network* (2010) was widely praised for its zappy portrayal of the rise of Facebook entrepreneur Mark Zuckerberg (Jesse Eisenberg), though it certainly makes everyone and everything in it look a lot cooler than they were in real life.

While Facebook is all about people invading their own privacy, governments and corporations aren't too pleased when hackers invade theirs:

2012

The Fifth Estate (2013)

Director: Bill Condon • Entertainment grade: C • History grade: B+

Wikileaks, an online organization publishing secret information, became internationally prominent by the end of the first decade of the twenty-first century.

Importance: *The Fifth Estate* begins grandly with a montage of the history of media, from people chipping hieroglyphics on pyramids through the printing press to the televised announcement of John F. Kennedy's assassination. The end result of this great sweep of events, it suggests, was a platinum blonde Australian bombshell, Julian Assange (Benedict Cumberbatch), leaking stuff on a website. As the film begins in 2012, his former BFF Daniel Berg (Daniel Brühl) is trying to send him a message, over and over again: 'Julian, are you there?' That would have made a good alternative title for this movie.

Leaks: The film flashes back to 2002. Berg attends some sort of rave-inflected nerd convention in Berlin, full of people who look like they could do with a hot bath and some vitamins, wiring bits of Lego up to Tesla coils and so forth. Assange refers to this lot as 'cypherpunks'. He talks about freedom of information and protecting the anonymity of whistleblowers. Berg is smitten. The two team up to leak information on Bank Julius Baer, in a complicated case, which the film does a decent job of making comprehensible. The leaks multiply: Tibet protests, Scientology secrets, Sarah Palin's emails.

People: The real Julian Assange deplores this film, writing to Cumberbatch claiming that it would 'depict me and my work in a negative light'. In fact, *The Fifth Estate* goes fairly soft on him. Cumberbatch's portrayal is brilliant: terrifically accurate in terms of speech and mannerisms, while skilfully capturing a sort of traumatized vulnerability beneath all the searing hostility. It would be possible for audiences to find the screen Assange sympathetic. Moreover, the film all but dodges the sexual assault allegations made against him in Sweden, mentioning them only in a title card at the end. Still, it seems like the real Assange would have been unhappy with any script unless it began 'INT. STABLE. BETHLEHEM. NIGHT. Shepherds and wise men gather round to adore the strikingly handsome newborn JULIAN ASSANGE while angels sing hosannas' and got ever more appreciative from there.

Plot: Historically speaking, it's fine that the film doesn't ever fully determine whether Assange is a hero, an antihero or a villain. It needn't patronize its audience with a didactic conclusion. As some reviews have noted, it takes cues from *The Social Network*. In both, a sweet, innocent nerd embarks upon a codependent bromance with a smarter, more ruthless nerd, and gets burned. *The Social Network* was written by *West Wing* creator Aaron Sorkin; *The Fifth Estate* was written by *West Wing* writer Josh Singer. And, for all these films' dash and style, they both face the fundamental narrative problem that nothing really happens in them.

Action: The significant action in *The Fifth Estate* boils down to a few keystrokes on a laptop. The filmmakers have tried to add excitement with the murders of Kenyan human rights activists in 2009, a State Department informant being exfiltrated from Libya before Wikileaks can blow his cover, and a few government-issue heavies glaring at Assange across Scandinavian cocktail bars. Even so, the principal characters face no tangible peril: just the amorphous threat of lawsuits and bad publicity. It would have taken substantially greater historical inaccuracies to turn this film into a genuine thriller. If it were theatre, of course, *The Fifth Estate* could have made a virtue of its own lack of action. They could have set the entire thing in the broom cupboard of the Ecuadorean Embassy, with Assange sitting under his sunlamp, explaining how important and wonderful he is to a sock on his hand with eyes drawn on it. Every single day. For years. Now that, one suspects, would be all too close to the truth.

The End

Index

Acknowledgements

I would like to thank Catherine Shoard at the *Guardian* for having the original idea for the Reel History column and nurturing it over the years, James Nightingale at Atlantic for having the vision and persistence to turn it into a book, and Natasha Fairweather and Sarah Thickett at United Agents for making it all come together. Many thanks to Claire Cock-Starkey for copyediting the book with an eagle eye, Mary Chamberlain for her excellent proofreading and to Chris Shamwana for designing the jacket so wittily.

Thanks also to many wonderful people from the worlds of history, journalism, cinema and my life who have helped along the way, including Henry Barnes, Xan Brooks, Nicholas Cole, Rachel Dwyer, Carol Dyhouse, Sarah Habberfield, Tom Holland, Saba Imtiaz, Greg Jenner, Faiza Sultan Khan, Benjamin Lee, Mike McCahill, Giles MacDonogh, Kate Phillips, Justin Pollard, Andrew Pulver, Imogen Robertson, Tim Robey, Mehul Srivastava, Eugénie von Tunzelmann, Nick von Tunzelmann, Alison Weir, Maddie West, Kate Williams, Mike Witcombe, Robyn Young, and all the witty, clever and charming readers of Reel History.

A Note About the Author

Alex von Tunzelmann is a historian and writer. She has published two books: *Indian Summer: The Secret History of the End of an Empire* (2007) and *Red Heat: Conspiracy, Murder and the Cold War in the Caribbean* (2011), and is the author of the long-running 'Reel History' column in the *Guardian*.